STUDY GUIDE FOR

Copi: INTRODUCTION TO LOGIC

FIFTH EDITION

STUDY GUIDE FOR

Copi:

INTRODUCTION TO LOGIC

FIFTH EDITION

Keith Emerson Ballard

B.A., Princeton Ph.D. (Philosophy), Yale J.D. (Law), Harvard

MACMILLAN PUBLISHING CO., INC.
New York
COLLIER MACMILLAN PUBLISHERS
London

Printed in the United States of America

Macmillan Publishing Co., Inc.
866 Third Avenue, New York, New York 10022

Collier Macmillan Canada, Ltd.

ISBN 0-02-305520-0

Printing: 4 5 6 7 8 Year: 0 1 2 3 4

Acknowledgments

I should like to express my gratitude to Professor Irving M. Copi, who had the kindness and patience to read both an early draft and the final draft of the manuscript and who offered a great many helpful comments and suggestions. Special thanks are due to Mr. Kenneth J. Scott, Mr. Ronald C. Harris, and other members of the staff of Macmillan Publishing Co., Inc., for their thoughtful advice and help in editing the manuscript. I also wish to thank Professors James Dickoff and Patricia James, who read an early version of the manuscript and offered many suggestions for its improvement. I am also grateful for the suggestions made by many of the nearly five hundred students who used the early version of the manuscript in class on an experimental basis. The Carnegie Corporation was most generous in providing a grant to support the writing of this study guide and the experimental use of it in class over a two-year period.

K. E. B.

Contents

PART ONE LANGUAGE

PART TWO DEDUCTION

PART THREE INTRODUCTION

Part One Language

Chapter 1 Introduction

How to Use This Study Guide

This self-instructional study guide is designed to help you to achieve complete mastery of *Introduction to Logic,* Fifth Edition, by Irving M. Copi. You should first thoroughly study each section of Professor Copi's text, then study the corresponding section of this book, and finally work on the exercises in Copi's text, doing as many as you feel are necessary in order to achieve complete mastery of the material.

After studying a section of Copi's text, you can turn to this study guide to find:

1. A preliminary self-quiz (with answers) to test your understanding of the material.
2. A brief, systematic review or summary of the essential points in the text, and a further explanation of certain points which may cause difficulty.
3. Complete solutions to approximately one fifth of the exercises in the text. A number of these solutions contain step-by-step analyses that should help with some common difficulties that may arise in your attempts to do the exercises on your own.
4. At the end of each chapter, a comprehensive examination (with answers) designed to test your mastery of the material.

This study guide is thus based on the assumption that what students need in studying logic is not only an excellent textbook, but also a means of summarizing and reviewing what they have learned, a test of their mastery of the theory and its applications, and some help with any special difficulties that they may have either in the theory or in the exercises. The material presented in this study guide can be used in a number of different ways, depending upon the individual student's needs. For example, the systematic review or summary can be used in the place of a second reading of the text (particularly for the easier sections), or it may be used as an aid in structuring and remembering the essential points, and it may be used as a final review before an examination. Similarly, the preliminary self-quizzes, the additional explanations, and the review examinations may be used in whatever way the individual student thinks will be most helpful. One thing to remember always is that this study guide is designed to help students in their work with Copi's text and is useful only as a supplement to that text, so that it should never be used to the exclusion of the main text.

If you are studying Copi's text in a regular course in logic where classroom work and individual help from an instructor are available, you can use the study guide to increase your understanding of the material before going to class. Or if you are one of the growing number of students, teachers, and others who are anxious to learn logic on their own, this study guide should enable you to master Copi's text by yourself, without the kind of classroom work or individual help from an instructor that has in the past usually been considered necessary in learning logic.

Although this book adds to the number of pages to be read in learning the material in Copi's text, the use of this study guide should actually save time and effort in the long run, because the brief systematic reviews and summaries in the study guide should replace to a large extent the need for rereading the text, which would otherwise be necessary in a subject like logic. The reviews and summaries in the study guide are a good deal shorter than the corresponding sections of the main text, because the review and summary need not contain those details which must be included when the various principles of logic are first explained but which soon become so obvious that they need not be repeated when the essential points of each section are being systematically summarized. Thus, the summaries in the study guide leave the student with a clearly structured understanding of the essential points in the text.

Moreover, reading two different explanations of the same point should produce a better understanding than would result from reading the same explanation twice. In other words, it is felt that a single thorough study of a section of Copi's text, followed by a reading of the summary in this study guide, will be the quickest, easiest, and most effective way of mastering the material.

The study guide can also help to reduce the time and effort that are sometimes wasted when one gets the wrong notion of some basic concept, or fails to understand an essential part of the exposition, or fails to distinguish the fundamental and important aspects of the theory being developed from the secondary details which are necessary only in expounding the theory for the first time, or struggles unsuccessfully for a long time with a set of exercises when one's difficulties could have been cleared up quite easily. It is hoped that by reducing these causes of wasted time and effort, this self-instructional study guide will make the student's learning process more efficient and thus actually decrease the total amount of work that the student will have to do in learning logic.

You can now begin your study of logic by reading carefully pages 3–44 of the text, *Introduction to Logic,* Fifth Edition, by Irving M. Copi. Study these pages now, before continuing your reading of this study guide.

READ PAGES 3–44 OF THE TEXT

From the first chapter of Copi's text you learned that logic is a study of the techniques and principles used to distinguish correct from incorrect arguments, and that an **argument** is a group of **propositions,** one of which (the **conclusion**) is claimed to follow from the others (the **premisses**).[1]

You can determine whether or not a particular passage contains an argument by determining whether or not one of the propositions in the passage is claimed to follow from some of the other propositions in the passage. The proposition that is claimed to follow from certain other propositions is called the **conclusion** of the argument; and the other propositions (from which the conclusion is claimed to follow) are called the **premisses** of the argument. The conclusion of an argument is sometimes (although not always) preceded by one of the following *conclusion-indicators:* "therefore," "hence," "so," "consequently," "it follows that," "we may infer that," and "we may conclude that." Similarly, the premisses of an argument are sometimes preceded by one of the following *premiss-indicators:* "since," "because," "for," "as," "inasmuch as," and "for the reason that."

To summarize: an argument is present whenever one proposition is claimed to follow from other propositions that are assumed as premisses.

[1] The printing of a word in **boldface** indicates that it is an important technical term whose precise definition must be accurately understood and remembered; otherwise, confusion is likely to result when the meaning of a passage depends upon a term being understood in its precise technical sense.

Arguments can be classified as **deductive** or **inductive, valid** or **invalid,** and **sound** or **unsound.** These six terms have precise, technical meanings that you should remember from your reading of the first chapter of the text.

SELF-QUIZ

You can test your understanding of these terms by answering the following multiple-choice questions. If you get all the questions correct, with no confusion or uncertainty, you should skip the next section of review in this study guide and go right on to the exercises in the first chapter of the text. But if you do miss a question, or even if you are uncertain about the correctness of a particular answer, you should study carefully the next section of review, since the understanding of logic is cumulative, and any confusion at the beginning is likely to produce greater confusion later on.

The answers to the questions are given after the last question, but you should not look at them until you have answered *all* seven of the questions for yourself. In each question choose the answer which finishes the sentence in a completely accurate way. An answer is wrong if it is incomplete or inaccurate in any respect.

Write your answers on a separate piece of paper. Do not write your answers in this book, because you may want to take this quiz again for review purposes.

1. A deductive argument can be distinguished from all other types of arguments by saying that it is an argument in which ______.
   a. It is impossible for the premisses to be true and the conclusion false.
   b. It is claimed that if the premisses are true then the conclusion cannot be false.
   c. The truth of the conclusion follows from the truth of the premisses.
   d. It is claimed that the premisses are true and that the conclusion is true.
   e. None of the above.

2. The conclusion of a particular argument must be true if the argument is ______.
   a. A valid argument not all of whose premisses are false.
   b. An argument in which the conclusion would have to be true if the premisses were all true.
   c. A deductive argument that neither is invalid nor has any false premiss.
   d. A correct (or highly probable) inductive argument all of whose premisses are true.
   e. None of the above.

3. A correct (or highly probable) inductive argument can be distinguished from all other types of arguments by saying that it is an argument in which ______.
   a. The probability of the conclusion being true is the same as the probability of the premisses being true.
   b. The premisses probably are true, and if they are as a matter of fact true, then the conclusion must be true also.
   c. Even if the premisses were false, the conclusion would probably still be true.
   d. It is claimed that if the premisses are true then the conclusion is probably true also; and the claim is correct.
   e. None of the above.

4. A valid argument can be distinguished from all other types of arguments by saying that it is an argument in which ______.
   a. If the conclusion is false then all the premisses must be false also.
   b. All the premisses and the conclusion are true.
   c. The conclusion is true.
   d. If the conclusion is true, then at least one of the premisses must be true also.
   e. If the conclusion is false, then at least one of the premisses must be false also.
   f. If the premisses are all false, then the conclusion must be false also.
   g. None of the above.

5. An argument is invalid only if ______.
   a. The premisses are true and the conclusion is false.
   b. It is claimed that if the premisses are true, then the conclusion must be true also; but as a matter of fact the premisses are false.
   c. If the premisses were true, then the conclusion would have to be false.
   d. The conclusion could be true even though the premisses were all false.
   e. None of the above.

6. An argument can be valid and have a true conclusion only if ______.
   a. All its premisses are true.
   b. It has at least one true premiss.
   c. It is a sound argument.
   d. Its conclusion not only is true but would have to be true if its premisses were all true.
   e. None of the above.

7. An unsound argument can be valid only if ______.
   a. It has a false conclusion.
   b. It has a true conclusion but at least one false premiss.

c. The truth of the conclusion does not necessarily follow from the truth of the premisses.
d. Not all its premisses are true.
e. None of the above.

ANSWERS

1. b.	5. e.
2. c.	6. d.
3. d.	7. d.
4. e.	

If you answered all the questions correctly, were sure of your answers, and were not confused or uncertain about any of the alternative choices, then you should skip the following review and proceed directly to the exercises of Chapter 1 of the text. Those who feel in need of some further clarification should study the following section carefully.

Deductive, Inductive, Valid, Invalid, Sound, Unsound

All arguments are either deductive or inductive. An argument is **deductive** if it is claimed that the conclusion follows *necessarily* or with certainty from the premisses; and an argument is **inductive** if it is claimed merely that the conclusion follows from the premisses with *probability,* but not necessarily or with certainty. Thus, whether an argument is deductive or inductive depends upon what is being *claimed* about the relationship between the premisses and the conclusion. In a deductive argument it is *claimed* that if the premisses are true then the conclusion *must* be true also; it is claimed that it is *impossible* for all the premisses to be true without the conclusion also being true. Whereas in an inductive argument it is *claimed* merely that if the premisses are true, then the conclusion is *probably* true, but it is admitted that it is possible for all the premisses to be true without the conclusion being true also.

It might be helpful at this point to illustrate the difference between deductive and inductive arguments with the following very simple examples:

INDUCTIVE ARGUMENT

This swan is white.
And that swan there is white.
And that other swan over there is white.
Therefore, all swans are white.

Notice in the case of this inductive argument that although the premisses do provide some evidence for the conclusion, it is possible that the conclusion might be false even though the premisses were all true. All that is being claimed in such an inductive argument is that if the premisses are true, then the conclusion is *probably* true. If the truth of the premisses makes it *very probable* that the conclusion is also true, then the inductive argument is said to be strong or highly probable; whereas if the truth of the premisses does not provide very much evidence for the truth of the conclusion, then the inductive argument is said to be weak or not very highly probable. Obviously the "correctness" or "incorrectness" of an inductive argument is a matter of degree.

In the case of a deductive argument, such as the following, it is being claimed that if the premisses are true then the conclusion *must* be true also.

DEDUCTIVE ARGUMENT

All humans are mortal.
Julius Caesar was a human.
Therefore, Julius Caesar was mortal.

In the case of this *valid* deductive argument, the conclusion follows *necessarily* (conclusively, with certainty) from the premisses. If the premisses are true then the conclusion *must* be true also; not even Julius Caesar could prevent that. What makes this argument **deductive** is that it is being *claimed* that if the premisses are true then the conclusion must be true also. If this claim is correct then the argument is **valid;** and if the claim is incorrect then the argument is **invalid.** In other words, deductive arguments are characterized as valid or invalid according to whether the conclusion does or does not follow necessarily from the premisses. A **valid deductive argument** is one in which the conclusion is not only claimed to but does follow necessarily from the premisses. That is, if the premisses are true then the conclusion *must* also be true. Whereas an **invalid deductive argument** is one in which the conclusion is claimed to follow necessarily from the premisses but does not do so. That is, the conclusion *could* be false even though the premisses were all true.

The terms "valid" and "invalid" are used to characterize correct and incorrect *deductive* arguments, but are not generally used in connection with inductive arguments, since no inductive argument even claims to be deductively valid.

Remember that in determining the validity or invalidity of a deductive argument you are not interested in whether the premisses and conclusions are *as a matter of fact* true or false. You are interested only in whether the conclusion *would have* to be true *if* the premisses *were* all true. An argument can have false premisses and a false conclusion and still be valid, so long as the conclusion *would have* to be true if the premisses were all true. Consider the following example from the text (page 42):

> All spiders have six legs.
> All six-legged creatures have wings.
> Therefore, all spiders have wings.

The premisses are not true, nor is the conclusion true. But *if* it were true that all spiders had six legs, and *if* it were true that all six-legged creatures had wings, then it would *have* to be true also that all spiders had wings. In this example we can see clearly how the question of the validity of the argument is separate from the question of the actual truth or falsity of the individual propositions that constitute the argument.

A valid argument can also have false premisses and a true conclusion, as in the following example:

> All human beings have six legs.
> All six-legged creatures are mammals.
> Therefore, all human beings are mammals.

Once again, the argument is valid because if the premisses were true then the conclusion would *have* to be true also. The fact that the premisses are not actually true is irrelevant to the question of validity. And the fact that the conclusion is actually true even though the premisses are false is equally irrelevant.

Perhaps we have reached the point where it is unnecessary to provide further examples. Suffice it to say that a valid argument can have any combination of true or false premisses and conclusion, so long as it is the case that *if* the premisses were true, then the conclusion would have to be true also. The only combination that a valid argument cannot have is, of course, true premisses and a false conclusion, since then it would not be the case that if the premisses were true then the conclusion would have to be true also.

Similarly, an invalid argument can have any combination of true or false premisses and conclusion, so long as it is *not* the case that if the premisses were true then the conclusion would have to be true also. Thus, an invalid argument can have a conclusion that is actually true, so long as that conclusion *could* be false even though the premisses were all true. The next to last argument on page 42 of the text is a good illustration of this case.

It should now be obvious that you can determine the validity or invalidity of an argument without ever raising the question of whether the premisses and conclusion are *as a matter of fact* true or false. To determine validity or invalidity you must answer the question, "If the premisses were true, would the conclusion *have* to be true also?" If so, the argument is valid. If not, it is invalid.

There is one more pair of terms whose definitions must be accurately understood and remembered. An argument is **sound** if it is valid and all its premisses are true. From this definition and the definition of validity, it follows that every sound argument has a true conclusion. Thus, we can know that a particular conclusion is true if we know that the argument is sound, that is, if we know that the argument is valid and that all its premisses are true. But it is not sufficient that the argument be valid, since a valid argument with a false premiss could have a false conclusion.

An argument is **unsound** if it is either not valid or has at least one false premiss. Thus, to demonstrate that a particular argument does not establish the truth of its conclusion, it suffices to show that the argument is unsound, that is, to show either that the argument is not valid or that one of its premisses is false.

Deductive logic is mainly concerned with developing techniques and principles for determining the validity or invalidity of arguments. Logic is not normally concerned with the soundness or unsoundness of arguments, since this requires a consideration of the truth or falsity of the individual propositions contained in the arguments, which is, in general, a matter for empirical science rather than logic.

SOLUTIONS
to selected exercises on pages 10–15

Professor Copi has provided at the back of his text solutions to about one fifth of the exercises (generally numbers 1, 5, 10, 15, 20, and so on, of each set). This self-instructional study guide provides solutions to an additional one-fifth of the exercises in the text (generally numbers 2, 6, 11, 16, 21, and so on, of each set). The study guide will also sometimes provide more detailed solutions and additional explanation for exercises for which the text provides only the final answer.

The solutions that are provided both in the text and in this study guide can be a great help if used wisely, but if used improperly they can seriously interfere with the process that you must go through in order to learn and retain the material.

In general, you should try to answer each question in the exercises to your own satisfaction before looking up the solution in the back of the text or in this study guide. A great deal of practice is necessary if you are going to be able to solve the various types of problems on your own, and genuine practice requires struggling with the problems that you may not be able to solve quickly. It is not enough to read over a problem, then look up the answer, and then try to analyze why the given answer is correct and other possible alternatives are wrong. Such a procedure would short-circuit the learning process and would be disastrous in the long run, not only in terms of your performance on examinations, but also in terms of your ability to use the principles of logic effectively in real-life situations.

Of course everyone's time is limited, and there is no reason to struggle with a problem beyond the point at which nothing further can be gained from the struggle. It is up to you to make a wise use of the solutions to the exercises, but it is essential that you at least *try* to solve each problem on your own before looking up the answer. Such a procedure will probably even save you time *in the long run,* and it will certainly lead to a higher level of mastery of the subject.

It should be remembered that the solutions given in this study guide are sometimes not the only possible solutions. Alternative solutions might in some cases be justifiable also. As Professor Copi has said in one of his solutions manuals: "I have given what seem to me to be the best answers, but ingenious students always surprise me with the variety of alternative answers for which intelligent justifications can be supplied, and I think it is entirely proper to 'give credit' for analyses and solutions that a student can defend."

Page 10, #2:

PREMISSES: (1) Employers, emerging from a recession, usually expand hours for their existing workers before they hire new ones.

(2) The average quality of those unemployed declines as the better educated among them are rehired first.

(3) These two factors combine to reduce the leverage of economic growth on the unemployment rate.

CONCLUSION: A growth rate of five per cent would reduce the unemployment rate by only one third of a percentage point.

Page 11, #6:

PREMISS: Large numbers of people in this country have never had to deal with the criminal justice system.

CONCLUSION: Large numbers of people in this country are unaware of how the criminal justice system works and of the extraordinarily detrimental impact it has upon many people's lives.

Page 12, #11:

PREMISSES: (1) The pattern of female employment follows the course of the role that women play outside industry.

(2) Women are almost always ancillary, handmaids in the more important work of men.

CONCLUSION: Equal pay for equal work will not make as great a difference as women might hope in these figures—that the average male employee in the United States earns $6,610 a year; his sister $3,157, less than half.

Page 12, #16:

PREMISSES: (1) Any attempt to base logical principles on something more ultimate, whether it be our system of contingent rules for the use of language or anything else, consists of deducing conclusions from premisses.

(2) For deduction to be possible the prior validity of logical laws is a prerequisite.

CONCLUSION: Any attempt to base logical principles on something more ultimate, whether it be our system of contingent rules for the use of language or anything else, must be self-defeating.

Page 14, #21:

PREMISSES: (1) During the school period the student has been mentally bending over his desk.

(2) At the University he should stand up and look around.

CONCLUSION: It is fatal if the first year at the University be frittered away in going over the old work in the old spirit.

SOLUTIONS
to selected exercises on pages 17–22

Page 17, #2:

First argument:

PREMISS: Socialism is a system built on belief in human goodness.

CONCLUSION: Socialism never works.

Second argument:

PREMISS: Capitalism is a system built on belief in human selfishness.

CONCLUSION: Given checks and balances, capitalism is nearly always a smashing, scandalous success.

Page 18, #6:

First argument:

PREMISS: The Buddha is everywhere.

CONCLUSION: To ask the question which part of the motorcycle, which grain of sand in which pile, is the Buddha, is to look in the wrong direction.

Second argument:

PREMISS: The Buddha is everywhere.

CONCLUSION: To ask the question which part of the motorcycle, which grain of sand in which pile, is the Buddha, is to look in the right direction.

Page 19, #11:

First argument:

PREMISSES: (1) That the people have an original right to establish, for their future government, such principles as, in their opinion, shall most conduce to their own happiness is the basis on which the whole American fabric has been erected.

(2) The exercise of this original right is a very great exertion, and neither can be nor ought to be frequently repeated.

CONCLUSION: The principles so established are deemed fundamental.

Second argument:

PREMISSES: (1) The first premiss of the first argument.

(2) The authority from which these principles proceed is supreme and can seldom act.

CONCLUSION: These principles are designed to be permanent.

Page 20, #16:

First argument:

PREMISS: The machine will not be provided with legs.

CONCLUSION: The machine could not be asked to go out and fill the coal scuttle.

Second argument:

PREMISSES: (1) The machine will not be provided with legs.

(2) The machine might not have eyes.

CONCLUSION: It will not be possible to apply exactly the same teaching process to the machine as to a normal child.

Third argument:

PREMISS: The example of Miss Helen Keller shows that education can take place provided that communication in both directions between teacher and pupil can take place by some means or other.

CONCLUSION: We need not be too concerned about the [machine's lack of] legs, eyes, etc.

Page 21, #21:

First argument:

PREMISS: A punishment which comes at the end of all things, when the world is over and done with, cannot have for its object either to improve or deter.

CONCLUSION: A punishment which comes at the end of all things, when the world is over and done with, is pure vengeance.

Second argument:

PREMISS: The preceding conclusion.

CONCLUSION: God, who prescribes forbearance and forgiveness of every fault, exercises none himself, but does the exact opposite.

SOLUTIONS
to selected exercises on pages 25–32

Page 26, #2: Arguments.

First argument:

PREMISS: Invariably, high-status parents will seek to pass on their positions either through the use of influence or simply by the cultural advantages their children would possess.

CONCLUSION: After one generation a meritocracy simply becomes an enclaved class.

Second argument:

PREMISS: The preceding conclusion.

CONCLUSION: There can never be a pure meritocracy.

Page 26, #6:

This passage may be interpreted in either of two ways: First, it may be interpreted as not an argument at all but a series of statements or asserted propositions. Or, second, it may be interpreted as containing two arguments. In the first argument, the first sentence of the passage, which predicts what will happen, may be regarded as inferred from the second and third sentences. In the second argument, the third sentence, which describes the readiness of women to act in certain ways, may be regarded as inferred from the second sentence, which explains why women have not yet lost such readiness to act.

Page 27, #11: Argument.

PREMISSES: All of the statements or asserted propositions in the passage except the last six words.

CONCLUSION: Nurture, not nature, is our guide.

Page 29, #16:

This passage may be interpreted in either of two ways: First, it may be interpreted as not an argument at all but a series of statements or asserted propositions. Or, second, it may be interpreted as containing an argument in which from the first sentence as premiss it is inferred that the proposal to inject women into the combat role in war is an extreme suggestion which exceeds the bounds of reason and logic.

Page 29, #21: Arguments.

First argument:

The first sentence *reports* the argument in which the conclusion that members of the Movement should not attack marriage is inferred from the premiss that most women are married.

Second argument:

The second sentence states the argument in which the conclusion that the first argument is fallacious is inferred from the premiss that the first argument is logically analogous to the obviously fallacious argument that members of the Movement should not attack oppression because all women are oppressed.

Third argument:
PREMISS: The third sentence.
CONCLUSION: The last sentence.

SOLUTIONS
to selected exercises on pages 35–41

Page 35, #2: Inductive argument.
PREMISSES: (1) Hamilton was at no time a rich man.
(2) At his death Hamilton left a small estate.
CONCLUSION: That Hamilton ever held any considerable sum in securities seems highly improbable.

The argument is inductive rather than deductive, because only probability is *claimed* for the conclusion. Notice that the argument assumes that a person can hold a considerable sum in securities without being rich, because otherwise the conclusion would follow *deductively* from the first premiss.

Page 36, #6: Inductive arguments.
First argument:
PREMISS: At an underprivileged school in Harlem, they used to test the intelligence of all the children at two-year intervals. They found that every two years each advancing class came out ten points lower in "native intelligence."
CONCLUSION: The combined efforts of home influencing and school education, a powerful combination, succeeded in making the children significantly stupider year by year.

Second argument:
PREMISS: The preceding conclusion.
CONCLUSION: If they had a few more years of compulsory home ties and compulsory education, all would end up as gibbering idiots.

The first argument is inductive because it is an argument from experimental data to an alleged cause. The second argument is inductive because it is an argument from the alleged cause to the future consequences if the cause were allowed to continue to operate. The conclusion that they all would end up as gibbering idiots is inferred inductively on the basis of a trend presented in the premiss. The conclusion is, in effect, based on the projection of a line of a graph into a region of the graph for which no experimental data are presented; and such a projection, or "extrapolation," is a conclusion that is at best only probable.

Page 37, #11: Deductive argument.

PREMISSES: (1) You cannot have a rational justification for your appeal to history till your metaphysics has assured you that there *is* a history to appeal to.

(2) Your conjectures as to the future presuppose some basis of knowledge that there *is* a future already subjected to some determinations.

CONCLUSION: Induction presupposes metaphysics. In other words, it rests upon an antecedent rationalism.

Although the argument is about induction, the conclusion is claimed to follow necessarily from the premisses, and thus the argument is deductive.

Page 38, #16: Deductive arguments.

In the following arguments, "they" refers to those who propose to establish the universal from the particulars by means of induction.

First argument:

PREMISS: If they review some of the particular instances, some of the particular instances omitted in the induction may contravene the universal.

CONCLUSION: If they review some of the particular instances, the induction will be insecure.

Second argument:

PREMISS: The particular instances are infinite and indefinite.

CONCLUSION: If they are to review all of the particular instances, they will be toiling at the impossible.

Third argument:

PREMISSES: (1) When they propose to establish the universal from the particulars by means of induction, they will effect this by a review either of all or of some of the particular instances.

(2) The conjunction of the two preceding conclusions.

CONCLUSION: Induction is invalidated, and the method of induction is easy to set aside.

Page 39, #21: Deductive argument.

PREMISS: There are more people on the earth than hairs on any one person's head.

CONCLUSION: There must be at least two people with the same number of hairs.

Although the premiss must be arrived at inductively, the argument is deductive because the conclusion is claimed to follow necessarily from the premiss.

SOLUTIONS
to selected exercises on pages 44–48

Page 44, #2:
First argument:
PREMISSES: (1) Mankind always act in order to obtain that which they think good.
(2) Communities are established by mankind. [This premiss is tacitly assumed but not explicitly stated.]
CONCLUSION: Every community is established with a view to some good.

Aristotle presumably regarded the second premiss as being so obvious that it could be "tacitly understood" instead of being explicitly stated. But is it so obvious? Perhaps some communities simply developed gradually without being deliberately *established* by mankind, and perhaps some communities arose through the power of a single individual or small group, in which case the final conclusion that communities aim at the highest good (rather than at some individual's or group's good) would be even more questionable than you may already believe it to be.

These comments indicate briefly the caution which must be exercised in judging the validity (and especially the soundness) of complex arguments expressed in ordinary language (as opposed to the symbolic notation to be developed later in the text). In this regard, notice also the subtle shift from "every community is established with a view to some good" (in the first sentence of the passage) to "all communities aim at some good" (in the second sentence). The change may appear trivial. But even if we admit (what is certainly questionable from an historical point of view) that every community was *at one time* established with a view to some good, does it follow that all communities *now* aim at some good? Perhaps the aims and functions of communities have changed over the years. And do communities (as opposed to individuals) have *aims?* Isn't an aim a conscious desire to pursue some goal? Do communities have *desires?*

The *second argument* in the passage uses the altered version of the conclusion of the first argument as a premiss:

PREMISSES: (1) All communities aim at some good.
(2) The state or political community is the highest of all and embraces all the rest.
CONCLUSION: The state or political community aims at good in a greater degree than any other, and at the highest good.

Is this argument valid? If we assume that all communities aim at some good, and that the state is the highest community, does it follow that the state aims at the highest good? Compare the argument: "All houses are buildings; therefore, the highest house is the highest building." This is obviously invalid. Perhaps Aristotle's second argument is invalid also. What do you think?

Furthermore, what does "highest" mean in Aristotle's context? He says that the state is the highest political community in the sense that it embraces all the rest. This looks like a reference to size, which might have nothing to do with the moral sense of the word "highest" as it occurs in the phrase "highest good." Perhaps there is an equivocation on the word "highest."

Enough has been said to point out the complexity of a full analysis of these arguments.

Page 45, #6:

The first sentence of the passage is a statement of the "principle" which in the second sentence is claimed to "involve a manifest contradiction." The third sentence contains two arguments which lead to this conclusion, with the conclusion of the first argument being a premiss of the second argument.

First argument:

PREMISSES: (1) Houses, mountains, rivers, and in a word all sensible objects, are things we perceive by sense.

(2) All that we perceive by sense [or are conscious of] are our own ideas or sensations.

CONCLUSION: Houses, mountains, rivers, and in a word all sensible objects, are our own ideas or sensations.

Second argument:

PREMISSES: (1) Houses, mountains, rivers, and in a word all sensible objects, are our own ideas or sensations [i.e., the conclusion of the first argument].

(2) None of our own ideas or sensations can exist unperceived [i.e., without some mind being conscious of them].

CONCLUSION: Houses, mountains, rivers, and in a word all sensible objects, cannot exist unperceived.

Third argument:

PREMISS: Houses, mountains, rivers, and in a word all sensible objects, cannot exist unperceived [i.e., the conclusion of the second argument].

CONCLUSION: It would involve a manifest contradiction to say that houses, mountains, rivers, and in a word all sensible objects, have an existence, natural or real, distinct from their being perceived by the understanding.

Are these arguments valid? Are they sound? A good deal of philosophy since the time of Berkeley has been devoted to an attempt to answer these questions.

Page 47, #11:
PREMISSES: The last three sentences.
CONCLUSION: The first sentence.

In a somewhat simplified version, the argument may be summarized as follows:

PREMISSES: (1) All talents of the mind (e.g., intelligence, wit, judgment) may be bad if not used with a good will.

(2) All qualities of temperament (e.g., courage, resolution, perseverance) may be bad if not used with a good will.

(3) All gifts of fortune (e.g., power, riches, honor, health, happiness) may be bad if not used with a good will.

CONCLUSION: Nothing can possibly be conceived in the world, or even out of it, which can be called good without qualification, except a good will.

SOLUTIONS
to selected exercises on pages 48–54

Some of the exercises in this section may seem rather difficult, and it is probably not worthwhile struggling with any of them beyond the point at which you seem to be hopelessly stuck, but you should try hard to make as much progress as possible on each one. The object is not only to arrive at a correct answer, but also to be able to trace clearly and completely the process of step-by-step reasoning which leads from the statement of the problem to the answer. In general, there is more than one chain of reasoning which will lead to the answer. The reasoning presented below was selected either for its simplicity and elegance or for its exemplification of standard types of argumentation.

Page 49, #2:

The third prisoner, even though he is blind, can deduce that his hat is white through the following sequence of arguments. Since there are only two red hats, if the second and third prisoners both had red hats, then the first prisoner would know that he had a white hat. But he does not know. Therefore, the second and third prisoners cannot both have red hats. One of them at least must have a white hat. Therefore, if the second prisoner saw a red hat on the third prisoner, the second prisoner would know that he himself had a white hat. But he does not know. Therefore, the second prisoner cannot have seen a red hat on the third prisoner. Therefore, the third prisoner must have a white hat, and he can know this through the above reasoning even though he is blind.

Page 50, #6:

Since Ms. Adams remained on the main floor where books are sold, *Ms. Adams bought a book.*

Of the seven people who entered the elevator, Ms. Ennis was the sixth person to get out, and so *Ms. Ennis bought a lamp* on the fifth floor.

The two women who got off at the second floor bought a necktie and a handbag. Ms. Catt was not the woman who bought the necktie, so *Ms. Catt bought a handbag.*

Ms. Fisk, who got off at the sixth floor, bought neither a book (first floor), a necktie (second floor), a handbag (second floor), a dress (third floor), nor a lamp (fifth floor). Therefore, *Ms. Fisk bought a hat.*

It follows from the conclusions already reached that Ms. Baker bought neither a book, a lamp, a handbag, nor a hat. Nor did she buy a necktie, since one of the other women bought it and gave it to Mr. Baker. Therefore, *Ms. Baker bought a dress.* Therefore, *Ms. Dodge bought the necktie.*

Page 52, #11:

Notice that there are six men, three married women, and two unmarried women. The following are men: the Third VP (a), the First VP (f), the Cashier (f), the Janitor (g), and the Teller (j). That makes five men, so there is only one other man. The Second VP and the Assistant Teller are of the same sex (c), and thus both women, so the Bookkeeper is the sixth man (i). Thus, the other women are the President, the First Stenographer and the Second Stenographer. The sex of each person as established above will be referred to as (l).

The President is a woman (l) and married (a) and so is either Mrs. Brown, Mrs. Ford, or Mrs. Kane, but she is not Mrs. Brown (a), nor Mrs. Kane (e), so *the President is Mrs. Ford (m).*

The Second Stenographer is a woman (l) and unmarried (h) and so is either Miss Dale or Miss Hill, but she is not Miss Hill (d), so *the Second Stenographer is Miss Dale (n).*

The Assistant Teller is a woman (l) and married (b) [otherwise she would have the same last name as her unmarried sister (h)], but she is not Mrs. Ford (m), nor Mrs. Brown (a), so *the Assistant Teller is Mrs. Kane (o).*

The First Stenographer is a woman (l) and married (j), but she is not Mrs. Ford (m), nor Mrs. Kane (o), so *the First Stenographer is Mrs. Brown (p).*

The Second VP is a woman (l), but she is not Mrs. Ford (m), nor Miss Dale (n), nor Mrs. Kane (o), nor Mrs. Brown (p), so *the Second VP is Miss Hill (q).*

Mr. Grant is either the President or the First VP (d and q), but he is not the President (m), so *the First VP is Mr. Grant (r).*

Mr. Grant lives at the Bachelor's Club (f and r), so the Cashier is one of the President's nearest neighbors (f and e), and so the Cashier is either Mrs. Kane or Mr. Long, but the Cashier is not Mrs. Kane (o), so *the Cashier is Mr. Long (s).*

The Bookkeeper is a man (l), but he is not Mr. Evans (k), nor Mr. Jones (k), nor Mr. Adams (h and k), nor Mr. Grant (r), nor Mr. Long (s), so *the Bookkeeper is Mr. Camp* (*t*).

The Teller is a man (l), but he is not Mr. Grant (r), nor Mr. Long (s), nor Mr. Camp (t), nor Mr. Adams (h and j), nor Mr. Evans (j and k), so *the Teller is Mr. Jones* (*u*).

The Third VP is a man (l), but he is not Mr. Grant (r), nor Mr. Long (s), nor Mr. Camp (t), nor Mr. Jones (u), nor Mr. Evans (a and k), so *the Third VP is Mr. Adams* (*v*).

And by elimination, *the Janitor is Mr. Evans.*

EXAMINATION
on Chapter 1

The point of this examination is to give you a chance to test yourself on some of the material which is *not* covered in the exercises of Chapter 1. Some of the following questions consist of a sentence with a blank to be filled in. Other questions can be answered yes or no, whereas some questions require a word or phrase or a short explanation. The seven multiple-choice questions posed earlier in the review section of this chapter are repeated here just to make sure that you have eliminated any confusions you may have had about the terms "deductive," "inductive," "valid," "invalid," "sound," and "unsound."

Write your answers on a separate piece of paper, then check them against the answers given at the end of the test. Do not write your answers in this book, because you may want to take this exam again for review purposes. If you miss a question, restudy the appropriate part of the text.

1. Logic is a study of the techniques and principles used to distinguish correct from incorrect ______.

2. A deductive argument can be distinguished from all other types of arguments by saying that it is an argument in which ______.
   a. It is impossible for the premisses to be true and the conclusion false.
   b. It is claimed that the premisses are true and that the conclusion is true.
   c. The truth of the conclusion follows from the truth of the premisses.
   d. It is claimed that if the premisses are true then the conclusion cannot be false.
   e. None of the above.

3. The conclusion of a particular argument must be true if the argument is ______.

a. A valid argument not all of whose premisses are false.
b. An argument in which the conclusion would have to be true if the premisses were all true.
c. A deductive argument which neither is invalid nor has any false premiss.
d. A correct (or highly probable) inductive argument all of whose premisses are true.
e. None of the above.

4. A correct (or highly probable) inductive argument can be distinguished from all other types of arguments by saying that it is an argument in which ______.
   a. The probability of the conclusion being true is the same as the probability of the premisses being true.
   b. The premisses probably are true, and if they are as a matter of fact true, then the conclusion must be true also.
   c. It is claimed that even if the premisses were false, the conclusion would probably still be true.
   d. The premisses are true and the conclusion is probably true.
   e. None of the above.

5. A valid argument can be distinguished from all other types of arguments by saying that it is an argument in which ______.
   a. If the conclusion is false then all the premisses must be false also.
   b. All the premisses and the conclusion are true.
   c. The conclusion is true.
   d. If the conclusion is true, then at least one of the premisses must be true also.
   e. If the conclusion is false, then at least one of the premisses must be false also.
   f. If the premisses are all false, then the conclusion must be false also.
   g. None of the above.

6. An argument is invalid only if ______.
   a. The premisses are true and the conclusion is false.
   b. It is claimed that if the premisses are true then the conclusion must be true also; but as a matter of fact the premisses are false.
   c. If the premisses were true, the conclusion would have to be false.
   d. The conclusion could be true even though the premisses were all false.
   e. It is claimed that if the premisses were true then the conclusion would have to be true also; but as a matter of fact the conclusion could be false even though the premisses were all true.
   f. None of the above.

7. An argument can be valid and have a true conclusion only if ______.
   a. All its premisses are true.

b. It has at least one true premiss.
c. It is a sound argument.
d. Its conclusion not only is true but would have to be true if its premisses were all true.
e. None of the above.

8. An unsound argument can be valid only if ______.
a. It has a false conclusion.
b. It has a true conclusion but at least one false premiss.
c. The truth of its conclusion does not necessarily follow from the truth of the premisses.
d. Not all of its premisses are true.
e. None of the above.

9. Why would it be incorrect to define logic as the science of the laws of thought?

10. Do the sentences "Bill is taller than Jim" and "Jim is shorter than Bill" assert the same proposition?

11. Is the logician mainly interested in the truth or falsity of individual propositions or in the relations between propositions?

12. Would it ever be correct to say of a proposition that it was either valid or invalid (in the logical sense of these terms)?

13. Would it ever be correct to say of an argument that it was either true or false?

14. Is it possible for a valid argument with a true conclusion to be unsound?

15. Is it true that an invalid argument can be defined as an argument in which it is claimed that if the premisses were true then the conclusion would have to be false?

16. Does an argument with a false conclusion have to be either invalid or else valid but unsound?

17. Does the conclusion of an unsound argument have to be false?

18. Can a false conclusion be validly deduced from premisses of which some are true?

19. Is it true that a valid argument can be unsound only if it has a false conclusion?

20. Is it true that if an argument has a false conclusion, this guarantees that either the argument is invalid or at least one of its premisses is false?

21. Does an unsound argument with true premisses have to have a false conclusion?

22. Can a true conclusion be validly deduced from false premisses?

23. Is it true that the conclusion of an unsound argument can be false only if the argument is invalid?

24. Does the conclusion of a valid argument have to be true?

25. Is it possible for an argument with true premisses and a true conclusion to be unsound?

26. Is it true that in order to establish the truth of a particular proposition it suffices to find a valid argument with that proposition as its conclusion?

27. Can an invalid argument have false premisses and a true conclusion?

ANSWERS

1. Arguments (or reasoning).
2. d.
3. c.
4. e.
5. e.
6. e.
7. d.
8. d.
9. Because logic is not *the* science of the laws of thought (since psychology is also a science dealing with laws of thought); nor does logic deal with *all* the laws of thought (since there are also psychological laws dealing with thought processes).
10. Yes.
11. In the relations between propositions.
12. No.
13. No.
14. Yes.
15. No.
16. Yes.
17. No.
18. Yes.
19. No.
20. Yes.
21. No.
22. Yes.
23. No.
24. No.
25. Yes.
26. No.
27. Yes.

Chapter 2
The Uses of Language

READ PAGES 55–59 OF THE TEXT

2.1 Three Basic Functions of Language

There are at least three different uses or purposes or functions of language:

1. The **informative** function, in which language is used to communicate information.
2. The **expressive** function, in which language is used to express or give vent to the feelings, emotions, or attitudes of the user, or to attempt to arouse or evoke certain feelings, emotions, or attitudes in others.
3. The **directive** function, in which language is used to cause (or prevent) certain overt actions.

Only insofar as a sentence is used to communicate information is it either true or false. Expressive and directive discourse as such are neither true nor false.

Examples of the *informative* function of language are: reporting an event; describing an object; reasoning about facts; presenting arguments; formulating a theory or hypothesis to explain an event; stating or declaring an opinion, a belief, or a conviction.

Examples of the *expressive* function of language are: thanking someone; cursing someone; greeting someone ("How are you?", "How do you do?", "I'm very glad to meet you.") ; reciting a prayer in order to express one's religious feelings; singing the national anthem; seeking oratorically to arouse feelings of patriotism in one's audience; courting a beloved with poetic language; trying to get someone to react aesthetically to a particular work of art.

Examples of the *directive* function of language are: giving the order to shoot to kill; preaching on the commandment "Thou shalt not kill"; saying to a child at dinner, "We don't eat with our elbows on the table"; ordering a cup of coffee; asking a question; inciting to riot; praying for God's help.

READ PAGES 59–61 OF THE TEXT

2.2 Discourse Serving Multiple Functions

Although some sentences are mainly informative, other sentences mainly expressive, and still others mainly directive, it is very common for a single sentence to serve more than one of these functions at the same time. For example, a sentence which communicates certain information (and therefore serves the informative function) may be intended also to arouse a particular emotion or to cause a particular overt action, and may thus be expressive or directive as well as informative. Similarly, a sentence would have a multiple function if it were designed to evoke a particular attitude in order ultimately to produce a certain overt action. The **ceremonial** use of language, for example, can serve both the expressive and directive functions.

Language can also serve functions other than the informative, expressive, and directive. For example, a **performative utterance** is an utterance that *performs* the very action that it reports or describes. Thus, when I say, "I apologize," not only do my words describe what I am doing, but also their utterance constitutes the doing of it.

READ PAGES 61–65 OF THE TEXT

2.3 The Forms of Discourse

Sentences can be classified according to their *grammatical form* as either **declarative, interrogative, imperative,** or **exclamatory.** These four grammatical *forms* of sentences should be carefully distinguished from the informative, expressive, and directive *functions* of sentences previously discussed. You should keep in mind the difference between form and function, and you should not assume that declarative sentences can serve only the informative function, or that exclamatory sentences can serve only the expressive function, or that interrogative and imperative sentences can serve only the directive function. The numerous examples given in the text show how any one of the four grammatical forms can serve any of the three functions. For example, "I had a very nice time at your party" is declarative in form, but it serves an expressive rather than an informative function. "I'd like some more coffee" is also declarative in form but it serves a directive function.

SOLUTIONS

to selected exercises on pages 65–67

You should regard each of the exercises in the text as a kind of self-quiz, by means of which you can check on the thoroughness of your understanding of the material. You should try to solve each problem *before* looking up the answer. In this way you can discover the gaps in your understanding and can determine which parts of the text you need to restudy.

Page 65, I, #2:

Informative: Judges do not know how to rehabilitate criminals, because no one knows how to rehabilitate criminals.

Directive: Let us learn how to rehabilitate criminals.

Expressive: To evoke a desire to learn how to rehabilitate criminals.

Page 65, I, #6:

Informative: The passage is a refutation of the philosophical theory that every human action is motivated by the pursuit of pleasure.

Page 66, I, #11:

Directive: Be armed!

Expressive: To evoke a desire to be armed.

Informative: Being unarmed causes you to be despised, which is evil.

Page 66, I, #16:

Directive: Don't be patriotic.

Expressive: To evoke feelings of disapproval for patriotism.

Informative: Patriotism prevents peace.

Page 67, I, #21:

Informative: All desires are directed toward particular objects rather than toward the pleasures arising from these objects, because a person would not derive any pleasure from a particular object unless that person had a desire for that object rather than for some other object.

SOLUTIONS
to selected exercises on pages 67–70

Page 67, II, #2:

Asserts that the government's classification of ice as a "food product" implies that Antarctica is one of the world's foremost food producers.

Intended to cause critical reappraisal of the government's classification of ice as a "food product."

Provides evidence that the speaker has a sense of humor, has a sense of the ridiculous, and does not assume that the government always acts wisely.

Page 68, II, #6:

Asserts that the writer has tried to understand human acts, and not to laugh at them, nor to lament them, nor to detest them.

Intended to cause a more "objective" approach to the study of human acts, and an acceptance of the writer's ideas as "objective."

Provides evidence that the writer has tried to study and to understand human acts objectively without being influenced by his own personal emotional reaction to these acts.

Page 68, II, #11:

Asserts that we are foolish to boast about the middle classes, for they (and not the lower classes) are the cause of the turbulence and every other evil temper of this evil age.

Intended to cause hostility toward the middle classes rather than toward the lower classes.

Provides evidence that the speaker is hostile toward the middle classes.

Page 69, II, #16:

Asserts that wisdom and understanding will be imputed to any silent man, even a fool.

Intended to cause people to talk less and understand more.

[Note the proverb that follows in the Bible two lines later: "A fool takes no pleasure in understanding, but only in expressing his opinion."]

Provides evidence that the speaker believes that incessant chattering is the sign of a fool.

Page 69, II, #21:

Asserts that when a person who has the basic material comforts of life does not enjoy life enough to value it, the reason is generally that he is totally selfish.

Intended to cause people to be less selfish and more altruistic.

Provides evidence that the speaker believes that complete selfishness is self-defeating and that altruism enhances the enjoyment and value of life.

READ PAGES 70–73 OF THE TEXT

2.4 Emotive Words

It was explained in an earlier section how a single sentence could have both an informative function and an expressive function. Similarly, a single word can have not only a literal or cognitive meaning but also an emotive significance or emotive meaning. In fact, the same object or event can be described in alternative ways by different words that have the same literal meaning but different emotive meanings.

EXERCISES
on page 73

The value of these exercises is to be obtained from actually creating what is called for, so no sample answers will be provided here. However, the following "conjugations of irregular verbs" might be found interesting:

I study conscientiously.
You get your work done.
He is a grind.

I am unique.
You are an individual.
He is different.

I am a gourmet.
You enjoy good food.
He is a glutton.

I am serious.
You are quiet.
He is dull.

READ PAGES 73–77 OF THE TEXT

2.5 Kinds of Agreement and Disagreement

There are at least two kinds of disagreement:

1. **Disagreement in belief** occurs when two people hold incompatible beliefs about the facts of the universe.
2. **Disagreement in attitude** occurs when two people have different attitudes (feelings, emotions) toward something.

If there is agreement in belief but disagreement in attitude, the same fact may be described in two different ways, the two descriptions having the same literal meaning but different emotive meanings.

Disagreements in belief can be resolved by ascertaining the facts. Disagreements in attitude can be resolved either by appealing to additional facts in order to persuade a person to change his or her attitude, or simply by employing expressive discourse to evoke a change of attitude.

Both disagreements in belief and disagreements in attitude are *genuine* disagreements, in the sense that they are not *merely verbal.* A good example of a merely verbal disagreement can be found in the text on page 135, #17. It would be helpful to you to read this example right now. The disagreement is merely verbal because it can be entirely resolved by the merely verbal device of pointing out the ambiguity in the word "sound" (which can mean either an auditory sensation or a vibration in the air). A disagreement in attitude is not merely verbal because it cannot be resolved by any merely verbal clarification. A disagreement in attitude is a perfectly *genuine disagreement,* even though it is quite different from a disagreement in belief.

SOLUTIONS
to selected exercises on pages 78–81

Page 78, #2:

Agreement in belief that Mr. Blank's thoughts are different from those of other people.

Disagreement in attitude toward Mr. Blank: *a* approves and *b* disapproves.

Page 78, #6:

Disagreement in belief: *a* believes that Ms. Roe spoke at the meeting, and *b* believes that Ms. Roe did not speak at the meeting.

Agreement in attitude: both disapprove of Ms. Roe's conduct at the meeting.

Page 78, #11:

Disagreement in belief: *a* believes that life presents a person with only one opportunity to do some particular thing, and *b* believes that there will always be another opportunity.

Disagreement in attitude: *a* disapproves, whereas *b* approves, of letting the first opportunity go by.

Page 79, #16:

Disagreement in belief: *a* believes that the most important thing is not whether you won or lost, and *b* believes that the most important thing (in fact, "the only thing") is whether you won or lost.

Disagreement in attitude: *a* is concerned with how you played the game, and *b* couldn't care less.

Page 80, #21:

Agreement in belief: Man's happiness is largely dependent upon improvements in agriculture.

Disagreement in attitude: Washington approves and Russell disapproves of an agricultural way of life without modern machinery.

Page 81, #26:

Disagreement in belief: *a* believes that nothing ever comes from farming, and *b* believes that happiness can come from farming.

Disagreement in attitude: *a* abhors farming, whereas *b* enjoys it.

READ PAGES 81–85 OF THE TEXT

2.6 Emotively Neutral Language

There are contexts in which emotive language is legitimate and valuable, but there are other contexts in which language should be made as literal and nonemotive as possible. If one is objectively trying to ascertain the facts, or to determine the validity or invalidity of an argument, or to communicate information, then emotive language is only distracting and confusing. Empirical science and logic require a language that is as literal and nonemotive as possible.

EXERCISE
on page 85

Once again, the value of this exercise is to be obtained from the student discovering a suitable passage and performing the extraction of literal meaning.

EXAMINATION
on Chapter 2

The point of this examination is to give you a chance to test yourself on some of the material which is *not* covered in the exercises of Chapter 2. Write your answers on a separate sheet of paper, then check them against the answers given at the end of the examination. Do not write your answers in this book, because you may want to take this exam again for review purposes. If you miss a question, restudy the appropriate part of the text.

1. If you simply described, as objectively as you could, someone else's feelings, emotions, or attitudes concerning some particularly contro-

versial situation, would you be using language expressively or informatively?

2. Language is used directively when it is designed to cause other people to perform certain overt actions, whereas language is used expressively when it is designed to cause other people to ______.

3. Besides the three *functions* of language, sentences can also be classified into four grammatical *forms:* declarative, interrogative, imperative, and ______.

4. When a person asks a question and expects an answer, is he using language informatively, expressively, or directively?

5. If two people disagree as to what *attitude* a third person has toward a certain situation, this is a
   a. disagreement in belief.
   b. disagreement in attitude.
   c. merely verbal dispute.
   d. type of disagreement basically different from any of the above.

6. What is the best method for resolving disagreements in belief?

7. Are disagreements in attitude merely verbal?

8. Can disagreements in attitude ever be resolved by appealing to facts?

9. "I accept," "I apologize," and "I promise" are all examples of a special use of language called ______.

10. Give an example of two words which have the same literal or cognitive meaning but different emotive meanings.

11. For what purposes is it preferable to employ emotively neutral language rather than emotively colored language?

What *one* language function (informative, expressive, directive) is *primarily* intended to be served by each of the following quotations?

12. "But I say unto you, that ye resist not evil: but whosoever shall smite thee on thy right cheek, turn to him the other also." (Matthew 5:39)

13. "Thus demandeth my great love to the remotest ones: *be not considerate of thy neighbor!* Man is something that must be surpassed." (Friedrich Nietzsche, *Thus Spake Zarathustra*)

14. "The Bourgeoisie has stripped of its halo every occupation hitherto honored and looked up to with reverent awe. It has converted the physician, the lawyer, the priest, the poet, the man of science, into its paid wage laborers." (Marx and Engels, *The Communist Manifesto*)

15. "Perhaps the movement of the perihelion of Mercury could be explained in part by the oblateness of the sun."
16. "I would like you to wash your hands before dinner." (mother to child)
17. "I would like to thank you for your help."
18. "I'd appreciate some help with this."
19. "I'm hungry." (petulant child at bedtime trying to trick his parents into letting him stay up longer)
20. "There isn't much time left." (wife to husband reading the paper when he should be getting dressed for a dinner party)
21. "I had a very nice time at your party." (same husband to hostess)
22. "How do you do?" (upon being introduced at a cocktail party)
23. "I would like that to be delivered as soon as possible." (shopper to salesman)
24. "I hope you'll be able to meet me after class at the library."
25. "Wha'd'ya know about that!" (upon hearing an astonishing piece of news)
26. "We don't eat with our elbows on the table." (mother to child)
27. "It's great to see you again!" (upon greeting a good friend whom you haven't seen for years)

ANSWERS

1. Informatively.
2. Have a certain feeling, emotion, or attitude.
3. Exclamatory.
4. Directively.
5. (a) Disagreement in belief.
6. Ascertain the facts.
7. No.
8. Yes.
9. Performative utterance.
10. "Bureaucrat" and "public servant," or any other such pair of words.
11. To ascertain the facts, *or* to determine the validity or invalidity of an argument, *or* to communicate information.
12. Directive.
13. Directive.
14. Directive. (Eliminate the evils of the Bourgeoisie!)
15. Informative.
16. Directive.
17. Expressive.
18. Directive.
19. Directive.
20. Directive.
21. Expressive.
22. Expressive.
23. Directive.
24. Directive.
25. Expressive.
26. Directive.
27. Expressive.

Chapter 3
Informal Fallacies

READ PAGES 86–87 OF THE TEXT

3.1 Classification of Fallacies

A **fallacy** is sometimes defined as any type of incorrect argument, but in the present chapter the word "fallacy" is used more specifically to refer to arguments which, although incorrect, may be psychologically persuasive.

There are basically two different reasons why an argument, although incorrect, may nevertheless be psychologically persuasive, and fallacies can be divided accordingly into two broad categories, called formal fallacies and informal fallacies.

A **formal fallacy** is a type of argument which may be psychologically persuasive because it bears a superficial resemblance to a valid pattern of reasoning, but which nevertheless is invalid because it violates the principles of valid reasoning. In Part Two of the text, formal fallacies are discussed in connection with the principles of valid reasoning which they violate. An example of a formal fallacy would be

> All Yalies are students.
> Not all students are good at logic.
> Therefore, not all Yalies are good at logic.

An **informal fallacy** is a type of argument which, although incorrect, may nevertheless be psychologically persuasive either because we are deceived by some ambiguity in the language used to state the argument or because we are misled by some technique designed to *cause* us to *accept* a particular conclusion, even though the truth of that conclusion is not established by the premisses of the argument.

Informal fallacies can be divided into two groups: fallacies of relevance and fallacies of ambiguity.

READ PAGES 87–101 OF THE TEXT

3.2 Fallacies of Relevance

An argument can be classified as a **fallacy of relevance** if its premisses are *logically* irrelevant to its conclusion and therefore incapable of establishing the truth of its conclusion. (Notice that the fallacy of *Petitio Principii,* or begging the question, is also classified as a fallacy of relevance because its premisses are likewise not relevant to the objective of *establishing* the truth of its conclusion.)

It may be difficult at first to understand how a person can be psychologically persuaded to accept the truth of a particular conclusion even though the premisses of the argument used are logically irrelevant to the conclusion. But if you reflect on the power of emotive language to produce such feelings as desire, hatred, fear, pity, reverence, enthusiasm, and approval and disapproval, you will realize that it is possible, through a clever use of language, to persuade a person to *accept* a particular conclusion, even though no logically correct argument has been used to *prove* the conclusion. The premisses of an argument may be psychologically or emotively relevant to the conclusion without being logically relevant. It is in this way that an argument can be persuasive without being correct. Psychological relevance is often confused with logical relevance when one is unaware that language is being used expressively or directively rather than informatively.

In studying the following review of the thirteen fallacies of relevance discussed in the text, you should pay particular attention to the way in which such fallacious arguments might seem persuasive and the way in which these fallacies can be easily recognized and avoided.

1. ***Argumentum ad Baculum* (*appeal to force*).** The fallacy of *argumentum ad baculum* is committed whenever one uses a threat of force or coercion to cause acceptance of a particular proposition. Obviously, a proposition is not proved *true* just because someone has the power to coerce you to assent to the proposition. When a parent says to a child, "It is right to do such and such," the parent

cannot prove this proposition true by arguing, "If you don't agree, I'll spank you." You can't prove that it is morally wrong to murder by arguing that if you do murder you will probably be caught and punished. You can't prove that Christianity is true by arguing that if you don't believe in it you'll be punished. You can't prove that a particular action is right by arguing simply that God will punish you if you don't do it. Just as might does not make right, so the threat of force does not prove the truth of a proposition.

2. ***Argumentum ad Hominem (abusive).*** The fallacy of *argumentum ad hominem* (abusive) is committed whenever, instead of presenting evidence to disprove the truth of a particular proposition, one tries to cause rejection of the proposition by attacking, insulting, criticizing, disparaging, or abusing in any other way the person who asserted the proposition. An *ad hominem* argument may seem persuasive if, through a psychological process of transference, you allow the hostility that you may feel toward the abused person to spill over into a rejection of what he or she asserts. You can avoid being persuaded by an *ad hominem* argument if you remember that *your attitude* toward the person is logically independent of the truth or falsity of what he or she asserts.

Although there is no doubt about the fact that an *argumentum ad hominem* (abusive) is fallacious, there may nevertheless be some legitimate doubt about the extent to which a particular argument commits the *ad hominem* fallacy. For example, one could argue, "Johnny is the stupidest kid in the class, so his answer to this complicated algebra problem is obviously false." If this is considered as an *inductive* argument, it certainly seems to have a high degree of probability, since if Johnny has continually made mistakes in the past there is a high probability that he will make a mistake this time also. But notice that the strength of this inductive argument depends upon the additional, tacitly assumed premiss that it is very unlikely that someone who had continually made mistakes in the past would suddenly cease to make them now.

In general, what we have to guard against in *ad hominem* arguments is assuming (without further proof) that there is some logical or causal connection (and not merely an emotive connection) between the *falsity* of a particular assertion and the despicable moral character, objectionable personality traits, dangerous political beliefs, fanatical, heretical, unpopular, or absurd religious faith, corrupt economic practices, race, national origin, and so on, of the person who made the assertion. Unless some relationship is objectively established between the truth or falsity of a particular assertion and a characteristic of the person who made the assertion, any argument which simply abused the person and then concluded that his or her assertion was false would commit the *ad hominem* (abusive) fallacy.

3. ***Argumentum ad Hominem* (*circumstantial*).** The fallacy of *argumentum ad hominem* (circumstantial) occurs when two people disagree about the truth of some proposition and when one person, instead of trying to prove his or her contention, tries simply to cause acceptance of the contention by appealing to the special circumstances of the opponent. The fallacy has two different forms:

(1) In its first form the fallacy is committed when one person tries to persuade his or her opponent to accept the truth of a particular proposition on the grounds that it follows from the opponent's basic beliefs (either in religion or politics or economics or other areas). But the fact that a proposition follows from the opponent's basic beliefs does not prove that proposition true, since the opponent's basic beliefs may be false.

Such an *argumentum ad hominem* (circumstantial) is a legitimate technique in debate if your objective is to force your opponent either to accept your contention or to admit an inconsistency in his or her position. But if you go further and conclude that your contention is *true,* you have committed a fallacy. In other words, an *ad hominem* (circumstantial) argument may be an effective technique in any debate where the object is to score points against your opponent, but no such argument ever establishes the truth or falsity of any proposition. Nevertheless, such arguments are sometimes psychologically persuasive with the audience as well as with your opponent, because the attitude of approval built up toward you as a result of your rhetorical skill may be transferred by a process of association to approval of what you are asserting.

(2) The second form of the *ad hominem* (circumstantial) fallacy is committed by a person who concludes that a particular proposition must be false on the grounds that his or her opponent asserts the proposition only because of his or her special circumstances (economic, political, religious, etc.) and not for any objective reason. But to show that self-interest rather than objective evidence is the only reason why your opponent asserts a particular proposition does not *prove the proposition false,* even though such an argument may be an effective technique in debate.

In both forms of the *ad hominem* (circumstantial) fallacy, one ignores the primary issue of whether the proposition in question is true or false, and one digresses to the logically independent issue of how the proposition in question is related to the opponent's other beliefs or special circumstances. But any attempt to use this digression as a basis for reaching a conclusion about the truth or falsity of the proposition in question is fallacious.

4. *Argumentum ad Ignorantiam* (*argument from ignorance*). The fallacy of *argumentum ad ignorantiam* is committed whenever one concludes that a particular proposition is true on the grounds that it has not been proved false, or whenever one concludes that a particular proposition is false on the grounds that it has not been proved true. From the *absence* of proof, no conclusion whatsoever should be drawn concerning the truth or falsity of the proposition.

Of course there are some arguments which might appear to commit the *argumentum ad ignorantiam* fallacy but which can be more fairly interpreted as correct inductive arguments with additional, tacitly assumed premisses. For example, the following could be interpreted as a highly probable inductive argument (with a suppressed premiss):

> The F.B.I., after a thorough investigation, has discovered no evidence that there is an elephant loose in the White House. Therefore, there is no elephant loose in the White House.

This argument *as it stands* certainly does commit the *argumentum ad ignorantiam* fallacy, but the argument is not really fallacious when one adds the tacitly assumed premiss that if there were an elephant loose in the White House, it would be highly probable that a thorough investigation by the F.B.I. would produce evidence of it.

The general conclusion to be drawn is that an *argumentum ad ignorantiam* is always fallacious *as it stands,* and can be made correct only if an additional premiss is supplied. Of course it may not be possible to supply a *plausible* additional premiss which would eliminate the fallacy, in which case the argument remains fallacious. A difficulty may arise in deciding when the required additional premiss is plausible. Perhaps it is our willingness to accept the additional premiss without special evidence which accounts for the psychological persuasiveness of some *argumentum ad ignorantiam* fallacies. After all, we have developed a very strong habit of expecting that if an event has occurred, then it should be easy to discover evidence of it. But some reflection upon the arguments for and against the existence of extrasensory perception ought to make us wary of this habit.

5. *Argumentum ad Misericordiam* (*appeal to pity*). The fallacy of *argumentum ad misericordiam* is committed whenever a person tries to prove the truth or cause acceptance of a particular factual conclusion by arousing a feeling of pity.

6. *Argumentum ad Populum.* The fallacy of *argumentum ad populum* is committed whenever a person tries to cause acceptance of a particular conclusion by using any of the emotively based techniques of advertising or propaganda to arouse the enthusiasm, approval, and desires of the multitude. There are a variety of such techniques, two of which are particularly common and effective:

(1) In the *snob appeal* argument one tries to associate acceptance of the conclusion with other desirable things. For example, one might try to cause acceptance of the conclusion that a particular product is best by surrounding that product with the kind of things that will stimulate the desire, arouse the admiration, and win the approval of the consumer.

(2) In the *band-wagon* argument one might argue that a particular proposition is true because everyone believes it; or that something is desirable (*worthy* of being desired) because everybody as a matter of fact desires it; or that a particular product is best because everyone is buying it.

7. *Argumentum ad Verecundiam* (*appeal to authority*). An appeal to authority is fallacious whenever someone tries to win assent to a particular proposition by appealing to the testimony of an authority, when in fact the person appealed to is not really a genuine authority concerning the subject matter dealt with by the proposition in question. In order to apply this definition in a particular case, we would have to determine whether the person appealed to is or is not a genuine authority concerning the subject matter in question. But what makes a person a genuine authority? And how can *we* know whether someone is a genuine authority concerning a particular subject matter? One plausible answer to these questions would be to hold that a person is a genuine authority concerning a particular subject matter if a very high percentage of his or her previous assertions concerning that subject matter have turned out to be true. Using this criterion, a legitimate appeal to authority could then be analyzed in the following way, where X stands for the person appealed to as an authority, and p stands for the proposition whose truth is claimed to be established by the appeal to authority.

X asserts p.
p is a part of the subject matter S.
A very high percentage of the assertions made by X concerning S have turned out to be true.
Therefore, p is true.

In this form, the argument is a very strong or highly probable inductive argument. Up to now X has usually been right about S, so he or she is probably right this time too. Notice, however, that in order to know whether an appeal to authority is legitimate or fallacious, we must first know whether or not the previous assertions made by X concerning S are true. This presents no difficulty, at least in principle, when applied to the areas of scientific and everyday knowledge. But if we turn to religion and ask whether it is legitimate to appeal to some religious leader (or sacred writing) as the *sole authority and source of knowledge* concerning the nature and actions of God, then we encounter an interesting problem. For if we claim that X is the sole authority and source of knowledge concerning S, then it follows that *we* can have no way of knowing whether X's previous assertions about S are indeed true, and thus any appeal to X would be fallacious. It does not help to invoke another authority to support the previous assertions of the first authority, for we would have no better grounds for regarding the new authority as genuine than we had for regarding the first authority as genuine. And we cannot use the authorities to justify each other, for such an argument would be ultimately circular, as in the following example:

A: What the Church says is true because the Church is an authority.
B: What grounds do you have for holding that the Church is a genuine authority?
A: The authority of the Church is implied in the Bible.
B: And why do you hold that the Bible is true?
A: Because the Church says that the Bible is an authority, and what the Church says is true.

We have now returned full circle to *A*'s original claim. There seems to be no way of breaking out of this vicious circle, because neither authority can be known to be genuine so long as it is held that they are the sole authorities and sources of knowledge concerning the subject matter in question.

It should be obvious that the above problem does not arise with respect to scientific authorities, since they are never claimed to be the sole authorities and sources of knowledge, because we can always appeal directly to the objective evidence which is in principle open to examination by any competent investigator.

Fallacious appeals to authority may sometimes be psychologically persuasive because of the feeling of respect that we may have for eminent people or even for our elders or professors, or because of the awe and reverence which we may feel in a place of worship or in the presence of a religious person. The basis of this persuasiveness may, of course, be only emotional.

8. *Accident.* The fallacy of accident is committed whenever one argues that because a certain generalization is usually true, it holds therefore for a particular case, even though, as a matter of fact, the particular case has "accidental" or individual characteristics which make the generalization inapplicable (and therefore not true for that case).

9. *Converse Accident* (*hasty generalization*). The fallacy of converse accident is committed whenever one argues that because a statement is true for some particular class of cases, it is therefore true in general, for all cases.

10. *False Cause*. The fallacy of false cause is committed whenever one concludes that a particular causal connection exists by arguing from premisses that do not actually establish the causal connection, because of a violation of the correct methods of induction (to be studied in Part Three of the text).

In the typical case, the premiss would assert that X was preceded by Y, and the conclusion would assert that X was caused by Y.

The fallacy of false cause is sometimes confused with the fallacy of converse accident (hasty generalization) if both arguments are characterized simply as the drawing of a fallacious generalization from insufficient evidence. But the two fallacies can be easily distinguished if you keep in mind that the fallacy of false cause argues that X causes Y because X precedes Y, which is not an inference from particular to general but an inference from a temporal relation to a causal relation. On the other hand, the fallacy of converse accident argues that some statement is true in general because it is true in a particular case, but the statement in question is not normally concerned with causal connections.

11. *Petitio Principii* (*begging the question*). The fallacy of *petitio principii* is committed whenever one tries to establish the truth of a particular conclusion by arguing from premisses which contain the very proposition that one is trying to prove. Such an argument is not fallacious in the sense of being invalid, for if the premisses were all true then the conclusion would have to be true also. But such an argument is fallacious in the sense of being an incorrect procedure for *establishing* the truth of the conclusion, since the argument asks us to *assume* as a premiss the very proposition whose truth we are trying to *establish* as the conclusion. We cannot legitimately assume the truth of what we are trying to prove, for if an argument is needed to establish the truth of a proposition, then it would be begging the question to assume that proposition without argument.

All circular arguments are instances of the fallacy of *petitio principii.*

In trying to determine whether an argument commits the fallacy of *petitio principii,* remember that the proposition asserted in the conclusion need not be stated in exactly the same words in the premisses so long as the two statements are equivalent in meaning.

12. ***Complex Question.*** One kind of complex question is a question which cannot be answered simply yes or no without implying that a certain answer has already been given to a prior (but unasked) question. The fallacy of complex question occurs whenever such a complex question is posed, a simple yes or no answer is given, and then an inference is drawn from the implied answer to the prior (but unasked) question. The fallacy can occur either in a dialogue where one person poses the complex question, a second person responds yes or no without being aware that he or she is by implication also conceding an unwanted answer to the prior, unasked question, and then the first person draws the conclusion which follows from the implied answer to the prior question; or the fallacy can occur when a person rhetorically poses a complex question, answers it either implicitly or explicitly, and then goes on to draw the fallacious inference.

There are two other kinds of complex questions which can also serve as the basis for the fallacy of complex question. One of these is the kind of complex question which can be divided into two separate questions: For example, "Are you in favor of giving women equal rights and thus letting them take over completely?" Another example would be, "Are you in favor of conserving energy and thus giving up all hope of further economic growth?"

The third kind of complex question involves the use of a question-begging epithet to formulate a question to which a simple yes or no answer may not be appropriate. For example, "Is the lowering of tariffs going to have a disastrous impact on certain American industries?" or "Are we heading straight toward a horrible welfare state?"

13. ***Ignoratio Elenchi (irrelevant conclusion).*** The fallacy of *ignoratio elenchi* is committed whenever one tries to establish a particular conclusion by arguing from premisses which are actually directed toward proving some other conclusion. Such an argument may be psychologically persuasive if the attitude of approval built up toward this other conclusion can be transferred to the conclusion that the speaker is trying to establish.

You must be careful not to confuse the fallacy of *ignoratio elenchi* with the other fallacies of relevance. All twelve of the fallacies discussed so far are fallacies of relevance, and in each of these fallacies (except *petitio principii*) the premisses are logically irrelevant to the conclusion. In this sense, each of these fallacies has an *irrelevant conclusion*. But the other fallacies of relevance should not for this reason be confused with *the* fallacy of irrelevant conclusion (*ignoratio elenchi*), which is specifically the fallacy of trying to prove a particular conclusion by arguing from premisses which are directed toward proving a different conclusion.

SOLUTIONS
to selected exercises on pages 101–110

In some of these exercises you may be able to identify more than one fallacy of relevance in a single argument, but in most cases one fallacy will be much more obvious and important than any others.

It might be helpful to make a list of the thirteen fallacies on a note card, so that you won't have to leaf back repeatedly through the text.

Page 101, #2: *Ignoratio Elenchi* (irrelevant conclusion).

Page 102, #6: *Argumentum ad Verecundiam* (appeal to authority). There may be some disagreement over whether this appeal to authority is legitimate or fallacious. It could be argued, perhaps with considerable justification, that there is no fallacy here because Freud is a genuine authority on psychology, and the possibility or impossibility of religious *belief* (which is the question at issue here) is properly a question of psychology rather than theology. Notice that the question does not concern the existence or nature of God or any other theological issue; the question is one of human *belief,* which is a psychological question on which Freud may very well be a genuine authority. At least the argument is not as obviously fallacious as it would be if Freud were appealed to as an authority on a theological issue.

Page 103, #11: *Petitio Principii* (begging the question).

Page 104, #16: *Petitio Principii* (begging the question).

Page 105, #21: *Argumentum ad Hominem* (circumstantial).

Page 105, #26: Accident.

Page 106, #31: *Argumentum ad Hominem* (circumstantial and/or abusive). Also, perhaps, *ignoratio elenchi* (irrelevant conclusion), because the premiss is directed toward proving merely that Nietzsche's philosophy was unphilosophical, whereas the conclusion actually drawn asserts that Nietzsche was personally more philosophical.

Page 107, #36: *Argumentum ad Hominem* (circumstantial), "Poisoning the well."

Page 107, #41: *Argumentum ad Misericordiam* (appeal to pity).

Page 108, #45: Notice that the text lists *argumentum ad verecundiam* (appeal to authority) as the fallacy committed in this argument. This is correct so long as you recognize that it was Galileo's adversary in the argument and not Galileo himself who accepted Aristotle as an authority on physics. Galileo's basic method in science is to avoid appeals to authority and instead to examine by himself the "great book of nature," which is open to investigation by any scientist who is not satisfied with merely appealing to authorities to settle questions of fact. Given this context, it might be plausible to accuse Galileo of an *argumentum ad hominem* (circumstantial) rather than an appeal to authority, since Galileo's adversary is in the special circumstances of being a convinced Aristotelian, and Galileo is trying to get him to accept the conclusion that air has weight by pointing out that to deny this would be inconsistent with his basic belief in Aristotle's physics.

Page 108, #46: *Argumentum ad Ignorantiam* (argument from ignorance).

READ PAGES 110–117 OF THE TEXT

3.3 Fallacies of Ambiguity

A word or phrase can be **ambiguous** in a particular context if it can have two or more different meanings in that context. Ambiguities can arise in several different ways: An **equivocation** occurs if a word or phrase purporting to have a single meaning in a particular context is used with two or more distinct meanings in that context. A phrase may also be ambiguous if it is **amphibolous,** that is, if it has an awkward or misleading grammatical structure which allows it to be understood in two different ways. A phrase can also be ambiguous if a different meaning is produced by giving a different **accent** to the individual words. And finally, an ambiguity can arise if there is confusion between the **collective** and **distributive** senses of a class term. Each of these kinds of ambiguity, when it occurs in an argument, can be the source of a fallacy of ambiguity.

A **fallacy of ambiguity** is a type of argument which contains an ambiguous word or phrase whose shift in meaning makes the argument fallacious. In the typical case, the ambiguous word or phrase must be given one meaning in order for the premisses to be acceptable, but it must be given a different meaning if the conclusion is to follow from the premisses. Such arguments may be psychologically persuasive if the shift in meaning passes unnoticed. There are (at least) five different ways in which a fallacy of ambiguity may be committed.

1. ***Equivocation.*** An **equivocation** occurs if a word or phrase purporting to have a single meaning in a particular context is used with

two or more distinct meanings in that context. The ambiguity that is then present is not the result of an amphibolous grammatical structure or of a change in the way the words are accented or of a confusion between the collective and distributive senses of a class term, but it is rather the result of the fact that in natural languages many words have more than one meaning, and these meanings are sometimes confused with one another.

A **fallacy of equivocation** occurs in an argument whenever there is an equivocation on a particular word or phrase whose shift in meaning renders the argument fallacious.

To see how an equivocation can produce a fallacy, consider the following argument:

All *A* are *B*.
All *B* are *C*.
Therefore, all *A* are *C*.

A, B, and *C* are to be understood as standing for words, in this case class terms. No matter what classes are designated by the words represented by *A, B,* and *C,* so long as each word designates the same class in each of its two occurrences, the argument is valid. But suppose, for example, that there is an equivocation on the word *B*. Suppose that in order for the premisses to be true, the word *B* must be given one meaning (say B_1) in its first occurrence and a different meaning (say B_2) in its second occurrence. When the ambiguity of the word *B* is made explicit, the argument actually reads as follows:

All *A* are B_1.
All B_2 are *C*.
Therefore, all *A* are *C*.

Now this argument is clearly invalid, and hence the original argument above is invalid if there is an equivocation on the word *B*.

The fallacy of equivocation can also occur in an argument when there is an equivocation on a **relative term** (such as "tall" or "good"). A relative term is a term whose meaning changes in relation to the context. Many adjectives are relative terms in the sense that their meaning changes in relation to the noun that they are used to modify. Thus, a tall man is tall in relation to average men; a tall mountain is tall in relation to average mountains. Hence, a tall man and a tall mountain are not tall in the same sense (since they are not the same height). The word "useful" is also a relative term in most contexts, since the usefulness of something is relative to the end desired. If there were no ends that we desired, then nothing would be useful as a means. "Good" is also a relative term in many contexts for the same reason. If an apple is good for cooking, it does not follow necessarily that it is good for eating uncooked. If a car is good around town, it does not follow necessarily that it is good at sustained high speeds. If a man is a good carpenter, it does not follow necessarily that he is a good neighbor. Most things are called good in relation to some *human desire or preference*. You may now be wondering whether there is anything that is good in a *nonrelative* or *absolute* sense, that is, anything whose goodness is not relative to human desires and preferences. Can you think of any evidence or good reason which would justify answering this question one way or the other?

2. ***Amphiboly.*** An **amphibolous** statement is ambiguous because its grammatical construction is so loose, or awkward, or misleading that it can be interpreted in two ways, and thus the statement can have two different meanings. The **fallacy of amphiboly** is committed in an argument when one of the premisses is an amphibolous statement and when one interpretation of that premiss is required in order to make it true, but another interpretation (which would make it false) is required if the conclusion of the argument is to follow from the premisses. In other words, the amphibolous statement must be interpreted one way if we are to assent to its truth, and it must be interpreted the other way if we are to assent to the inference from premisses to conclusion.

3. ***Accent.*** The meaning of some sentences can be changed by changing the way in which individual words or phrases are accented. The **fallacy of accent** is committed in an argument when one of the premisses is such a sentence, and when one accenting of that sentence is required in order to make it true, but another accenting (which would make it false) is required if the conclusion of the argument is to follow from the premisses. In other words, the sentence must be accented one way if we are to assent to its truth, and it must be accented the other way if we are to assent to the inference from premisses to conclusion.

The fallacy of accent is also committed in an argument when the meaning of the conclusion can be changed by changing the accenting, and when the conclusion must be accented one way in order to produce its intended meaning but must be accented the other way if it is to follow from the premisses.

The ambiguity of the conclusion can also be the source of a fallacy of equivocation or amphiboly.

Common instances of the fallacy of accent are misquoting, quoting out of context, inserting or deleting italics in a quotation (without so indicating), and deleting a part of a quotation without so indicating with three dots.

4. ***Composition.*** The **fallacy of composition** can occur in two different ways:

(1) The fallacy of composition occurs when one starts with a premiss which asserts that some particular attribute belongs to each of the individual parts of a whole, and then concludes that the attribute must therefore belong to the whole. For example,

> Atoms are invisible to the unaided human eye.
> Tables and chairs are composed of atoms.
> Therefore, tables and chairs are invisible to the unaided human eye.

(2) The fallacy of composition occurs also when one starts with a premiss which asserts that some particular attribute belongs to each of the individual members of a collection (taken **distributively** or individually; that is, one at a time), and then concludes that the attribute must therefore belong to the collection or totality of those members (taken **collectively;** that is, as a group). For example,

> *A, B, C, D,* and *E* are the best players.
> Therefore, they will compose the best team.

The fallacy of composition is sometimes confused with the fallacy of converse accident (hasty generalization) if both arguments are thought of simply as proceeding from particular statements to general statements. But the two fallacies can be easily distinguished if you keep in mind that the fallacy of converse accident is not concerned with a whole made up of parts or with a collection made up of elements, but simply with some statement that is asserted to be true in general because it is true in some particular case. On the other hand, the fallacy of composition is always concerned with a whole made up of parts or with a collection made up of elements, and the fallacy of composition always argues that some particular attribute belongs to a whole because it belongs to each part, or that it belongs to a collection because it belongs to each element of the collection.

5. ***Division.*** The **fallacy of division** is exactly the reverse of the fallacy of composition. Once again there are two different ways in which the fallacy of division can occur:

(1) The fallacy of division occurs when one starts with a premiss which asserts that some particular attribute belongs to a whole, and then concludes that the attribute must therefore belong to each of

the individual parts of the whole, or to some particular part or parts of the whole. For example,

> The United States Army is powerful.
> Therefore, each soldier in it is powerful.

(2) The fallacy of division occurs also when one starts with a premiss which asserts that some particular attribute belongs to a collection or totality of elements (taken **collectively;** that is, as a group), and then concludes that the attribute must therefore belong to each of the individual elements of the collection (taken **distributively** or individually; that is, one at a time), or to some particular element or elements of the collection. For example,

> Gerald Ford was rejected by the voters.
> Senator Robert Dole was a voter.
> Therefore, Gerald Ford was rejected by Senator Robert Dole.

The fallacy of division is sometimes confused with the fallacy of accident if both arguments are thought of simply as proceeding from general statements to particular statements. But the two fallacies can be easily distinguished if you keep in mind that the fallacy of accident is not concerned with a whole made up of parts or with a collection made up of elements, but simply with some statement which is asserted to be true in some particular case because it is true "in general." On the other hand, the fallacy of division is always concerned with a whole made up of parts or with a collection made up of elements, and the fallacy of division always argues that some particular attribute belongs to some part or parts of a whole because it belongs to the whole, or that it belongs to some element or elements of a collection because it belongs to the collection.

SOLUTIONS
to selected exercises on pages 117–125

Page 117, #2: Equivocation (on "poor").

Page 118, #6: Amphiboly.

Page 118, #11: Equivocation (on "no news").

Page 119, #16: Division.

Page 120, #2: *Argumentum ad Hominem* (abusive).

Page 120, #6: Accent (no *more* money).

Page 121, #11: *Argumentum ad Hominem* (abusive).

Page 122, #16: Division.

Page 122, #21: *Argumentum ad Hominem* (circumstantial).

Page 122, #26: Equivocation (on "found").

Page 123, #31: Converse accident (hasty generalization).

Page 123, #36: Composition *or* accident.

Page 124, #41: Accident.

Page 124, #46: *Ignoratio Elenchi* (irrelevant conclusion).

EXAMINATION
on Chapter 3

The point of this examination is to give you a chance to test yourself on some of the material which is *not* covered in the exercises of Chapter 3, and also to give you another group of informal fallacies (with answers) so that you can have a fairly accurate measure of your ability to identify the various informal fallacies.

Write your answers on a separate sheet of paper, then check them against the answers given at the end of the examination. If you miss a question, restudy the appropriate part of the text.

The first twenty-eight questions consist of arguments which commit informal fallacies. Identify the fallacy in each argument.

1. Water extinguishes fire.
   Oxygen is a part of water.
   Therefore, oxygen will extinguish fire.

2. Aquinas's rational proofs of the existence of God are fallacious, for he was just trying to justify through reason what he already believed through faith.

3. Priests take a vow of poverty.
   The Church is a corporate body composed of priests.
   Therefore, the Church should not own property.

4. The Church condemns the pill.
   Therefore, the pill is wrong.

5. "Why is this the right thing to do?"
   "Because it is morally obligatory."
   "But why should I do what is morally obligatory?"
   "Because it is the right thing to do."

6. I ought always to do what is right.
   I have a right to say what I think.
   Therefore, I ought always to say what I think.

7. Any farmer who now grows potatoes could make more money if he grew artichokes, since artichokes are a luxury food and the profit margin is higher. Therefore, if all farmers who now grow potatoes were to grow artichokes, they would all make more money.

8. The existence of a Creator is implied by scientific terminology, for the phrase "law of nature" is constantly used in science, and whenever there is a law there must be a law-giver.

9. AMBASSADOR: "Mr. Prime Minister, it would be fairer if your country increased its contribution to our mutual defense costs, for in order for us to continue paying our present contribution without hurting our balance of payments we would have to raise the tariff on imports such as those we have been purchasing from your country."

10. Boiling an egg for six minutes will give you a hard-boiled egg. Therefore, someone in Mexico City can make a hard-boiled egg by boiling an egg for six minutes.

11. The "Abominable Snowman" obviously doesn't exist, since no one has ever produced convincing evidence of him.

12. According to the law, a man is innocent until proved guilty. So Mr. Mafia must be innocent of the charge of bribery, since he has not yet been proved guilty. Therefore, since Mr. Mafia is innocent, it would be wrong to convict him.

13. General Jack D. Ripper believes that it is absolutely essential to our future security that we immediately start mass production of the new RS-101 long-range bomber. But his arguments are hardly deserving of careful consideration, for in a couple of weeks General Ripper will retire from the Air Force and become chairman of the board and be given large stock options in the Hawk Corporation, which manufactures the RS-101.

14. Harvard produces the best Ph.D.'s in the country, so any Harvard Ph.D. is better than any other Ph.D.

15. No one has discovered any limits to the universe. In fact, it is impossible to discover any limits to the universe, since to know that the universe had a limit one would have to go beyond the limit and make sure that nothing was there, which would be impossible in the case of a limit to the universe, since the universe by definition contains everything that exists, so no one by definition can go outside the

universe to verify that nothing exists there. Therefore, the universe must be infinite.

16. All fraternity members are playboys.
John is a member of Phi Beta Kappa.
Phi Beta Kappa is a fraternity.
Therefore, John is a playboy.

17. The Constitution guarantees freedom of speech. Therefore, if a person believes that the only way to achieve certain reforms is through rioting, he should have the freedom of inciting to riot.

18. In some countries where atheism has spread in recent years the suicide rate has also gone up. Therefore, loss of belief in God is a cause of suicide.

19. Insane people and criminals are locked up against their will. Therefore, our country is not truly committed to the principle that all men are free and that one of their inalienable rights is liberty.

20. All the angles of a triangle are equal to two right angles. *B* is an angle of this triangle. Therefore, *B* is equal to two right angles.

21. The Constitution guarantees freedom of speech, so it would be unconstitutional to outlaw the filibuster in the Senate.

22. The flights to New York are cancelled. Therefore, we'll have to take the train.

23. A great many charges of corruption have been brought against Senator Porkbarrel, and he has had numerous opportunities to refute them, but he has never done so. Therefore, he must be guilty as charged.

24. The welfare program is totally unnecessary. Why, I know a guy who runs a very lucrative illegal gambling operation and who drives his new Cadillac down every week to collect his welfare check.

25. "Why should I do this?"
"Because it is right."
"Why is it right?"
"Because God commands it."
"Why does God command it?"
"Because it is right."

26. Conscientious students will study even without the threat of impending examinations, and hopelessly lazy students won't study even with the threat of impending examinations, so examinations are useless as devices for getting students to study.

27. The word "God" is not meaningless. It means, by definition, a supreme being. Therefore, since the meaning of the word exists, and the meaning of the word is a supreme being, it follows that a supreme being must exist.

Answer the following questions in as brief a way as possible:

28. Can an argument which commits the fallacy of *petitio principii* (begging the question) be sound?
29. The "band-wagon" argument is usually an instance of the *argumentum ad* ______.
30. If your answer to a question has the effect of conceding an implied answer to a prior but unasked question, you may be about to fall for the fallacy of ______.
31. Misquoting may be the basis of a fallacy of ______.
32. State clearly the two different forms of the fallacy of division.
33. There are really two different ways in which an *argumentum ad hominem* (circumstantial) can occur. In one way, the fallacy is committed by a person who concludes that a particular proposition must be false on the grounds that his or her opponent asserts the proposition only because of his or her special circumstances and not for any objective reason. What is the other way in which an *argumentum ad hominem* (circumstantial) can occur?
34. Advertising "testimonials" may be interpreted as instances of either of two fallacies: (1) ______ and (2) ______.
35. Common to all arguments which commit fallacies of relevance is the characteristic that their premisses are *logically irrelevant* to, and therefore incapable of establishing the truth of, their conclusions. But the specific fallacy of *ignoratio elenchi* (irrelevant conclusion) has an additional characteristic which distinguishes it from all other fallacies of relevance. What is that additional characteristic?
36. Explain specifically how an *argumentum ad hominem* (abusive) may be psychologically persuasive in spite of its logical incorrectness.
37. Relative terms (like "tall" and "good") may be the source of the fallacy of ______.
38. Explain why an *argumentum ad ignorantiam* (argument from ignorance) may not be fallacious if used by a defense attorney in a court of law.
39. An advertiser who relies on snob appeal is using an *argumentum ad* ______.

40. Which of the fallacies of relevance is committed by a "circular argument"?

41. In parliamentary procedure, the motion "to divide the question" is closely related to which of the fallacies of relevance?

ANSWERS

1. Division.
2. *Argumentum ad Hominem* (circumstantial).
3. Composition.
4. *Argumentum ad Verecundiam* (appeal to authority).
5. *Petitio Principii* (begging the question).
6. Equivocation (on "right," which can mean either "morally obligatory" or "a privilege").
7. Composition.
8. Equivocation (on "law," which can mean either "descriptive, scientific law" or "prescriptive, legislative law").
9. *Argumentum ad Baculum* (appeal to force).
10. Accident (because of the altitude of Mexico City).
11. *Argumentum ad Ignorantiam* (argument from ignorance).
12. Equivocation (on "innocent," which can mean either "legally not guilty" or "factually not guilty").
13. *Argumentum ad Hominem* (circumstantial).
14. Division.
15. *Argumentum ad Ignorantiam* (argument from ignorance).
16. Equivocation (on "fraternity," which can mean either "undergraduate social organization" or "academic honor society").
17. Accident.
18. False cause.
19. Converse accident (hasty generalization).
20. Division.
21. Accident.
22. *Ignoratio Elenchi* (irrelevant conclusion).
23. *Argumentum ad Ignorantiam* (argument from ignorance).
24. Converse accident (hasty generalization).
25. *Petitio Principii* (begging the question).
26. Converse accident (hasty generalization).
27. Equivocation (on "meaning," which can mean either "the attributes connoted by the word" or "the things denoted by the word." For a full explanation of this distinction see the next chapter of the text.)
28. Yes.
29. *Populum.*
30. Complex question.
31. Accent.

32. (1) Arguing that because a whole has a certain attribute, each part must have that attribute.
    (2) Arguing that because a collection has a certain attribute, each member of that collection must have that attribute.
33. The other way in which the fallacy of *argumentum ad hominem* (circumstantial) is committed is when one person tries to persuade his or her opponent to accept the truth of a particular proposition on the grounds that it follows from the opponent's basic beliefs.
34. *Argumentum ad Populum; Argumentum ad Verecundiam* (appeal to authority).
35. The premisses are directed toward proving a conclusion different from the conclusion actually drawn.
36. The attitude of disapproval built up toward the man is transferred, by a process of psychological association, into rejection of what he asserts.
37. Equivocation.
38. Because according to the law the accused is to be presumed innocent *unless proved guilty*.
39. *Populum.*
40. *Petitio Principii* (begging the question).
41. Complex question.

Chapter 4
Definition

READ PAGES 126–132 OF THE TEXT

4.1 Five Purposes of Definition

Although we learn our native language primarily by observing and imitating the way other people use the language rather than by being given a definition of each word, there are various occasions when definitions can serve a useful purpose, and we can distinguish at least **five purposes of definition:**

1. ***To Increase Vocabulary.*** That is, to convey the meaning of a term to a person who does not yet know it.

2. ***To Eliminate Ambiguity.*** The purpose here might be to resolve a merely verbal dispute or to expose a fallacy of equivocation.

3. ***To Reduce Vagueness.*** That is, to eliminate or at least to reduce the vagueness of a term whose general meaning is known but whose exact range of application is not precisely specified. Here we are concerned with a **vague** term, which is a term whose range of application contains "borderline cases" such that common usage does not determine whether the term applies to them or not. For example, the term "wealthy" is vague because common usage does not specify precisely the exact borderline between wealthy people and middle-income people. The concept of a vague term must not be confused with the concept of an ambiguous term. A term is ambiguous in a given context if it has *two* or more *distinct* meanings and it is not clear from the context which meaning is intended. On the other hand, a term is vague if it has *one* meaning but with an unspecified, imprecise borderline to that meaning.

4. *To Explain Theoretically.* A definition of a term serves this purpose if it provides a useful theoretical (usually scientific) description of the entities to which the term is applied. For example, a scientific definition of "electron" would have as its purpose to explain theoretically, because the definition would describe electrons in terms of those attributes which in the context of the latest atomic theory were most useful for understanding or explaining theoretically the behavior of electrons. A definition likewise serves the purpose of explaining theoretically if it states how one concept is defined in terms of other concepts within the context of a theory. Newton's definition of "force" as the product of mass and acceleration is an excellent example of this kind of definition, in which a part of a scientific theory is actually embodied in the definition of one of the basic concepts of the theory.

5. *To Influence Attitudes.* Here the purpose of the definition is not to convey the literal meaning of a term but rather to influence someone's attitude toward something by phrasing the "definition" in language designed to have a certain emotive impact. For example, if someone disapproved of psychedelic drugs and wanted to produce a similar attitude of disapproval in other people, he could "define" psychedelic drugs as "substances which corrupt the mind and distort its perception of reality by producing weird and confusing hallucinations, illusions, fantasies, and other abnormal psychic states, often leading to a dangerous alienation from the world and a crippling destruction of the person's ability to adjust to reality." Whereas if someone approved of psychedelic drugs and wanted to produce a similar attitude of approval in other people he could "define" psychedelic drugs as "substances which liberate the human mind from the limitations and distortions of ordinary experience and which expand consciousness until it rises to an appreciation of the truth, beauty, and goodness at the heart of ultimate reality." The purpose of these definitions is obviously to influence attitudes rather than to provide a literal definition of "psychedelic drugs" in terms of their chemical structure and physiological effects.

4.2 Verbal Disputes and Definition

In a previous section of the text we distinguished two kinds of *genuine* disagreements: disagreements in belief, in which two people disagree about a question of fact; and disagreements in attitude, in which two people have different attitudes toward something.

We can also distinguish two kinds of *verbal* disputes:

A **merely verbal dispute,** in which there is no genuine disagreement present, and in which the apparent disagreement results from confusing two different senses of an ambiguous term, so that the dispute can be resolved by the merely verbal device of eliminating the ambiguity;

An **apparently verbal dispute that is really a genuine disagreement in attitude,** in which there is an ambiguity present, which can be removed, but behind this ambiguity (and in some sense accounting for its presence in the dispute) there is a genuine disagreement in attitude, which cannot be resolved by merely removing the ambiguity.

SOLUTIONS

to selected exercises on pages 132–135

In this set of exercises you are asked to determine which of the three following types of dispute is present in each case: (1) disagreement in belief, (2) merely verbal dispute, (3) apparently verbal dispute (there is an ambiguity present, but there is also an underlying disagreement in attitude).

Page 133, #2: An apparently verbal dispute that is really genuine. The ambiguous word "relevant" is used by Daye in the sense of *dealing with eternally recurring problems and values such as love and sacrifice, the conflict of generations, life and death,* and by Knight in the sense of *dealing with the pressing and immediate issues of our time such as inflation, unemployment, the population explosion, and the energy crisis.* Behind the verbal dispute there is very probably a disagreement in attitude, Daye appreciating the plays of Sophocles more than Knight does.

Page 133, #6: An apparently verbal dispute that is really genuine. The ambiguous phrase "excellent student" is used by Daye in the sense of *student who takes a lively interest in everything and asks very intelligent questions in class,* and by Knight in the sense of *student who gets assignments in on time.* They disagree in attitude toward Ann as a student, Daye approving and Knight disapproving.

Page 134, #11: A merely verbal dispute. The ambiguous phrase "long way" is used by Daye in the sense of *taking nearly two hours to walk* and by Knight in the sense of *taking more than ten minutes to drive.*

Page 135, #16: This is a genuine disagreement in belief. Daye is affirming and Knight is denying the proposition that *the average intelligence of college graduates is higher than that of college freshmen.* It should be pointed out that the arguments offered by Daye and Knight are both quite weak. Daye asserts that "it takes more intelligence to graduate from college than to be admitted to college." This is doubtful for two reasons: first, because with the keen competition for admission to good colleges, it may actually take more intelligence to be admitted to a particular college than it does to graduate from that college; and second, because with the increasing numbers of college applicants (and therefore, presumably, the increasing average intelligence of those accepted), the present freshmen may actually have a higher average intelligence than those students who have already graduated from college. On the other hand, Knight's argument is also doubtful. Knight asserts that "every college graduate was once a college freshman and a person's intelligence does not change from year to year." But this does not prove that the average intelligence of college graduates is not higher than that of college freshmen, because some freshmen may flunk out, leaving a higher average intelligence group to graduate. Just because every college graduate was once a college freshman, it does not follow that every college freshman will be a college graduate.

READ PAGES 135–142 OF THE TEXT

4.3 Five Types of Definition

A definition is always a statement of the meaning of a *symbol* (words are one type of symbol). The symbol being defined is called the **definiendum,** and the symbol or group of symbols asserted by the definition to have the same meaning as the definiendum is called the **definiens.** Note carefully that the definiens is not the *meaning* of the definiendum, but is simply some other symbol or group of symbols which, according to the definition, has the same meaning as the definiendum. There are **five types of definition** (not to be confused with the five *purposes* of definition discussed in the first section of this chapter):

1. ***Stipulative Definitions.*** If we want to introduce a new symbol and give it a particular meaning, or if we want to assign a new meaning to an already existing symbol, then we use a stipulative definition, which is, in effect, a kind of resolution or proposal to attach a certain meaning to the symbol. Since proposals are like requests or subtle commands in not being either true or false, a stipulative definition is neither true nor false. A stipulative definition does not either truly or falsely report a previously accepted usage; rather it creates a new usage. Stipulative definitions may nevertheless be evaluated on the basis of their usefulness, clarity, and so on.

2. ***Lexical Definitions.*** Whereas a stipulative definition assigns to a symbol a meaning that that symbol did not previously have, a

lexical definition merely purports to state or report the meaning that a symbol already has according to established usage. If a lexical definition does, as a matter of fact, correctly report established usage, then the definition is true; whereas if a lexical definition is an erroneous or incorrect report of established usage, then the definition is false. The definitions found in dictionaries are lexical definitions. The purpose of a lexical definition is often to increase vocabulary or to eliminate ambiguity.

3. ***Precising Definitions.*** A term may have a meaning according to established usage, yet the term may be *vague;* that is, there may be borderline cases such that established usage does not specify to which of these borderline cases (if any) the term should be applied. The vagueness of such a term can be reduced by a precising definition, which is a definition that specifies whether or not certain borderline cases are to be included within the range of application of the term. It is important to understand both the similarity and the difference between a precising definition on the one hand and a stipulative definition or a lexical definition on the other hand. A precising definition *stipulates* where the borderline is to be drawn in the application of a vague term, and in this respect a precising definition is similar to a stipulative definition and different from a lexical definition, which merely reports an already established meaning rather than creating a more precise meaning. On the other hand, a precising definition should conform to the established usage so far as it goes, and in this respect a precising definition is similar to a lexical definition and different from a stipulative definition, which arbitrarily creates a wholly new meaning rather than reporting or conforming to an already established meaning.

4. ***Theoretical Definitions.*** A theoretical definition of a term is a definition which attempts to provide a theoretically adequate description of the entities to which the term is applied. In other words, a theoretical definition defines an X in terms of those attributes which in the context of a certain theory are most useful for understanding and predicting the behavior or additional attributes of X. A theoretical definition could also state how one concept is defined in terms of other concepts within the context of a certain theory. The adequacy of a theoretical definition is, in general, determined by the adequacy or usefulness of the theory of which it is a part.

5. ***Persuasive Definitions.*** A definition is called a persuasive definition insofar as its purpose is not to report or stipulate the literal meaning of a term but rather to influence someone's attitude toward something by phrasing the "definition" in language designed to have a certain emotive impact. Insofar as a definition is persuasive

it is functioning expressively (or perhaps directively) but not informatively.

Before going on to the next set of exercises, you should reread the paragraph in the middle of page 142 of the text, which provides an excellent summary of the relationship between the five purposes of definition and the five types of definition discussed in this chapter.

EXERCISE
on page 142

The value of this exercise can be obtained only if the student actually looks for and finds examples of each type of definition; so no sample answers will be provided here.

READ PAGES 142–146 OF THE TEXT

4.4 Various Kinds of Meaning

In the case of class terms (terms which are applicable to more than a single object, such as the term "table"), we can distinguish two kinds of meaning: extension or denotation, and intension or connotation.

In the sense of **extension** or **denotation,** the meaning of a term can be specified by referring to the collection or class of objects to which the term correctly applies. This class of objects is said to constitute the term's extension or denotation and to determine its meaning in the referential sense.

In the sense of **intension** or **connotation,** the meaning of a term can be specified by listing the set of attributes which an object must have in order to be included within the term's extension. This set of attributes is said to constitute the term's intension or connotation and to determine its meaning in the intensional or connotative sense. The connotative meaning of a term is in a sense a criterion for determining whether or not a given object is to be included within the term's extension.

There are three different senses in which the term "connotation" may be used:

1. The **subjective connotation** of a term is the set of attributes which a particular person believes to be possessed by the objects within the term's extension. Thus, the subjective connotation may differ from one person to another, and it may be thought of as the

subjective criterion by which a particular person judges whether or not a given object is to be included within the term's extension.

2. The **objective connotation** of a term is the set of *all* those attributes which are, as a matter of objective fact, possessed by all the objects within the term's extension. Thus, the objective connotation of a term does not differ at all from one person to another, as does the subjective connotation. Since it would require omniscience to know the objective connotation of a term, it is clear that no person's subjective connotation includes *all* those attributes which constitute a term's objective connotation.
3. The **conventional connotation** of a term is the set of attributes established by common usage as the criterion for determining whether or not a given object is within the term's extension. It is the conventional connotation of terms that makes language public and communication possible.

SOLUTIONS
to selected exercises on page 147

Page 147, I, #2: Beverage, alcoholic beverage, wine, white wine, fine white wine, champagne.

Page 147, II: Domestic animal, beast of burden, horse, foal, filly.

READ PAGES 147–150 OF THE TEXT

4.5 Techniques for Defining

We can divide the various techniques for defining into two separate groups, one of which (denotative definition) is discussed in this section and the other (connotative definition) in the next section.

A **denotative definition** is given by referring to the objects denoted by the term being defined. This can be done in any one of three ways:

1. By naming examples of the objects denoted by the term.
2. By enumerating the subclasses of the term (for example, a parent is either a father or a mother).
3. By actually pointing at an object denoted by the term. This is called an **ostensive definition.**

SOLUTIONS
to selected exercises on page 150

The object of these exercises is to demonstrate that a definition of a class term by the partial enumeration of examples is never complete, that it never fully determines the intension of a term, that two terms with different intensions may nevertheless have overlapping extensions, and finally that every object has many different attributes and is therefore within the extension of many different terms.

Page 150, I, #2: Joe Louis, Floyd Patterson, Joe Frazier.

Page 150, I, #6: Gardenia, hyacinth, lilac.

Page 150, II, #2: American.

Page 150, II, #6: Fragrant thing.

READ PAGES 150–153 OF THE TEXT

The various techniques for defining can be divided into two separate groups: denotative definitions (which were discussed in the previous section) and **connotative definitions,** of which there are (at least) three different kinds:

1. ***Synonymous Definition.*** In the synonymous definition the definiens is usually a single word which is asserted to have the same meaning as the definiendum.

2. ***Operational Definition.*** An operational definition states the meaning of a term by specifying that the term correctly applies to a given object if and only if the performance of a certain *operation* on that object would produce a certain *result.* For example, an operational definition of the word "fragile" could be given by specifying a certain operation which could be performed on a given object (for example, striking the object lightly) and by specifying a certain result (the object's breaking) the occurrence or nonoccurrence of which would determine whether or not the term "fragile" correctly applied to the given object. Such an operational definition of "fragile" would then read as follows: "An object is fragile if and only if it would break if struck lightly." Notice that such an operational definition consists essentially of specifying an operation (or procedure) which can be used to determine to which particular objects a term correctly applies.

3. ***Definition by Genus and Difference.*** For our present purpose in classifying the various techniques for defining, we shall understand the genus *X* to be the class of all those entities and only those entities which possess the attribute connoted by the term *X;* and we shall say that *Y* is a species of *X* if and only if *Y* is a subclass of *X* (that is, all members of class *Y* are members of class *X*) and there is some attribute (called the specific difference) which is possessed by all members of *Y* but is not possessed by any other members of *X*. We can then say that a **definition by genus and difference** conveys

the meaning of a term by stating (a) some *genus* which has among its members all those entities denoted by the term being defined and (b) some specific *difference* which is possessed by all those entities denoted by the term being defined, but which is not possessed by any other members of the genus used in the definition. Obviously, this technique for defining can be used only where the definiendum connotes a complex attribute which is analyzable into (at least) two other attributes. The genus is then defined by one of these attributes and the specific difference is defined by another of these attributes. Remember that the specific difference must always be an attribute possessed by all the members of the class designated by the definiendum but by no other members of the genus in question. An example of a definition by genus and difference would be: "A filly is a female foal." Here the genus is the class of all foals and the specific difference is the attribute of being female.

SOLUTIONS
to selected exercises on pages 153–154

Page, 153, I, #2: Clown.

Page 153, I, #6: Banquet.

Page 153, I, #11: Cows.

Page 153, I, #16: Cure-all.

Page 154, II, #2: Very large meal.

Page 154, II, #6: Young horse.

Page 154, II, #11: Young woman.

Page 154, II, #16: Female parent.

Page 154, II, #21: Male offspring.

READ PAGES 154–158 OF THE TEXT

4.6 Rules for Definition by Genus and Difference

There are five rules to which a definition by genus and difference should adhere:

Rule 1: A definition should state the essential attributes of the species. Because these five rules for definition by genus and difference are intended to apply primarily to *lexical* definitions, the attributes which are considered *essential* are those which constitute the *con-*

ventional connotation of the term being defined. Thus, Rule 1, in effect, simply imposes the obvious requirement that a good lexical definition should state the conventional connotation of the definiendum.

Rule 2: A definition must not be circular. This rule is intended to prohibit the definiendum, or any synonym or antonym of the definiendum, from appearing in the definiens. This rule, of course, applies only to definition by genus and difference and is not intended to exclude synonymous definitions as such, which are not of the genus-difference form. The reason for imposing this second rule on definition by genus and difference is that if the definiendum itself appears in the definiens, the definition will not be intelligible to anyone who does not already know the meaning of the definiendum; and if a synonym of the definiendum appears in the definiens, the definition will be intelligible only if one knows the meaning of the synonym, in which case a synonymous definition would be possible, and the definition by genus and difference, which is more complicated, would be unnecessary.

Rule 3: A definition must be neither too broad nor too narrow. This rule simply requires that a lexical definition must be accurate or true to established usage. The same entities must be denoted by the definiens as are denoted by the definiendum. If there are entities denoted by the definiens which are not denoted by the definiendum, then the definition is said to be too broad; whereas if there are entities denoted by the definiendum that are not denoted by the definiens, then the definition is said to be too narrow. A definition may, of course, be both too broad in one respect and at the same time too narrow in another respect.

Rule 4: A definition must not be expressed in ambiguous, obscure, or figurative language. In other words, a definition should be as unambiguous, clear, and literal as possible.

Rule 5: A definition should not be negative where it can be affirmative. A definition should positively state the meaning of the definiendum, rather than merely exclude other meanings. For example, Baudelaire's definition of a superior man as "not a specialist" fails to state positively how a *superior* man is to be distinguished from all other men who are not specialists.

SOLUTIONS
to selected exercises on pages 158–162

Page 158, I, #2: A buffoon is a person who acts in a manner that might be variously described as comically ridiculous or grotesque, foolish, rude or ill-bred, boorish, jesting, or exaggerated.

Page 158, I, #6: A feast is a very large, elaborate meal.

Page 158, I, #11: Kine [plural of "cow"] are mature female cattle (genus *Bos*).

Page 158, I, #16: A panacea is a remedy which cures all ills.

Page 158, II, #2: The definition is too broad and therefore violates Rule 3. In order to constitute knowledge, an opinion must not only be true but must also be supported by good grounds. Otherwise, my opinion that Fermat's last theorem is provable would, if true, be knowledge; whereas I cannot *know* that Fermat's last theorem is provable until someone proves it.

Page 159, II, #6: The definition violates Rule 5 because it is negative where it could be affirmative.

Page 159, II, #11: The definition is too broad and therefore violates Rule 3, because it includes acts of violence by individuals not engaged in war.

Page 159, II, #16: The definition violates Rule 3 because it is too broad (since some education also has for its purpose the transmission to others of the highest and best feelings to which men have risen) and because it is too narrow (since some art does not have for its purpose the transmission to others of the highest and best feelings to which men have risen).

Page 160, III, #2: The definition violates Rule 3 because it is too narrow (since faith may exist when you believe something without knowing whether or not it is true), and it is also too narrow because the definiens does not denote any entity (since if you really know something is not true you cannot believe it to be true).

Page 160, III, #6: The definition violates Rule 4 because it uses figurative language.

Page 161, III, #11: The definition violates Rule 2 because it is circular, unless "economic activities" has already been defined beforehand.

Page 161, III, #16: The definition could be criticized for violating Rule 4 because it uses figurative language. The definition could also be criticized for being too narrow (Rule 3) on the grounds that not all beliefs are products of our *intellectual* life. Perhaps some beliefs are based on attitudes, emotions, or feelings, and perhaps other beliefs are the product of habit rather than thought.

Page 161, III, #21: The definition could be criticized for using figurative language and thus violating Rule 4.

EXAMINATION
on Chapter 4

The point of this examination is to give you a chance to test yourself on some of the material *not* covered in the exercises of Chapter 4. Write your answers on a separate sheet of paper, then check them against the answers given at the end of the examination. If you miss a question, restudy the appropriate part of the text.

1. The conventional connotation of a term is
   a. The set of attributes which a particular individual believes is commonly (conventionally) used as the criterion for determining whether or not a given object is within the term's extension.
   b. The set of attributes that is generally acknowledged to be possessed by all objects within the term's extension.
   c. The set of attributes established by common (conventional) usage as the criterion for determining whether or not a given object is within the term's extension.
   d. The set of all attributes possessed by all objects within the term's extension.
   e. None of the above.

2. If the attributes which constitute the conventional connotation of class term *A* are all included within the set of attributes which constitute the conventional connotation of class term *B*, then
   a. The denotation of *B* must include fewer entities than are included in the denotation of *A*.
   b. The denotation of *A* must include fewer entities than are included in the denotation of *B*.
   c. The denotation of *B* cannot include more entities than are included in the denotation of *A*.
   d. The denotation of *A* cannot include more entities than are included in the denotation of *B*.
   e. None of the above.

3. A precising definition may be considered as partially, but not wholly, stipulative because
   a. It is not possible to stipulate completely the meaning of a symbol
   b. In stipulating the meaning of any symbol, one must always conform to some extent to conventional usage.
   c. Only a partially stipulative definition can be completely precise.
   d. A precising definition is one which reduces the vagueness of a term which already has a conventional connotation, and the precising definition should stay within the range of this conventional connotation.
   e. None of the above.

4. If two people genuinely disagree on what attitude a third person has toward a certain state of affairs, this is a
   a. Disagreement in belief.
   b. Disagreement in attitude.
   c. Merely verbal dispute.
   d. Apparently verbal dispute, with an underlying disagreement in attitude.
   e. Type of disagreement basically different from any of the above.

5. William James's story about the disagreement which arose over the squirrel going around the tree is an example of a
   a. Disagreement in belief.
   b. Disagreement in attitude.
   c. Merely verbal dispute.
   d. Apparently verbal dispute.
   e. None of the above.

6. A stipulative definition can legitimately be attacked on which of the following grounds? List *all* correct answers.
   a. The definition is so complex as to be unusable for the purpose for which it was introduced.
   b. The definition is unclear.
   c. The definition is false.
   d. The definition is arbitrary.
   e. None of the above.

7. Which of the three language functions (informative, expressive, directive) is most often served by each of the following types of definition?
   a. A stipulative definition most often serves a (n) ______ function.
   b. A lexical definition most often serves a (n) ______ function.
   c. A theoretical definition most often serves a (n) ______ function.
   d. A persuasive definition most often serves a (n) ______ function.

8. The objective connotation of a term includes
   a. More attributes than are included in the conventional connotation but fewer attributes than are included in some person's subjective connotation.
   b. More attributes than are included in anyone's subjective connotation but fewer attributes than are included in the conventional connotation.
   c. More attributes than are included in either the conventional connotation or anyone's subjective connotation.
   d. Fewer attributes than are included in either the conventional connotation or anyone's subjective connotation.
   e. None of the above.

9. Can two terms with different connotations nevertheless have *exactly* the same extension?

10. Is the definiendum of a stipulative definition necessarily a new symbol never before used?

11. If you have an accurate criterion for deciding of any given object whether or not it falls within the denotation of a certain class term, do you thereby know the conventional connotation of that term?

12. Is it true that a definition by genus and difference is possible only if the definiendum is a word whose connotation is composed of more than one attribute?

13. Would it be correct to say that stipulative definitions are similar to lexical definitions in that they both report that the definiendum and the definiens have the same meaning?

14. Is a class term meaningless if its extension is empty?

15. Can two terms with different extensions have identical connotations?

16. Is the maker of a precising definition free to assign any meaning he chooses to the definiendum?

17. Are disagreements in attitude classified (according to Copi) as genuine or nongenuine disagreements?

18. Which of the following types of definition would normally be said to be either true or false: stipulative, lexical, theoretical, persuasive?

19. What does an apparently verbal dispute have that a merely verbal dispute does not have?

20. Suppose that the foreign aid bill stipulated that aid could be given only to "democratic" governments. Which one of the following types of definition would be required before it could be determined exactly which countries could receive aid?
    a. A stipulative definition.
    b. A lexical definition.
    c. A precising definition.

21. Among the five purposes of definition listed by Copi, four are concerned with communicating something about the literal meanings of words, whereas the fifth is concerned with ________.

22. Which of the five types of definition would be required in order to create a secret code?

23. Is it true that it is impossible to give a definition by genus and difference for words connoting universal attributes (that is, attributes

possessed by everything in the universe), such as the words "being," "entity," "existent," and so on?

24. Why is the following statement false? In a definition, the definiens is the meaning of the definiendum.

25. An "operational definition" can be used to convey the meaning of a term by specifying *two things* which are sufficient for determining the application of the term. What are these two things?

26. Explain why it would be wrong to say that one of the purposes of definition is to resolve apparently verbal disputes.

27. State the essential difference between a vague term and an ambiguous term.

28. Although a precising definition may be considered as partly stipulative, it may nevertheless be false. Explain how a precising definition may be false.

ANSWERS

1. c.
2. c.
3. d.
4. a.
5. c.
6. a, b.
7. (a) directive, (b) informative, (c) informative, (d) expressive.
8. c.
9. Yes.
10. No.
11. No. ["Having three equal sides" is an accurate criterion for deciding of any given object whether or not it falls within the denotation of the class term "equiangular triangle," but you do not *thereby* know the conventional connotation of "equiangular triangle," for you do not necessarily know that having three equal sides entails having three equal angles.]
12. Yes.
13. No.
14. No.
15. No.
16. No.
17. Genuine disagreements.
18. Lexical; theoretical.
19. An underlying disagreement in attitude.
20. (c) A precising definition.

21. Influencing attitudes.
22. A stipulative definition.
23. Yes.
24. The definiens is *a symbol which has the same meaning as* the definiendum. Therefore, it is false to say that the definiens *is* the meaning of the definiendum.
25. The two things are (i) an *operation* which can be performed on an object and (ii) a *result,* the occurrence or nonoccurrence of which determines whether or not the term being defined correctly applies to the object.
26. Because a definition can only help to eliminate an ambiguity; it cannot resolve the disagreement in attitude which underlies an apparently verbal dispute.
27. A vague term has borderline cases in its range of application, whereas an ambiguous term has two or more distinct meanings.
28. A precising definition is false if the definiens is not true to conventional usage so far as it goes.

Part Two Deduction

Chapter 5
Categorical Propositions

READ PAGES 165–169 OF THE TEXT

5.1 Categorical Propositions and Classes

In Part Two of the text we study deductive arguments. An argument is **deductive** if it is claimed that it is impossible for the premisses of the argument to be true without the conclusion also being true. If this claim is correct, then the argument is **valid;** whereas if the claim is incorrect, then the argument is **invalid.** One of our main objectives in Part Two of the text is to understand the principles and techniques that can be used to determine the validity or invalidity of deductive arguments.

We begin with a consideration of categorical propositions, which occur in many common types of deductive arguments. For example, the argument at the top of page 166 of the text is composed entirely of categorical propositions. This argument is an example of a categorical syllogism, a type of argument that we study in detail in the next chapter of the text. Besides categorical syllogisms, there are various other types of deductive arguments involving categorical propositions, and we study many of these arguments in the present chapter.

If we define a **class** as a collection of all objects which have some specified attribute, or set of attributes, in common, then we can regard a **categorical proposition** as a proposition about the relationship between two classes, either affirming or denying that one class is included, either wholly or partially, in the other class. Thus, we can distinguish four different forms of categorical propositions, one of which *affirms* that one class is *wholly* included in some other class, another of which *affirms* that one class is *partially* included in some other class, another of which *denies* that one class is *wholly* included in some other class, and the last of which *denies* that one class is *partially* included in some other class. If we use *S* and *P* to stand for any two class terms, then we can represent these four different *standard forms* of categorical propositions as follows:

1. All *S* is *P*.
2. No *S* is *P*.
3. Some *S* is *P*.
4. Some *S* is not *P*.

The first form is called **universal affirmative,** because it *affirms* of all *S universally* that they are also members of the class *P*. The second form is called **universal negative,** because it *denies* of all *S universally* that any of them are members of the class *P*. The third form is called **particular affirmative,** because it *affirms* of some *particular S* that it is also a member of the class *P*. The fourth form is called **particular negative,** because it *denies* of some *particular S* that it is a member of the class *P*.

We are using the letters *S* and *P* as variables to stand for any class terms whatever. *S* and *P* are introduced so that the four different *forms* of categorical propositions can be clearly revealed schematically. In the four standard forms just listed, *S* stands for the **subject term** and *P* stands for the **predicate term.** The subject term and the predicate term in standard-form categorical propositions may be either single words or extended phrases. The only requirement is that each term designate a class of objects.

In order to avoid all ambiguity and vagueness in our discussion, and in order to be able to examine all the various logical relationships between categorical propositions, we shall find it useful to adopt the following two stipulations:

1. For purposes of analyzing the logical relationships between various categorical propositions, we shall stipulate that a proposition of the form "Some *S* is *P*" is to be interpreted as saying that *at least one* member of the class *S* is also a member of the class *P*. Similarly, "Some *S* is not *P*" is to be understood as saying that *at least one* member of the class *S* is not a member of the class *P*. You must be careful not to misunderstand the intent of this stipulation. We are not claiming that every proposition of the form "Some *S* is *P*" *really means* that at least one *S* is also a *P*. Such a claim would obviously be false, for there are contexts in which the word "some" is clearly intended to mean "at least two" (for example, "Some friends of yours have just arrived"). What we are stipulating is that whenever in the

next three chapters we say that there are certain logical relationships between a proposition of the form "Some *S* is *P*" and various other propositions, we shall be talking about "Some *S* is *P*" in the sense of "At least one *S* is *P*." After we have studied these logical relationships, we could then go on to study the logic of propositions of the form "At least two *S*'s are *P*'s," although such a study would be not only more complex, but perhaps also of less theoretical interest.

2. Likewise, for purposes of analyzing the logical relationships between various categorical propositions, we shall stipulate that a proposition of the form "Some *S* is *P*" is to be interpreted as saying *only* that some member of the class *S* is also a member of the class *P*. According to this stipulation, "Some *S* is *P*" is to be understood as saying nothing whatever about whether or not all *S* is *P*. Thus, in saying that some *S* is *P*, we are *not* also to be understood as affirming that all *S* is *P*, nor are we to be understood as denying that all *S* is *P*. We are to be understood as saying nothing whatever about the truth or falsity of "All *S* is *P*." Similarly, in saying that some *S* is *P*, we are to be understood as neither affirming nor denying that some *S* is not *P*. A similar stipulation is to be made for propositions of the form "Some *S* is not *P*." According to this stipulation, "Some *S* is not *P*" is to be understood as saying nothing whatever about whether or not no *S* is *P* and nothing whatever about whether or not some *S* is *P*. It may be helpful to point out once again that we adopt these conventions not because we believe that they accord with common usage in all contexts, but because we must have a precise, unambiguous interpretation of a categorical proposition before we can examine its logical relationships with other propositions.

SOLUTIONS

to selected exercises on page 169

Page 169, #2: *S* = athletes who have ever accepted pay for participating in sports; *P* = amateurs. Form: universal negative.

Page 169, #6: *S* = paintings produced by artists who are universally recognized as masters; *P* = works of genuine merit that either are or deserve to be preserved in museums and made available to the public. Form: particular negative.

READ PAGES 169–172 OF THE TEXT

5.2 Quality, Quantity, and Distribution

It is customary to use the letters ***A, E, I,*** and ***O*** as names for the four standard forms of categorical propositions. In the following table the name of each form is on the left and the description of the form is on the right.

A	All *S* is *P*.	universal affirmative
E	No *S* is *P*.	universal negative
I	Some *S* is *P*.	particular affirmative
O	Some *S* is not *P*.	particular negative

Each of these four standard-form categorical propositions is said to have a **quantity** (either universal or particular) and a **quality** (either affirmative or negative). The quantity and quality of each form are indicated in the right-hand column of the preceding table and should be remembered for future use.

We shall also find it useful to know which terms are distributed in the four standard-form categorical propositions. A proposition is said to **distribute** a certain term if the proposition says something about *all* members of the class designated by the term. Otherwise, the term is said to be undistributed in the proposition; that is, the proposition does not say anything about *all* members of the class designated by the term, even though it may say something about *some* members.

Which terms are distributed and which terms are undistributed in the four standard forms of categorical propositions?

In an ***A*** proposition of the form "All *S* is *P*," something is said about every member of the class *S*, namely, that every member of *S* is also a member of *P*. Therefore, the subject term (*S*) is distributed in an ***A*** proposition. But nothing is said about every member of the class *P*. Even though all *S* is *P*, there may be some *P* which is not *S*, or it may be the case that all *P* is *S*, but nothing is said about this one way or the other. Therefore, nothing is said about every member of *P*. Therefore, the predicate term (*P*) is undistributed in an ***A*** proposition.

In an ***E*** proposition of the form "No *S* is *P*," something is said about every member of the class *S*, namely, that every member of *S* is excluded from the whole of the class *P*. Therefore, the subject term (*S*) is distributed in an ***E*** proposition. Moreover, since an ***E*** proposition says that the classes *S* and *P* do not share any members in common, it says in effect that every member of the class *P* is excluded from the whole of the class *S*, and thus it says something about every member of the class *P*. Therefore, the predicate term (*P*) is also distributed in an ***E*** proposition.

In an ***I*** proposition of the form "Some *S* is *P*," nothing is said about every member of the class *S*. The proposition is only about some (at least one) member of *S*. Therefore, the subject term (*S*) is undistributed in an ***I*** proposition. Similarly, nothing is said about every member of the class *P*. The proposition is only about some (at least one) member of *P*, namely, that member of *P* which is identical with the member of *S* referred to. Therefore, the predicate term (*P*) is undistributed in an ***I*** proposition.

In an ***O*** proposition of the form "Some *S* is not *P*," nothing is said about every member of the class *S*. The proposition is only about some (at least one) member of *S*. Therefore, the subject term (*S*) is undistributed in an ***O*** proposition. But now (contrary perhaps to your first impression) something *is* said about every member of the class *P*, because it is said that some *S* is excluded from the whole of the class *P*, in other words, that there is some *S* which is not identical with any member of the class *P*. In order to see clearly that every member of *P* is referred to in an ***O*** proposition, let the members of *P* be named P_1, P_2, P_3, and so on. Now, the ***O*** proposition in effect says that there is some *S* which is not identical with P_1, nor identical with P_2, nor identical with P_3, etc.; and this proposition, when completed, makes reference to (says something about) every member of *P*. Therefore, the predicate term (*P*) is distributed in an ***O*** proposition.

The results of this analysis are summarized as follows, where the distributed terms are underlined:

A All $\underline{S}$ is P.
E No $\underline{S}$ is $\underline{P}$.
I Some S is P.
O Some S is not $\underline{P}$.

You might study the table again, reviewing in your own mind *why* each term is or is not distributed.

SOLUTIONS
to selected exercises on page 173

Page 173, #2: Affirmative, universal. Subject term distributed, predicate term undistributed.

Page 173, #6: Affirmative, universal. Subject term distributed, predicate term undistributed.

READ PAGES 173–177 OF THE TEXT

5.3 The Traditional Square of Opposition

According to the traditional or Aristotelian view of categorical propositions, there are certain logical relationships between ***A, E, I,*** and ***O*** propositions having the same subject and predicate terms. The traditional or Aristotelian account of these relationships is perfectly correct so long as we make a certain assumption, which will be mentioned briefly below and then discussed in detail in Section 5.5 of this chapter.

The traditional Square of Opposition is a diagram which displays the various logical relationships between ***A, E, I,*** and ***O*** propositions, when interpreted from the traditional or Aristotelian point of view. Based on the logical relationships displayed in the traditional Square of Opposition, there are certain immediate inferences that can be made from one categorical proposition to another. The following are the various logical relationships displayed in the traditional Square of Opposition and the immediate inferences based upon them.

Contradictories. An ***A*** proposition (All *S* is *P*) and the corresponding ***O*** proposition (Some *S* is not *P*) are contradictories, which means that one is the denial or negation of the other, that if one is true the other must be false and if one is false the other must be true; that is, they cannot both be true and they cannot both be false. That ***A*** and ***O*** are contradictory is immediately apparent, since if all *S* is *P,* it must be false that some *S* is not *P;* and if some *S* is not *P,* it must be false that all *S* is *P*. Either the ***A*** or the ***O*** proposition must be true, and whichever one is true, the other one must then be false. In other words, ***A*** being given as true, it follows that ***O*** is false. And ***O*** being given as true, it follows that ***A*** is false. Moreover, ***A*** being given as false, it follows that ***O*** is true; and ***O*** being given as false, it follows that ***A*** is true.

The same logical relationship holds between the ***E*** and the ***I*** propositions, and the same immediate inferences can be made as a result of this relationship. An ***E*** proposition (No *S* is *P*) and the corresponding ***I*** proposition (Some *S* is *P*) are contradictories, which means that one is the denial or negation of the other, that if one is true the other must be false and if one is false the other must be true; that is, they cannot both be true and they cannot both be false. That ***E*** and ***I*** are contradictory is immediately apparent, since if no *S* is *P,* it must be false that some *S* is *P;* and if some *S* is *P,* it must be false that no *S* is *P*. Either the ***E*** or the ***I*** proposition must be true, and whichever one is true, the other one must then be false. In other words, ***E*** being given as true, it follows that ***I*** is false. And ***I*** being given as true, it follows that ***E*** is false. Moreover, ***E*** being given as false, it follows that ***I*** is true; and ***I*** being given as false, it follows that ***E*** is true.

Subcontraries. An ***I*** proposition (Some *S* is *P*) and the corresponding ***O*** proposition (Some *S* is not *P*) are said to be subcontraries, which means simply that they can both be true (unless, of course, one of them is *necessarily* false) but they cannot both be false, as is immediately apparent, since an *S* must be either *P* or not *P*, there being no other alternative. If an ***I*** proposition and the corresponding ***O*** proposition cannot both be false, then the following immediate inferences can be made: If an ***I*** proposition is false, then the corresponding ***O*** proposition must be true. And if an ***O*** proposition is false, then the corresponding ***I*** proposition must be true. However, if an ***I*** proposition is given as true, nothing whatever can be inferred concerning the truth or falsity of the corresponding ***O*** proposition; and if an ***O*** proposition is given as true, nothing whatever can be inferred concerning the truth or falsity of the corresponding ***I*** proposition.

At this point it may be helpful to mention the assumption which underlies the traditional or Aristotelian account of the Square of Opposition. An ***I*** proposition and the corresponding ***O*** proposition are subcontraries (that is, cannot both be false) *only if we assume that the class S has at least one member,* for if the class *S* is empty (examples of empty classes are the class of unicorns or the class of men over twenty feet tall), then both the ***I*** and the ***O*** propositions would be false, because it would be false that some *S* is *P,* and it would also be false that some *S* is not *P* (there being no *S*'s at all). An example will make this clear: Since there are no unicorns, it is false that some unicorns are good swimmers, and it is also false that some unicorns are not good swimmers. Hence, ***I*** and ***O*** propositions can both be false and thus are not subcontraries, *unless we assume that* S *designates a class which is not empty.*

As a matter of fact this same assumption must be made for all of the relationships in the traditional Square of Opposition, with the exception of the contradictories. The necessity of this assumption and the difficulties and confusions that arise when one is not clear about the need for the assumption are matters which are discussed fully in Section 5.5 of this chapter. But if you reflect now on what has just been said, the later discussion will be easier to understand.

Contraries. An ***A*** proposition (All *S* is *P*) and the corresponding ***E*** proposition (No *S* is *P*) are said to be contraries, which means simply that they can both be false (unless, of course, one of them is *necessarily* true) but they cannot both be true. If an ***A*** proposition and the corresponding ***E*** proposition cannot both be true, then the following immediate inferences can be made: If an ***A*** proposition is true, then the corresponding ***E*** proposition must be false. And if an ***E*** proposition is true, then the corresponding ***A*** proposition must be false. However, if an ***A*** proposition is false, nothing whatever follows concerning the truth or falsity of the corresponding ***E***

proposition; and if an ***E*** proposition is false, nothing whatever follows concerning the truth or falsity of the corresponding ***A*** proposition.

It may be helpful to point out here also that this traditional or Aristotelian account of the relationship between *A* and ***E*** propositions depends on the assumption that the class *S* has at least one member, for if class *S* is empty then ***A*** and ***E*** are both true. In order to explain this, it will be helpful to analyze the *A* and ***E*** propositions in the following way: The ***E*** proposition (No *S* is *P*) really means that there is nothing in the universe which is both an *S* and a *P*, so that if there are no *S*'s at all, then the ***E*** proposition is true, because if there are no *S*'s at all, then there is certainly no *S* which is a *P*. Moreover, the ***A*** proposition (All *S* is *P*) says that there are no *S*'s which fail to be *P*'s, that there is nothing in the universe which is both an *S* and yet not a *P*, so that if there are no *S*'s at all, then the ***A*** proposition is true, since if there are no *S*'s at all, then there is certainly no *S* which fails to be a *P*. Hence, an ***A*** proposition and the corresponding ***E*** proposition are both true where there are no *S*'s; and thus ***A*** and ***E*** are not contrary *unless we assume that* S *designates a class which is not empty.*

Subalternation. The relationship of subalternation is said to hold between *A* and ***I*** and between ***E*** and ***O***. According to this relationship, if an ***A*** proposition (All *S* is *P*) is true, then it follows that the corresponding ***I*** proposition (Some *S* is *P*) is true also; and if an ***E*** proposition (No *S* is *P*) is true, then it follows that the corresponding ***O*** proposition (Some *S* is not *P*) is true also. But the truth of ***I*** does not imply the truth of ***A***, nor does the truth of ***O*** imply the truth of ***E***. Moreover, from the falsity of an *A* proposition, nothing whatever follows concerning the truth or falsity of the corresponding ***I*** proposition; and from the falsity of an ***E*** proposition, nothing whatever follows concerning the truth or falsity of the corresponding ***O*** proposition.

When discussing the relationship of subalternation, the ***A*** or ***E*** proposition can be referred to as the superaltern and the ***I*** or ***O*** proposition as the *subaltern.*

The relationship of subalternation also depends on the assumption that the class *S* is not empty. To see this, consider the inference from an ***E*** proposition (No *S* is *P*) to the corresponding ***O*** proposition (Some *S* is not *P*). Let *S* designate the class of unicorns (which is empty) and let *P* designate the class of good swimmers. The ***E*** proposition then says in effect that there is nothing in the universe that is both a unicorn and a good swimmer, which is true, because there are no unicorns. Therefore, the ***E*** proposition is true where the class *S* is empty. But does the corresponding ***O*** proposition follow validly by subalternation from the truth of the ***E***? Certainly not, for the ***O*** proposition is false where *S* is empty; and no valid argument can have all true premisses and a false conclusion. Why is the corresponding ***O*** proposition false? Because it says that some members (at least one) of the class of unicorns are not members of the class of good swimmers, and this can be true only if there *are* some members of the class of unicorns, which there are not. Therefore, the ***O*** proposition is false. So the truth of the ***O*** proposition does *not* follow from the truth of the ***E*** proposition where the class *S* is empty. Therefore, the validity of subalternation depends on the assumption that the class *S* is not empty.

A similar explanation could be constructed to show that the relationship of subalternation between ***A*** and ***I*** also depends on the assumption that the class *S* is not empty.

Much more is said concerning this assumption later in this chapter of the text in the section entitled "Existential Import." In the meantime, you may simply assume that all classes discussed have members and that the inferences based on the traditional Square of Opposition may therefore be made.

The best way to check your understanding of this section before going on to the exercises is to restudy the traditional Square of Opposition on page 176 of the text to see if you can remember precisely what is involved in each relationship. Then restudy the table on page 177 of the text to see if you can remember (without checking back through the text) which relationship justifies each inference. If you can do this with complete understanding, you are ready for the exercises. It may take you ten minutes or more, but it will be time well spent.

SOLUTIONS
to selected exercises on pages 177–178

Page 178, #2:

If (a) is true: (b) is false (contradictories)
(c) is true (subalternation)
(d) is false (contraries)

If (a) is false: (b) is true (contradictories)
(c) is undetermined
(d) is undetermined

READ PAGES 178–183 OF THE TEXT

5.4 Further Immediate Inferences

Besides the immediate inferences based on the traditional Square of Opposition, there are other types of immediate inference, among which are conversion, obversion, and contraposition. You will find it easy to remember the principles of inference studied in this section and to apply them in the exercises if you concentrate on understanding the definition of conversion, the definition of obversion, and the definition of contraposition, and then learn which inferences are valid and which are not valid.

Conversion. The converse of a given proposition is the proposition obtained by interchanging the subject and predicate terms of the given proposition. The inference from a proposition to its converse is valid for ***E*** and ***I*** propositions.

Conversion is a valid immediate inference in the case of an ***E*** proposition because if an ***E*** proposition (No *S* is *P*) is given as true, it follows that the converse (No *P* is *S*) must also be true. To see in detail why this is the case, simply recall that the ***E*** proposition (No *S* is *P*) means that there is nothing in the universe that is both an *S* and a *P*, which means (by conversion) that there is nothing in the universe which is both a *P* and an *S*, which means that no *P* is *S*, which is the converse of the original proposition.

Conversion is also a valid immediate inference in the case of an ***I*** proposition, since from an ***I*** proposition (Some *S* is *P*) it follows that something is both an *S* and a *P*, which is to say (by conversion) that something is both a *P* and an *S*, which means that some *P* is *S*, which is the converse of the original ***I*** proposition.

Conversion is not, however, a valid immediate inference in the case of an ***O*** proposition, since from an ***O*** proposition (Some *S* is not *P*) it does not follow that some *P* is not *S*, as can be seen in an example such as the following: From the proposition that some animals are not dogs, it obviously does not follow validly that some dogs are not animals, since the first proposition is true and the second proposition is false.

Nor is conversion a valid immediate inference in the case of an ***A*** proposition, since from an ***A*** proposition (All *S* is *P*) it does not follow that all *P* is *S*, as can be seen in an example such as the following: From the proposition that all dogs are animals, it obviously does not follow validly that all animals are dogs, since the first proposition is true and the second proposition is false.

Nevertheless, according to the traditional or Aristotelian view of categorical propositions, there is a valid form of immediate inference, called **conversion by limitation,** which does apply to an ***A*** proposition. In conversion by limitation the subject and predicate terms of an ***A*** proposition are interchanged and the quantity of the proposition is changed from universal to particular. According to the traditional or Aristotelian view, if an ***A*** proposition (All *S* is *P*) is given as true, then it follows that the converse by limitation

(Some *P* is *S*) must be true also. Conversion by limitation can be explained in terms of the immediate inferences already discussed, since if all *S* is *P*, then it follows (by subalternation) that some *S* is *P*, from which it follows (by conversion) that some *P* is *S*.

It may be helpful to point out here that this traditional or Aristotelian account of conversion by limitation depends on the assumption that the class *S* has at least one member, for if class *S* is empty, then the ***A*** proposition (All *S* is *P*) would be true whereas "Some *P* is *S*" would be false, and a false proposition cannot be validly inferred from a true proposition. Why would the ***A*** proposition be true and its converse by limitation false where the class *S* is empty? As explained in the previous section of this study guide, an ***A*** proposition (All *S* is *P*) says that there are no *S*'s which fail to be *P*'s, that there is nothing in the universe that is both an *S* and yet not a *P*, so that if there are no *S*'s at all, then the ***A*** proposition is true, since if there are no *S*'s at all then there is certainly no *S* which fails to be a *P*. On the other hand, if the class *S* is empty then "Some *P* is *S*" is false, since if there are no *S*'s at all then there is certainly nothing which is both a *P* and an *S*. Therefore, if class *S* is empty then the ***A*** proposition (All *S* is *P*) would be true, whereas its converse by limitation (Some *P* is *S*) would be false, so that conversion by limitation is a valid immediate inference only on the assumption that *S* designates a class which is not empty. This matter is discussed more fully in the next section of this chapter.

If we adopt the traditional or Aristotelian view of categorical propositions and assume that class *S* is not empty, then the validity of conversion by limitation can be explained as follows: If all *S* is *P*, and if we assume that class *S* is not empty, then there is at least one *S* and that *S* is *P*. In other words, it is true that some *S* is *P*, which means (by conversion) that some *P* is *S*, which is the converse by limitation of the original ***A*** proposition.

The immediate inferences based on conversion are summarized in the table on page 179 of the text. This table should now be reviewed once again, not simply to memorize it, but to make sure that you can reconstruct in your mind the reasoning which went into the formulation of the table.

Obversion. The obverse of a given proposition is the proposition obtained by replacing the predicate by its complement and changing the quality of the given proposition. The inference from a proposition to its obverse is valid for ***A, E, I,*** and ***O*** propositions.

In using obversion it is important to understand exactly what is meant by the complement of a term. The term non-*P* is the **complement** of the term *P* in the sense that non-*P* designates the class of all those entities that are not members of the class designated by *P*. In other words, every entity in the universe is either a member of the class *P* or a member of the class non-*P*, and no entity is a member of both classes. You should be careful not to confuse the *complement* of a term with the *contrary* of a term. The terms "hero" and "coward" are contraries in the sense that nothing can be both a hero and a coward, but they are not complements because there are many things in the universe that are neither heroes nor cowards (for example, all inanimate objects), whereas two terms are complements only if every entity in the universe is a member of one class or the other.

Obversion is a valid immediate inference in the case of an ***A*** proposition, because if an ***A*** proposition (All *S* is *P*) is given as true, then every member of the class *S* is also a member of the class *P*, which means that no member of the class *S* is a member of the class non-*P*, which means that no *S* is non-*P*, which is the obverse of the original ***A*** proposition.

Obversion is also a valid immediate inference in the case of an ***E*** proposition, because an ***E*** proposition (No *S* is *P*) means that no member of the class *S* is a member of the class *P*, which means that every member of the class *S* is a member of the class non-*P*, which means that all *S* is non-*P*, which is the obverse of the original ***E*** proposition.

Obversion is also a valid immediate inference in the case of an ***I*** proposition, because if an ***I*** proposition (Some *S* is *P*) is given as true, then there is some member of the class *S* which is also a member of the class *P*, which means that there is some member of the class *S* which is not a member of the class non-*P*, which means that some *S* is not non-*P*, which is the obverse of the original ***I*** proposition.

Obversion is also a valid immediate inference in the case of an ***O*** proposition, since an ***O*** proposition (Some *S* is not *P*) means that there is some member of the class *S* which is not a member of the class *P*, which means that there is some member of the class *S* which is a member of the class non-*P* (since every entity is a member of either *P* or non-*P*), which means that some *S* is non-*P*, which is the obverse of the original ***O*** proposition.

Obversion is summarized in the table on page 181 of the text, which you should now review once again, with the object of reconstructing in your own mind the reasoning which went into the formulation of the table.

Contraposition. The contrapositive of a given proposition is the proposition obtained by replacing the subject term by the complement of the predicate term and replacing the predicate term by the complement of the subject term. The inference from a proposition to its contrapositive is valid for ***A*** and ***O*** propositions.

Contraposition is a valid immediate inference in the case of an ***A*** proposition, because if an ***A*** proposition (All *S* is *P*) is given as true, then every member of *S* is a member of *P*, which means that no member of *S* is a member of non-*P*, which means (by conversion) that no member of non-*P* is a member of *S*, which means that every member of non-*P* is a member of non-*S*, which means that all non-*P* is non-*S*, which is the contrapositive of the original ***A*** proposition.

Contraposition is also a valid immediate inference in the case of an ***O*** proposition, since from an ***O*** proposition (Some *S* is not *P*) it follows that some member of *S* is not a member of *P*, which means that some member of *S* is a member of non-*P*, which means (by conversion) that some member of non-*P* is a member of *S*, which means that some member of non-*P* is not a member of non-*S*, which means that some non-*P* is not non-*S*, which is the contrapositive of the original ***O*** proposition.

Contraposition is not, however, a valid immediate inference in the case of an ***I*** proposition, since from an ***I*** proposition (Some *S* is *P*) it does not follow that some non-*P* is non-*S*, as can be seen in an example such as the following: From the proposition that some citizens are nonvoters, it obviously does not follow validly that some voters are noncitizens, since the first proposition is true and the second proposition is presumably false.

Nor is contraposition a valid immediate inference in the case of an ***E*** proposition, since from an ***E*** proposition (No *S* is *P*) it does not follow that no non-*P* is non-*S*, as can be seen in an example such as the following: From the proposition that no dogs are cats, it obviously does not follow validly that no noncats are nondogs, since the first proposition is true and the second proposition is false (because most of the entities in the universe are both noncats and nondogs).

Nevertheless, according to the traditional or Aristotelian view of categorical propositions, there is a valid form of immediate inference, called **contraposition by limitation,** which does apply to an ***E*** proposition. In contraposition by limitation the subject term is replaced by the complement of the predicate term, the predicate term is replaced by the complement of the subject term, and the quantity of the ***E*** proposition is changed from universal to particular. According to the traditional or Aristotelian view, if an ***E*** proposition (No *S* is *P*) is given as true, then it follows that the contrapositive by limitation (Some non-*P* is not non-*S*) must be true also. Contraposition by limitation can be explained in terms of the immediate inferences already discussed, for if no *S* is *P*, then it follows (by subalternation) that some *S* is not *P*, from which it follows (by contraposition) that some non-*P* is not non-*S*.

It may be helpful to point out here that this traditional or Aristotelian account of contraposition by limitation depends on the assumption that the class *S* has at least one member, for if class *S* is empty, then the ***E*** proposition (No *S* is *P*) is true, whereas "Some non-*P* is not non-*S*" is false, and a false proposition cannot be validly inferred from a true proposition. Why would the ***E*** proposition be true and its contrapositive by limitation false where the class *S* is empty? As explained in the preceding section of this study guide, an ***E*** proposition (No *S* is *P*) says that there is nothing in the universe which is both an *S* and a *P*, so that if there are no *S*'s at all, then the ***E*** proposition is true, since if there are no *S*'s at all then there is certainly no *S* which is a *P*. On the other hand, if the class *S* is empty then "Some non-*P* is not non-*S*" is false, since it is equivalent (by obversion) to "Some non-*P* is *S*," which is clearly false, since if there are no *S*'s at all then there is certainly nothing which is both a non-*P* and an *S*. Therefore, if class *S* is empty then the ***E*** proposition (No *S* is *P*) would be true, whereas its contrapositive by limitation (Some non-*P* is not non-*S*) would be false, so that contraposition by limitation is a valid immediate inference only on the assumption that *S* designates a class that is not empty. This matter is discussed more fully in the next section of this chapter.

If we adopt the traditional or Aristotelian view of categorical propositions and assume that class *S* is not empty, then the validity of contraposition by limitation can be explained as follows: If no *S* is *P*, and if we assume that class *S* is not empty, then there is at least one *S* and that *S* is not *P*. In other words, it is true that some *S* is not *P*, which means (by obversion) that some *S* is non-*P*, which means (by conversion) that some non-*P* is *S*, which means (by obversion) that some non-*P* is not non-*S*, which is the contrapositive by limitation of the original ***E*** proposition.

Contraposition is summarized in the table on page 183 of the text, which you should now review once again, with the object of reconstructing in your own mind the reasoning which went into the formulation of the table.

It is now time to review all three types of immediate inference studied in this section. There is probably no easy and foolproof method for memorizing the various valid immediate inferences, and in any case rote memorization is obviously inferior to complete theoretical understanding, which in this case is not as difficult to achieve as the complex details of this section might indicate at first glance. Nevertheless, if you are looking for a systematic way to remember what you have learned about conversion, obversion, and contraposition, perhaps the easiest thing to do is to learn first the definition of conversion, the definition of obversion, and the definition of contraposition; then remember that obversion is valid for all four standard-form categorical propositions, that conversion is valid for ***E*** and ***I*** (the middle two in the list ***A, E, I, O***), and that contraposition is valid for ***A*** and ***O*** (the first and last in the list ***A, E, I, O***). Then, of course, you must also remember that conversion by limitation is valid for ***A*** (the first in the list) and that contraposition by limitation is valid for ***E*** (the second in the list). Of course, if you simply know the definitions of conversion, obversion, and contraposition, and if you can think logically, you can always determine by yourself (rather quickly and easily) which inferences are valid and which are invalid; and it is this kind of ability to think clearly and logically which will become increasingly important in mastering the material in the text. Rote memorization of a formula is no substitute for an understanding of the theory. Mere memorization is not sufficient for solving many of the exercises in the text, nor is it as long-lasting or as useful in the long run as thorough comprehension of basic principles.

You should make a conscientious effort to master the section of the text just completed before going on to the following set of exercises, and if in working on the exercises you find it necessary to refer back constantly to the text, you have not yet mastered even the basic principles developed in this section.

SOLUTIONS
to selected exercises on pages 183–187

Try to do these exercises without referring back to the last section of the text. If you do have to refer back to the text to check some specific item, learn that item thoroughly enough so that you do not have to refer back again for the same reason. If you find that a whole segment of the material is so vague in your mind that you cannot do the exercises with confidence, learn that whole segment so thoroughly that you do not have to refer back to it again. Several days after you first do these exercises (and again about a week later) retest your ability to do the exercises without referring back to the text.

Page 183, I, #2: All commissioned officers in the United States Army are graduates of West Point. Not equivalent.

Page 184, II, #2: All organic compounds are nonmetals.

Page 184, III, #2: Some nonofficers are not nonsoldiers. Equivalent.

Page 184, IV, #2: True (use obversion).

Page 184, IV, #6: True (use contraposition).

Page 184, V, #2: True (use contraposition by limitation).

Page 185, V, #6: False (we may infer by conversion that "No philosophers are scientists" is true, from which it follows by the relationship of contraries in the traditional Square of Opposition that "All philosophers are scientists" must be false).

Page 185, VI, #2: Undetermined.

Page 185, VI, #6: Undetermined.

Page 185, VI, #11: Undetermined.

Page 185, VI, #16: Undetermined.

Page 185, VI, #21: Undetermined.

Page 185, VI, #26: False.

Page 186, VII, #2: Undetermined.

Page 186, VII, #6: Undetermined.

Page 186, VII, #11: Undetermined.

Page 186, VII, #16: Undetermined.

Page 186, VII, #21: Undetermined.

Page 186, VII, #26: False.

READ PAGES 187–189 OF THE TEXT

5.5 Existential Import

A proposition is said to have **existential import** if it affirms the existence of some entity. From now on we shall be using the **Boolean interpretation of existential import,** according to which ***I*** and ***O*** propositions have existential import, whereas ***A*** and ***E*** propositions do not have existential import.

An ***I*** proposition is said to have existential import in the sense that in saying "Some *S* is *P*" we are affirming the existence of some entity which is both an *S* and a *P*.

An ***O*** proposition is said to have existential import in the sense that in saying "Some *S* is not *P*" we are affirming the existence of some entity which is an *S* but not a *P*.

An ***E*** proposition is said not to have existential import in the sense that in saying "No *S* is *P*" we are not affirming the existence of any entity. We are saying merely that there is nothing in the universe that is both an *S* and a *P*, and such a statement is purely negative. We are denying the existence of entities of a certain kind rather than affirming the existence of some entity. For example, when we say "No suspicious persons were seen trespassing," we are not affirming the existence of anything. We are saying merely that there is nothing in the universe that is both a suspicious person and someone seen trespassing; and such a statement is purely negative. We are denying the existence of entities of a certain kind rather than affirming the existence of some entity.

An ***A*** proposition is also said not to have existential import in the sense that in saying "All *S* is *P*" we are not necessarily affirming the existence of any entity. For example, in saying "All trespassers are subject to prosecution" we are not affirming that there are any trespassers. We are merely saying that nobody could be a trespasser without being subject to prosecution, in other words, that there is nothing in the universe that is both a trespasser and yet not subject to prosecution. Such a statement is purely negative; we are denying the existence of entities of a certain kind rather than affirming the existence of some entity. Hence, an ***A*** proposition, like an ***E*** proposition, has no existential import.

What we have just reviewed in the last four paragraphs is the **Boolean interpretation of existential import,** according to which ***I*** and ***O*** propositions have existential import (that is, in an ***I*** or an ***O*** proposition, we are affirming the existence of some entity), whereas ***A*** and ***E*** propositions do not have existential import (that is, in an ***A*** or an ***E*** proposition, we are not necessarily affirming the existence of any entity).

Of course, we could adopt the traditional or Aristotelian view of categorical propositions and assume or presuppose that every class term occurring in a categorical proposition designates a class that is not empty. But there are a number of reasons why it is not useful to make this blanket presupposition. In the first place, the blanket presupposition conflicts with ordinary usage. For example, when we say "All trespassers are subject to prosecution," we are certainly not presupposing the existence of a trespasser. Another reason for not making the blanket presupposition is that we often want to be able to examine the logical relationships between propositions without making any assumptions about whether the class terms involved denote (which is a matter of fact and not of logic). For example, in physics we want to be able to draw the logical consequences from Newton's First Law of Motion (every body not acted upon by external forces perseveres in its state of rest or of uniform motion in a straight line) without presupposing that there actually are bodies not acted upon by external forces. For these reasons we shall not make the blanket presupposition that every class term occurring in a categorical proposition designates a class that is not empty.

We shall *presuppose nothing* regarding the existence of various entities, and we shall simply adhere to the Boolean interpretation of existential import, according to which ***I*** and ***O*** propositions have existential import, whereas ***A*** and ***E*** propositions do not have existential import. We shall now explore the consequences of the Boolean interpretation.

When we say that an ***I*** proposition has existential import, we mean that in an ***I*** proposition (Some *S* is *P*) we are affirming the existence of an entity of a certain kind, namely, an *S* which is also a *P*. Thus, if the class *S* is empty (has no members), then the ***I*** proposition is thereby false.

Similarly, when we say that an ***O*** proposition has existential import, we mean that in an ***O*** proposition (Some *S* is not *P*) we are affirming the existence of an entity of a certain kind, namely, an *S* which is not a *P*. Thus, if the class *S* is empty, then the ***O*** proposition is thereby false.

But when we say that an ***E*** proposition has no existential import, we mean that in an ***E*** proposition (No *S* is *P*) we are not necessarily affirming the existence of any entity, so that if the class *S* is empty the ***E*** proposition is *not* thereby false. On the contrary, if the class *S* is empty, then the ***E*** proposition is thereby true, since the ***E*** proposition (No *S* is *P*) says that there is nothing in the universe that is both an *S* and a *P*, and if there is no *S* at all, then there is certainly no *S* that is a *P*. Thus, an ***E*** proposition is true if the class *S* is empty.

Similarly, when we say that an ***A*** proposition has no existential import, we mean that in an ***A*** proposition (All *S* is *P*) we are not necessarily affirming the existence of any entity, so that if the class *S* is empty the ***A*** proposition is *not* thereby false. On the contrary, if the class *S* is empty, then the ***A*** proposition is thereby true, since the ***A*** proposition (All *S* is *P*) in effect says that there is no *S* which fails to be a *P*, that there is nothing in the universe that is both an *S* and yet not a *P*, so that if there is no *S* at all, then the ***A*** proposition is true, since if there is no *S* at all then there is certainly no *S* which fails to be a *P*. Thus, an ***A*** proposition is true if the class *S* is empty.

We can summarize the results of the last four paragraphs by saying simply that if the class *S* is empty, then ***I*** and ***O*** propositions are false, whereas ***A*** and ***E*** propositions are true. Of course, if we adopted the traditional or Aristotelian view of categorical propositions and made the blanket presupposition that every class term occurring in a categorical proposition designates a class that is not empty, then we would always be presupposing that class *S* is not empty. But we have decided, for good reasons, to examine the logical relationships between categorical propositions without making this blanket presupposition, and thus the class *S* could be empty, and if it were empty then ***I*** and ***O*** propositions would be false and ***A*** and ***E*** propositions would be true, according to the Boolean interpretation of existential import. From the fact that corresponding ***I*** and ***O*** propositions can be false while corresponding ***A*** and ***E*** propositions are true, we can draw a number of conclusions concerning certain of the immediate inferences studied in traditional or Aristotelian logic:

Subcontraries. Since "Some *S* is *P*" and "Some *S* is not *P*" can both be false (where *S* is empty), they are not subcontraries, for by definition subcontrary propositions cannot both be false.

Contraries. Since "All *S* is *P*" and "No *S* is *P*" can both be true (where *S* is empty), they are not contraries, for by definition contrary propositions cannot both be true.

Subalternation. Since "All *S* is *P*" can be true while "Some *S* is *P*" is false (where *S* is empty), the latter does not validly follow from the former, and thus the relationship of subalternation does not hold between an ***A*** proposition and its corresponding ***I*** proposition. Moreover, since "No *S* is *P*" can be true while "Some *S* is not *P*" is false (where *S* is empty), the latter does not validly follow from the former, and thus the relationship of subalternation does not hold between an ***E*** proposition and its corresponding ***O*** proposition.

Conversion by Limitation. Since "All *S* is *P*" can be true while "Some *P* is *S*" is false (where *S* is empty), the latter does not validly follow from the former, and thus the inference based on conversion by limitation of an ***A*** proposition is not valid.

Contraposition by Limitation. Since "No *S* is *P*" can be true while "Some non-*P* is not non-*S*" is false (where *S* is empty), the latter does not validly follow from the former, and thus the inference based on contraposition by limitation of an ***E*** proposition is not valid. Perhaps it will be helpful to explain that "Some non-*P* is not non-*S*" is false where *S* is empty because it is equivalent (by obversion) to "Some non-*P* is *S*," which affirms the existence of some *S* and so is false where *S* is empty.

We can summarize the results of the last five paragraphs by saying simply that having decided not to make the blanket presupposition that every class term occurring in a categorical proposition designates a class that is not empty, and having decided to adopt the Boolean interpretation of existential import, according to which

I and ***O*** propositions have existential import whereas ***A*** and ***E*** propositions do not have existential import, then it is no longer valid to make the immediate inferences based on the relationships of contrariness, subcontrariness, subalternation, conversion by limitation, and contraposition by limitation.

The other inferences studied in previous sections of this chapter remain perfectly valid. For example, ***A*** and ***O*** propositions are still contradictory, since where *S* is empty ***A*** is true while ***O*** is false. Similarly, ***E*** and ***I*** propositions are still contradictory, since where *S* is empty ***E*** is true while ***I*** is false. Moreover, as you can check for yourself, obversion is still valid for all four standard-form categorical propositions, conversion is still valid for ***E*** and ***I***, and contraposition is still valid for ***A*** and ***O***.

But it is invalid, in general, to infer a proposition that has existential import (***I*** or ***O***) from a proposition that does not have existential import (***A*** or ***E***). This is one instance of the **Existential Fallacy,** and it can be explained in several ways. First, we can show that an argument composed of a premiss that does not have existential import and a conclusion that does have existential import is an argument in which the premiss could be true and the conclusion false, and is therefore an invalid argument. To prove this, consider an argument in which the conclusion is a proposition that does have existential import. Then the conclusion would be false if the subject term of the conclusion designated a class which was empty. But if the premiss is a proposition that does not have existential import, then the premiss could be true no matter what particular class was empty. So the premiss could be true even though the conclusion was false, which means that the argument is invalid.

There is another way of explaining why an argument is, in general, invalid if its premiss does not have existential import and its conclusion does have existential import. In order for an argument to be valid, what is affirmed by the conclusion must follow from what is affirmed by the premiss. If the conclusion affirms more than what is affirmed by the premiss, then the conclusion cannot follow validly from the premiss. But a conclusion with existential import affirms more than a premiss without existential import. Thus, a conclusion which affirms the existence of some entity cannot, in general, follow validly from a premiss which does not affirm the existence of that entity. An argument in which the premiss does not have existential import while the conclusion does have existential import is said to commit the Existential Fallacy.

The **Existential Fallacy** can be defined in a more general way as the fallacy of assuming that a class has members when this is not explicitly affirmed. For example, if we argue

It is true that all *S* is *P*.
Therefore, it is false that no *S* is *P*.

we have committed the Existential Fallacy, because we are assuming corresponding ***A*** and ***E*** propositions to be contraries, which requires us to assume that *S* has members, which is not explicitly affirmed in the premiss. Similarly, if we argue

It is false that some *S* is not *P*.
Therefore, it is true that some *S* is *P*.

we have committed the Existential Fallacy, because we are assuming corresponding ***O*** and ***I*** propositions to be subcontraries, which requires us to assume that *S* has members, which is not explicitly affirmed in the premiss.

SOLUTIONS
to selected exercises on pages 190–191

The directions ask you to explain at which step in each argument the Existential Fallacy is committed. It is committed whenever a conclusion having existential import is inferred from a premiss which does not have existential import, and it is committed whenever it is assumed that a class has members when this is not explicitly affirmed in the premiss.

Page 190, II: Step (2) follows validly from step (1) by conversion. Step (3) follows validly from step (2) by obversion. But the inference from step (3) to step (4) commits the Existential Fallacy because (3) is an ***A*** proposition (and therefore has no existential import) whereas (4) is an ***I*** proposition (and therefore has existential import). Step (4) is the subaltern of (3), but subalternation is no longer a valid immediate inference on the Boolean interpretation of existential import. The Existential Fallacy is not committed in arguing from (4) to (5) because both propositions have existential import. Step (5) follows validly from (4) by conversion.

READ PAGES 191–197 OF THE TEXT

5.6 Symbolism and Diagrams for Categorical Propositions

This section of the text consists essentially of the introduction and explanation of a number of special symbols and diagrams which are used extensively in subsequent chapters of the text. On the left in the following list are the symbols and diagrams whose meaning you must know. Listed on the right opposite each item is an explanation of the meaning of that item. Cover up the right-hand column with a piece of paper until you have recalled to your own satisfaction what each item means. Restudy in the text the explanation of any item you fail to explain correctly.

S	The name of the class of all entities which have the attribute (or set of attributes) connoted by the term S.
$S = 0$	The class S is empty (has no members).
$S \neq 0$	The class S is not empty (has at least one member).
SP	The name of the class of all entities which have all the attributes connoted by the terms S and P. In other words, the name of the class of all entities which are members both of class S and of class P.
$SP = 0$	The class SP is empty (has no members). In other words, there is nothing which is a member both of class S and of class P. In other words, no S is P.
$SP \neq 0$	The class SP is not empty (has at least one member). In other words, there is something which is a member both of class S and of class P. In other words, some S is P.
$\bar{S}$	The name of the class non-S, the complement of S. In other words, the name of the class of all those entities which are not members of class S.
$S\bar{P} = 0$	The class $S\bar{P}$ is empty (has no members). In other words, there is nothing which is a member both of class S and of class $\bar{P}$, which means (by obversion) that everything which is a member of class S is a member of class P. In other words, all S is P.

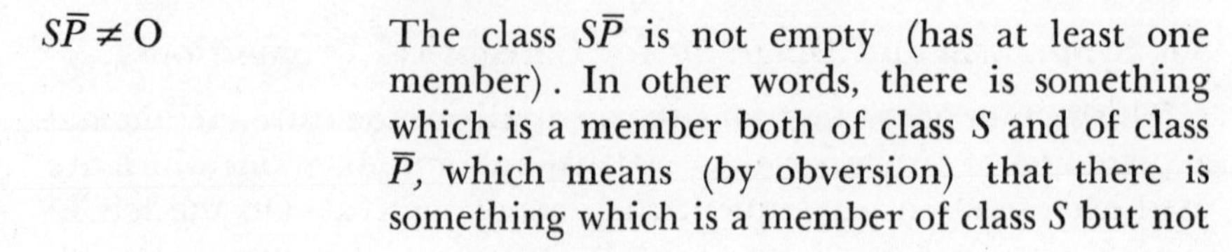

$S\bar{P} \neq 0$	The class $S\bar{P}$ is not empty (has at least one member). In other words, there is something which is a member both of class S and of class $\bar{P}$, which means (by obversion) that there is something which is a member of class S but not

a member of class *P*. In other words, some *S* is not *P*.

$PS = O$ No *P* is *S*.

$PS \neq O$ Some *P* is *S*.

$P\bar{S} = O$ All *P* is *S*.

$P\bar{S} \neq O$ Some *P* is not *S*.

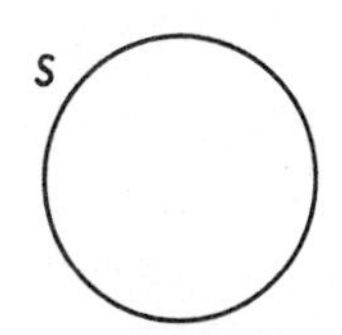

The class *S*. This diagram does not *affirm* (or represent the affirmation of) any proposition. It merely represents the class *S* but says nothing about the class *S*.

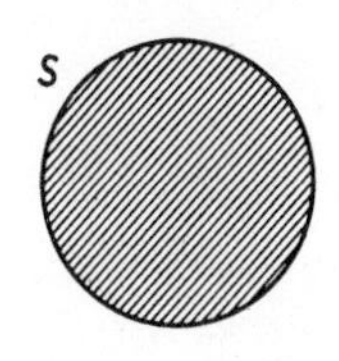

The class *S* is empty (has no members). This is indicated by blacking out the interior of the circle which represents the class *S*.

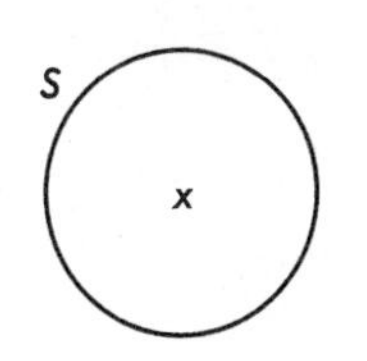

The class *S* is not empty (has at least one member). This is indicated by representing that member with an *x* within the interior of the circle which represents the class *S*.

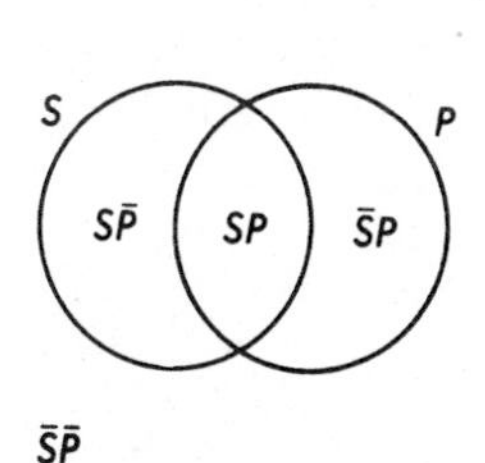

The class *S* and the class *P*. This diagram does not affirm (or represent the affirmation of) any proposition. It merely represents the class *S* and the class *P* together, but says nothing about their relationship. However, because the diagram is set up with the circles partially overlapping, it can be used for representing any of the standard-form categorical propositions that can be asserted about the relationship between *S* and *P*. The left area within the circles (labeled $S\bar{P}$) represents the class of all entities which are members of *S* but not members of *P*. The middle area within the circles (labeled *SP*) represents the class of all entities which are members both of *S* and of *P*. The right area within the circles (labeled $\bar{S}P$) represents the class of all entities which are members of *P* but not members of *S*. And the whole area outside of both circles (labeled $\overline{S}\overline{P}$) represents the class of all entities which are not members of *S* and also not members of *P*.

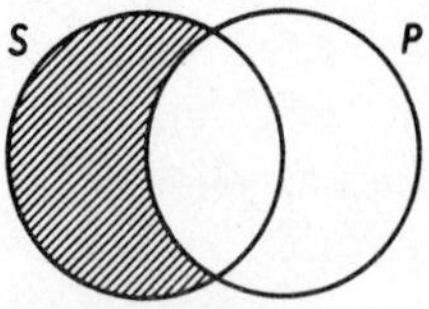

All *S* is *P*. In other words, everything within circle *S* is also within circle *P;* there is nothing within circle *S* which is outside circle *P*. Hence, the left area is blacked out.

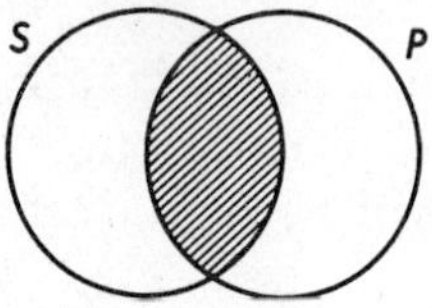

No *S* is *P*. *or*

No *P* is *S*.

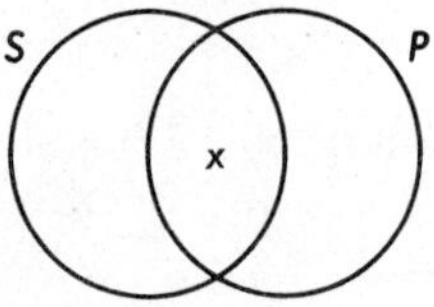

Some *S* is *P*. *or*

Some *P* is *S*.

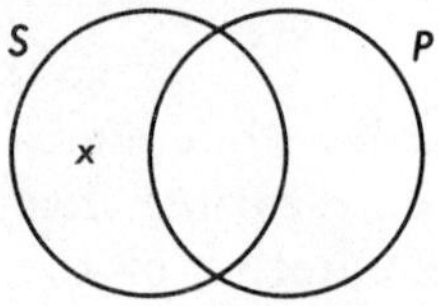

Some *S* is not *P*.

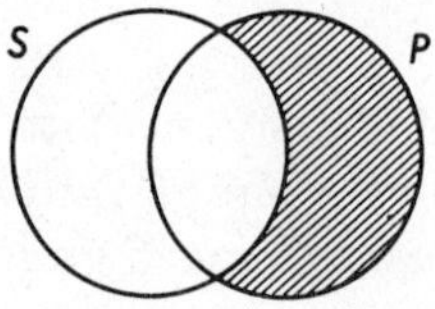

All *P* is *S*.

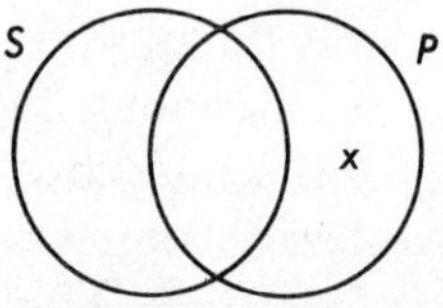

Some *P* is not *S*.

It is interesting to note that the diagrams and symbolic equations introduced in this section reflect the Boolean interpretation of existential import. In the following table the standard-form ***A, E, I,*** and ***O*** propositions are listed in the middle with their diagrams on the left and their symbolic equations on the right. Notice that the Boolean interpretation of existential import is reflected in the fact that the ***A*** and ***E*** propositions are represented by diagrams in which an area is blacked out (thus indicating that a certain class is empty, but not implying the existence of anything) ; whereas the ***I*** and ***O*** propositions are represented by diagrams in which there is an x in a certain area (thus implying the existence of something). The Boolean interpretation of existential import is also reflected in the symbolic equations, where ***A*** and ***E*** propositions are translated into symbolic equations which indicate that a certain class is empty (and thus do not imply the existence of anything); whereas ***I*** and ***O*** propositions are translated into symbolic equations which indicate that a certain class is not empty (thus implying the existence of something).

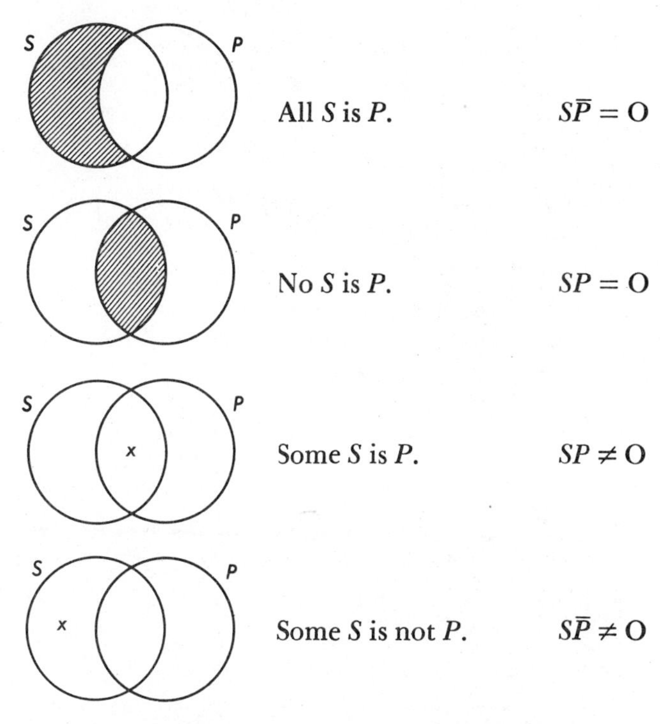

Notice also that the preceding diagrams and symbolic equations reflect clearly the fact that ***A*** and ***O*** propositions are contradictory, since the same area which is blacked out for an ***A*** proposition has an x inserted in it for an ***O*** proposition; and the symbolic equations for ***A*** and ***O*** propositions are identical except for the diagonal line indicating that one is the denial of the other. ***E*** and ***I*** propositions are also seen to be contradictory, since the same area which is blacked out for an ***E*** proposition has an x inserted in it for an ***I*** proposition; and the symbolic equations for ***E*** and ***I*** propositions are identical except for the diagonal line indicating that one is the denial of the other.

As a final (and very useful and important) test of your ability to use the symbols and diagrams introduced in this section, you should represent each of the following propositions by a symbolic equation *and* by a diagram. After you are all through, check your equations and diagrams against the figures on page 196 of the text.

All *S* is *P*.
No *S* is *P*.
Some *S* is *P*.
Some *S* is not *P*.
All *P* is *S*.
No *P* is *S*.
Some *P* is *S*.
Some *P* is not *S*.

SOLUTIONS
to selected exercises on page 197

Page 197, #2:

P M

$PM = O.$

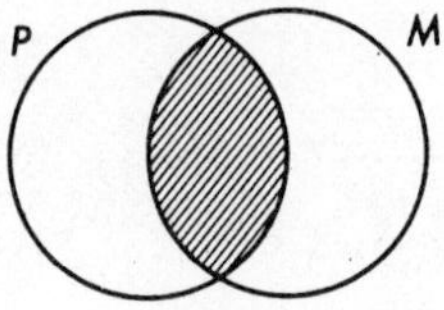

Page 197, #6:

P S x

$PS \neq O.$

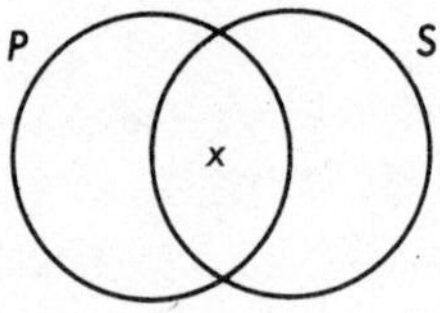

Page 197, #11:

S M x

$SM \neq O$

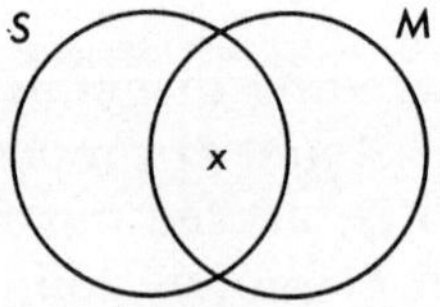

Page 197, #16:

P S x

$P\overline{S} \neq O$

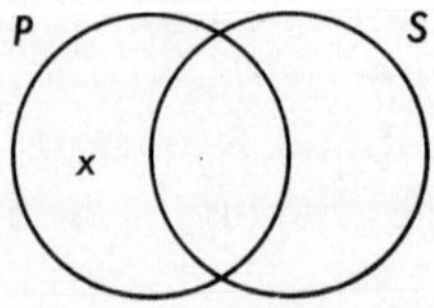

EXAMINATION
on Chapter 5

Write your answers on a separate sheet of paper, then check them against the answers given at the end of the examination. If you miss a question, restudy the appropriate part of the text.

1. There are six different ways in which we can mark the following diagram, corresponding to the six different ways in which the classes *S* and *P* can be related to one another. Thus, we could (1) black out the left area, indicating that all *S* is *P*, or (2) black out the middle area, indicating that no *S* is *P*, or (3) black out the right area, indicating that all *P* is *S*, or (4) insert an *x* in the left area, indicating that some *S* is not *P*, or (5) insert an *x* in the middle area, indicating that some *S* is *P*, or (6) insert an *x* in the right area, indicating that some *P* is not *S*. But if there are *six* different ways in which two classes can be related to one another, how can it be true that there are only *four* different standard forms of categorical propositions?

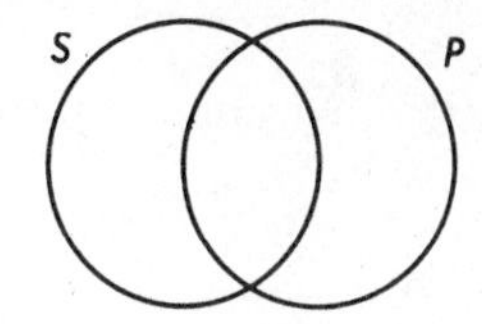

2. A standard-form categorical proposition can be either universal or particular and either affirmative or negative. Which of these characteristics do ***A*** and ***O*** propositions share?

3. Name the *quantity* and *quality* of each of the following propositions:
   a. Some non-*S* is non-*P*.
   b. No *P* is non-*S*.
   c. Some non-*P* is not *S*.

4. Which of the following statements are true and which are false?
   a. All universal propositions, whether affirmative or negative, distribute their subject terms.
   b. All negative propositions, whether universal or particular, distribute their predicate terms.
   c. No affirmative propositions, whether universal or particular, distribute their predicate terms.
   d. No particular propositions, whether affirmative or negative, distribute their subject terms.

5. State whether the subject and predicate terms are distributed or undistributed in the following propositions:
   a. Some incumbents are destined not to win in the next election.

b. Some events are not destined to happen.
c. Some ambassadors are persons who are not career diplomats.
d. Some ambassadors are not career diplomats.

For purposes of answering the following questions, you should assume the traditional or Aristotelian view of categorical propositions, according to which conversion by limitation, contraposition by limitation, and all the immediate inferences based on the traditional Square of Opposition are valid. Do *not* assume the Boolean interpretation of existential import until you are told to do so later in this exam.

6. You know that if you are given the truth value of one of the four propositions in the traditional Square of Opposition, you can determine the truth or falsity of some of the other three propositions. Supply the missing words in each of the following sentences in a way similar to the sample answer given for (a). Write your answers on a separate sheet of paper, *not in the book.*
   a. If an ***O*** proposition is given as true, it follows that the corresponding ***A*** proposition is ______, ***E*** is ______, and ***I*** is ______.

   ANSWER: false, undetermined, undetermined.

   b. If an ***I*** proposition is given as false, it follows that the corresponding ***A*** proposition is ______, ***E*** is ______, and ***O*** is ______.
   c. If an ***E*** proposition is given as false, it follows that the corresponding ***A*** proposition is ______, ***I*** is ______, and ***O*** is ______.
   d. If an ***A*** proposition is given as true, it follows that the corresponding ***E*** proposition is ______, ***I*** is ______, and ***O*** is ______.

7. Are two propositions necessarily contradictory if one is true and the other is false?

8. State the conditions which two propositions have to fulfill in order to be contraries of one another.

9. Since corresponding ***I*** and ***O*** propositions are subcontraries, why are the following two propositions not subcontraries?

   Some soldiers are nonheroes.
   Some soldiers are not cowards.

10. Which *one* of the following designates the complement of the class of all selfish men?
    a. The class of all selfish women.
    b. The class of all unselfish men.
    c. The class of all unselfish women.
    d. The class of all things which are neither selfish nor men.
    e. The class of all things which are either not selfish or not men.

11. When it is said that contraposition is not a valid immediate inference in the case of an ***I*** proposition, does this mean that if "Some *S* is *P*" is true then "Some non-*P* is non-*S*" must be false?

12. For which of the four standard-form categorical propositions is it the case that neither conversion nor conversion by limitation is a valid immediate inference?

13. The contrapositive of any ***A*** proposition is the obverse of the converse of the ______ of the original ***A*** proposition.

14. If *SP* designates the class of all those entities which have both the attribute connoted by *S* and the attribute connoted by *P*, then the complement of the class *SP* is
    a. The class $\bar{S}\bar{P}$.
    b. The class of all those entities which are members either of $\bar{S}$ or of $\bar{P}$.
    c. The class of all those entities which are members neither of *S* nor of *P*.
    d. None of the above.

15. If "All *S* is *P*" is given as true, what may be inferred about the truth or falsity of each of the following propositions? Remember that there are three possible answers: "true," "false," and "undetermined."
    a. All *P* is non-*S*.
    b. No non-*S* is *P*.
    c. Some non-*S* is not *P*.
    d. Some non-*P* is not non-*S*.
    e. Some *P* is non-*S*.

16. If "No *S* is *P*" is given as true, what may be inferred about the truth or falsity of each of the following propositions?
    a. All non-*S* is non-*P*.
    b. No non-*S* is non-*P*.
    c. Some non-*P* is not non-*S*.
    d. Some non-*S* is non-*P*.
    e. No non-*P* is *S*.

For purposes of answering the remaining questions, you should assume the Boolean interpretation of existential import, according to which ***I*** and ***O*** propositions have existential import whereas ***A*** and ***E*** propositions have no existential import.

17. State whether each of the following arguments is valid or invalid:
    a. It is false that all *P* is non-*S*.
       Therefore, it is true that some *S* is not non-*P*.
    b. It is false that some *P* is non-*S*.
       Therefore, it is false that all *P* is non-*S*.

c. It is false that some non-P is not non-S.
   Therefore, it is true that all non-P is non-S.
d. It is false that some P is not non-S.
   Therefore, it is true that some non-P is not non-S.

18. Express each of the following propositions by means of a symbolic equation. For example, "Some non-S is P" can be expressed as $\bar{S}P \neq 0$.
    a. No non-P is non-S.
    b. All P is non-S.
    c. Some non-S is not P.
    d. Some S is non-P.

ANSWERS

1. Since S and P are variables standing for any class terms whatever, "All S is P" and "All P is S" are really the same *form* of proposition. Similarly, "Some S is not P" and "Some P is not S" are the same *form* of proposition. Thus, although there are *six* different ways in which any two given classes may be related to one another, only *four* different forms of proposition are required to express these six ways.
2. None.
3. a. Particular affirmative.
   b. Universal negative.
   c. Particular negative.
4. a. True.
   b. True.
   c. True.
   d. True.
5. a. Subject and predicate both undistributed.
   b. Subject undistributed, predicate distributed.
   c. Subject and predicate both undistributed.
   d. Subject undistributed, predicate distributed.
6. b. False, true, true.
   c. Undetermined, true, undetermined.
   d. False, true, false.
7. No. ["The sky is blue" is true and "The grass is blue" is false, but they are not contradictory because they *could* both be true (or both false) if the facts of nature were different from what they are. Two propositions are contradictory only if they *cannot* both be true and *cannot* both be false, that is, only if one is the denial or negation of the other.]
8. Two propositions are contraries of one another if they cannot both be true although they may both be false.
9. Because the predicate terms are not synonymous. "Hero" is the contrary but not the complement of "coward."

10. e.
11. No.
12. ***O.***
13. Obverse.
14. b.
15. a. False. [If "All *S* is *P*" is true, then by conversion by limitation "Some *P* is *S*" is true, whence by obversion "Some *P* is not non-*S*" is true, whence by contradictories "All *P* is non-*S*" is false.]
    b. Undetermined.
    c. True. [If "All *S* is *P*" is true, then by contraposition "All non-*P* is non-*S*" is true, whence by conversion by limitation "Some non-*S* is non-*P*" is true, whence by obversion "Some non-*S* is not *P*" is true.]
    d. False. [If "All *S* is *P*" is true, then by contraposition "All non-*P* is non-*S*" is true, whence by contradictories "Some non-*P* is not non-*S*" is false.]
    e. Undetermined.
16. a. False. [If "No *S* is *P*" is true, then by conversion "No *P* is *S*" is true, whence by contraposition by limitation "Some non-*S* is not non-*P*" is true, whence by contradictories "All non-*S* is non-*P*" is false.]
    b. Undetermined.
    c. True. [If "No *S* is *P*" is true, then by contraposition by limitation "Some non-*P* is not non-*S*" is true.]
    d. Undetermined.
    e. False. [If "No *S* is *P*" is true, then by contraposition by limitation "Some non-*P* is not non-*S*" is true, whence by obversion "Some non-*P* is *S*" is true, whence by contradictories "No non-*P* is *S*" is false.]
17. a. Valid.
    b. Invalid.
    c. Valid.
    d. Invalid.
18. a. $\overline{P}\overline{S} = 0$
    b. $PS = 0$
    c. $\overline{S}\overline{P} \neq 0$
    d. $S\overline{P} \neq 0$

Chapter 6
Categorical Syllogisms

READ PAGES 198–201 OF THE TEXT

6.1 Standard-Form Categorical Syllogisms

In order to analyze standard-form categorical syllogisms and to develop techniques for determining their validity or invalidity, we must introduce some additional terminology.

A **syllogism** is simply an argument with two premisses and a conclusion. An argument is said to be a **standard-form categorical syllogism** if it has the following characteristics:

1. It consists of three standard-form categorical propositions.
2. Exactly three class terms occur in the three propositions.
3. Each class term occurs in exactly two of the propositions.
4. The three propositions are arranged in the following order:
   a. First is the **major premiss,** which is the premiss containing the **major term,** which is the class term that appears also as the predicate term of the conclusion.
   b. Second is the **minor premiss,** which is the premiss containing the **minor term,** which is the class term that appears also as the subject term of the conclusion.
   c. Third is the conclusion.

The **mood** of a standard-form categorical syllogism is stated by listing in order the forms (***A, E, I,*** or ***O***) of the three propositions occurring in the syllogism. Thus, the mood of the syllogism at the top of page 199 of the text is ***EIO*** because the major premiss is an ***E*** proposition, the minor premiss is an ***I*** proposition, and the conclusion is an ***O*** proposition.

For brevity, we shall refer to standard-form categorical syllogisms simply as syllogisms, wherever no confusion will arise from this abbreviation. In order to state completely the form of any syllogism, it is necessary to state not only its mood but also its figure. The **figure** of a syllogism is determined by the location in the two premisses of the **middle term,** which is the term that appears once in each premiss. The naming of the four possible figures is an arbitrary stipulation which can be easily memorized. If the middle term is the subject term of the major premiss and the predicate term of the minor premiss, the syllogism is said to be in **first figure.** If the middle term is the predicate term of both premisses, the syllogism is said to be in **second figure.** If the middle term is the subject term of both premisses, the syllogism is said to be in **third figure.** And if the middle term is the predicate term of the major premiss and the subject term of the minor premiss, the syllogism is said to be in **fourth figure.** In order to remember easily where the middle term is in each figure, look at the table near the bottom of page 200 of the text. In the first figure the two occurrences of the middle term are on a line slanted like this:

Remember this line. Now, to get from the first figure to the second figure, swing the top of the line to the right without moving the bottom of the line:

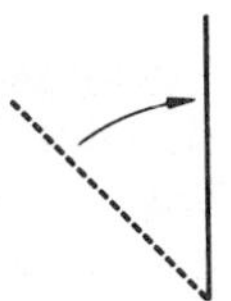

To get from the second figure to the third figure, move the whole line to the left:

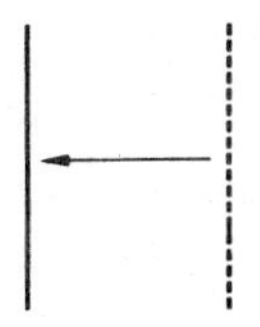

And to get from the third figure to the fourth figure, swing the top of the line to the right again:

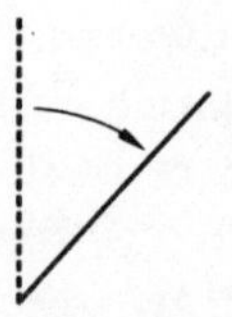

If you can picture in your mind the starting position of the line and the way it moves to get from one figure to another, you can easily remember the four figures.

In order to state completely the form of a given syllogism, you must name both its mood and its figure. Since there are sixty-four different moods and each mood can occur in each of the four figures, there are 256 different forms of syllogism, of which only fifteen are valid (on the Boolean interpretation of existential import), as you will discover for yourself when you solve exercise #11 on page 223 of the text.

SOLUTIONS
to selected exercises on pages 201–202

In naming the figure of each argument, try not to refer back to the table near the bottom of page 200 of the text.

Page 201, #2:
Some objects of worship are fir trees.
All fir trees are evergreens.
Therefore, some evergreens are objects of worship.
IAI-4

Page 202, #6:
No expensive and delicate mechanisms are suitable toys for children.
All hi-fi sets are expensive and delicate mechanisms.
Therefore, no hi-fi sets are suitable toys for children.
EAE-1

READ PAGES 202–204 OF THE TEXT

6.2 The Formal Nature of Syllogistic Argument

In the preceding section of the text you learned that there are 256 forms of syllogism. Fifteen of these forms are valid and the other

241 forms are invalid (on the Boolean interpretation of existential import). To say that a *form* of syllogism is valid means that every argument of that form is valid. Thus, if we examine the form ***AAA*-1**

All *M* is *P*.
All *S* is *M*.
Therefore, all *S* is *P*.

we can see that any argument of this form must be valid, for no matter what specific class terms are substituted for *S, P,* and *M,* if all *S* is *M* and all *M* is *P* then it follows necessarily that all *S* is *P*. In general, the validity or invalidity of a syllogism is determined by its *form* alone and not by its specific content (assuming the restrictions mentioned in the footnote on page 203 of the text). Thus, a particular syllogism is valid if and only if it has a valid form, and a form of syllogism is valid if and only if *all* syllogisms of that form are valid, from which it follows that a form of syllogism is invalid if there is any invalid syllogism of that form. Thus, if we know that a certain syllogism is invalid (because we know that its premisses are true and its conclusion false), then we can be sure that its *form* is invalid, from which it follows that any other syllogism of the same form must be invalid also, for a syllogism is valid only if its form is valid. Thus, if we are given a syllogism whose validity or invalidity is in question, we can prove the given syllogism to be invalid if we can find another syllogism which is of the same form and which has true premisses and a false conclusion (and is thus invalid). This technique for proving the invalidity of a syllogism is called **refutation by logical analogy,** and the rationale behind the technique can be summarized as follows: A given syllogism is valid only if its form is valid, and its form is valid only if every syllogism of that form is valid, so that if we can find a syllogism of that form which is invalid (because it has true premisses and a false conclusion) then we have proved the original syllogism to be invalid. Thus, to refute a given syllogism by the method of constructing a logical analogy, we must find another syllogism which

1. has the same form as the given syllogism, and
2. has obviously true premisses and an obviously false conclusion.

SOLUTIONS
to selected exercises on pages 204–205

Page 204, #2: This argument is valid because it is of the following valid form:

No *M* is *H*.
Some *N* is *M*.
Therefore, some *N* is not *H*.

Page 205, #6: This argument is valid because it is of the following valid form:

All *B* is *I* [safe investments].
Some *B* is *S*.
Therefore, some *S* is *I*.

READ PAGES 205–214 OF THE TEXT

6.3 Venn Diagram Technique for Testing Syllogisms

In this section you learned an effective method for determining the validity or invalidity of any standard-form categorical syllogism. This method can be summarized as follows:

1. *Draw a three-circle Venn Diagram and label the circles with the syllogism's three terms.* A model of the three-circle Venn Diagram is given on page 206 of the text. Notice that the three circles overlap in such a way that the diagram can be marked to represent any standard-form categorical proposition involving the terms occurring in the syllogism.

2. *Diagram each premiss of the syllogism.* In the preceding chapter of the text you learned how to diagram each of the four standard-form categorical propositions, so you should have no difficulty diagramming the premisses of a standard-form categorical syllogism. One of the premisses says something about *P* and *M*, and you can diagram what that premiss says by marking the circles *P* and *M* in the appropriate way without paying any attention to the circle *S*. The other premiss says something about *S* and *M*, and you can diagram what that premiss says by marking the circles *S* and *M* in the appropriate way without paying any attention to the circle *P*. There are, however, two special rules which must be followed in diagramming both premisses together on a three-circle Venn Diagram, and these two special rules are listed as items (3) and (4).

3. *If there is one universal premiss (**A** or **E**) and one particular premiss (**I** or **O**), diagram the universal premiss first.* For example, in the argument

All *M* is *P*.
Some *S* is *M*.
Therefore, some *S* is *P*.

the universal premiss is represented by blacking out the areas labeled 2 and 3 in the following diagram; whereas the particular premiss is represented by putting an *x* somewhere in the areas labeled 1 and 2. The *only* way to do *both* of these things is, of course, first to black out areas 2 and 3 and then to put the *x* in area 1. If we tried to represent the particular premiss first, we would not know whether to put the *x* in area 1 or in area 2 or on the line in between. But if we represent the universal premiss first, then we shall find that the *x* has to be in area 1.

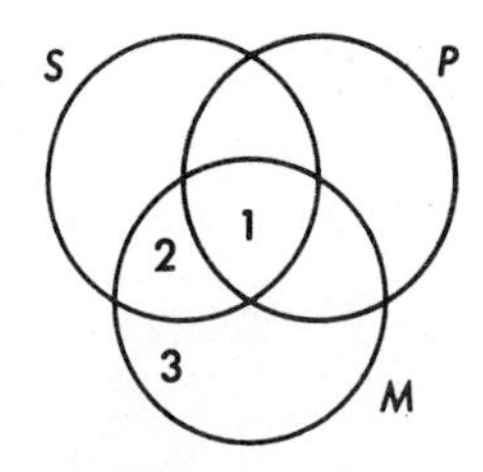

4. *If in diagramming a particular premiss (**I** or **O**) you are required to insert an* x *somewhere within two adjoining regions but the premiss does not definitely determine in which of the two regions the* x *must be inserted, then put the* x *on the line between the two regions.* The reason for this special rule is that your diagram should represent no more than what is definitely affirmed by the premisses. Thus, if a particular premiss does not specifically determine in which of two possible regions an *x* should be inserted, you would be wrong to place an *x* in one region rather than the other (or in both regions), because in doing so you would be representing in the diagram more than what is actually affirmed by the premiss. Put the *x* on the line, thus indicating that, as far as the premiss is concerned, there is something somewhere within the two regions but it need not be in one region rather than the other. If you ignore this rule, your diagram will represent more than what is actually affirmed by the premisses, and thus your diagram will not help you to answer accurately the final question: If the premisses were true would the conclusion have to be true also?

5. *After you have finished diagramming both premisses, study the diagram to determine whether what is affirmed by the conclusion is already represented in the diagram. If it is, then the argument is valid; if it is not, then the argument is invalid.* For example, if the conclusion of a syllogism is "Some *S* is *P*," then the syllogism is valid if and only if the diagram of the premisses contains an *x* somewhere within the overlapping region of the two circles *S* and *P*. And if the conclusion of a syllogism is "All *S* is *P*," then the syllogism is valid if and only if in the diagram of the premisses the region which is within the circle *S* but outside the circle *P* is *entirely* blacked out.

Similarly, if the conclusion of a syllogism is "No *S* is *P*," then the syllogism is valid if and only if in the diagram of the premisses the overlapping region of the two circles *S* and *P* is entirely blacked out. And if the conclusion of a syllogism is "Some *S* is not *P*," then the syllogism is valid if and only if the diagram of the premisses contains an *x* somewhere within the region which is within the circle *S* but outside the circle *P*.

You must be careful in applying this test to an argument whose diagram contains an *x* on a line. For example,

All *P* is *M*
Some *S* is *M*.
Therefore, some *S* is *P*.

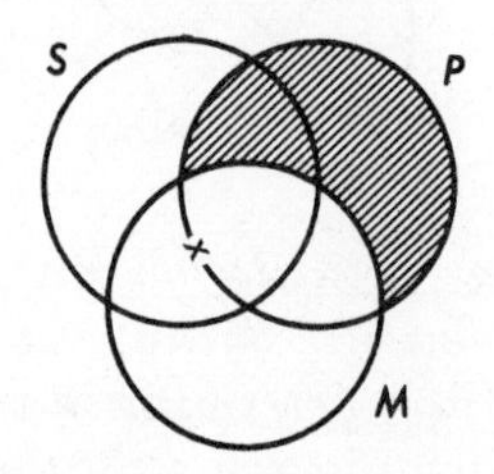

Here the *x* was put on the line because the minor premiss does not definitely determine in which of the two regions the *x* must be put. But the conclusion affirms that there *must* be an *x* within the overlapping regions of the two circles *S* and *P*. Therefore, the conclusion affirms more than what is affirmed by the premisses, and thus the conclusion does not follow validly from the premisses. Another way of explaining this is to show how it is possible for the premisses to be true and the conclusion false. The premisses would be true if something were an $S\bar{P}M$ even though nothing was an *SPM*, but the conclusion would then be false. Thus, the premisses could be true and the conclusion false, which means that the argument is invalid.

The principles explained here in theory will become much clearer as you work on the following exercises.

SOLUTIONS
to selected exercises on pages 214–215

Page 214, I, #2:
No *P* is *M*.
Some *S* is *M*.
. . Some *S* is not *P*.

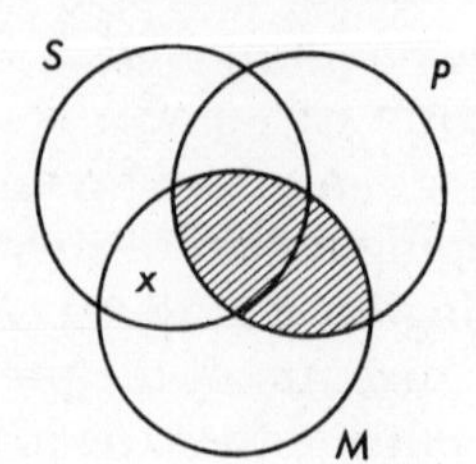

valid.

Page 214, I, #6:
Some *P* is not *M*.
All *S* is *M*.
∴ Some *S* is not *P*.

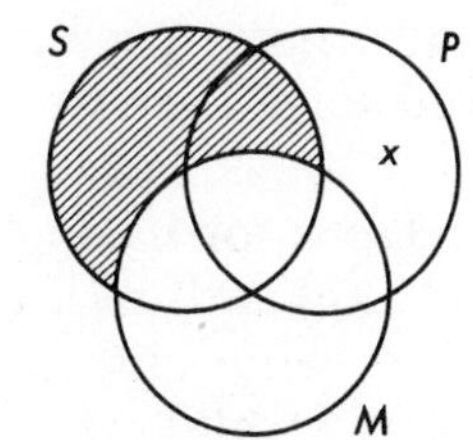

invalid.

Page 214, I, #11:
All *M* is *P*.
Some *M* is not *S*.
∴ Some *S* is not *P*.

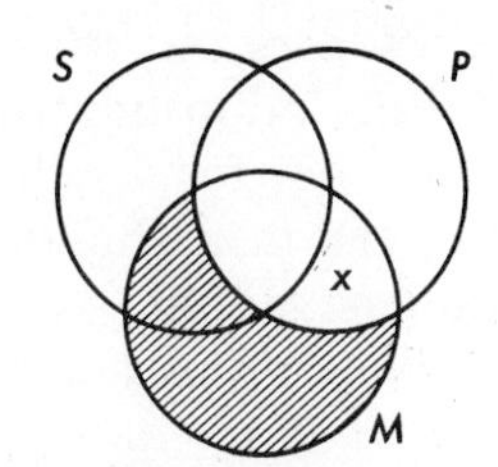

invalid.

Page 214, II, #2:
Some philosophers are mathematicians.
All scientists are mathematicians.
Therefore, some scientists are philosophers.

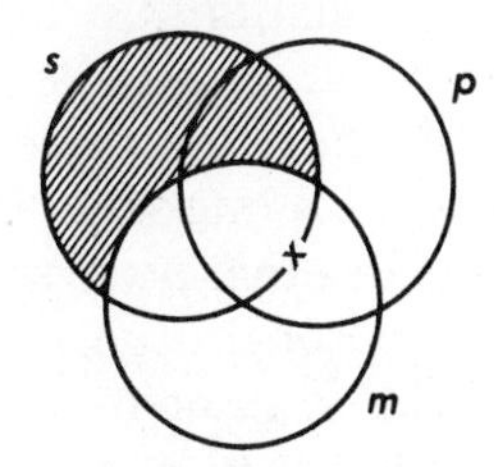

***IAI*-2**
invalid.

Page 215, II, #6:
No pioneers were unsavory persons.
All criminals are unsavory persons.
Therefore, no criminals were pioneers.

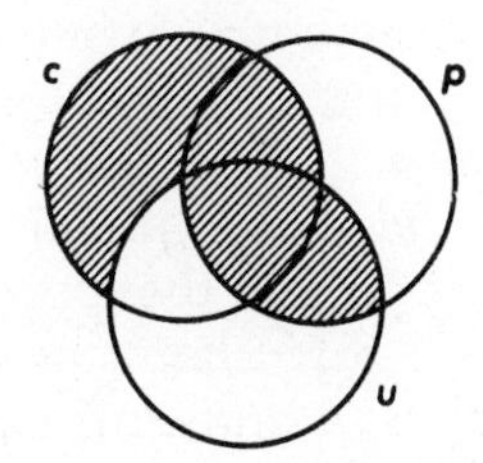

***EAE*-2**
valid.

READ PAGES 215–220 OF THE TEXT

6.4 Rules and Fallacies

In this section you learned another method for determining the validity or invalidity of a syllogism. If a syllogism violates any one of the six rules, it is invalid. If it conforms to all six rules, it is valid. (The latter statement is not proved in the text, although you can prove it easily after you solve exercise #11 on page 223 of the text.)

There are at least two reasons for having this additional method for distinguishing between valid and invalid syllogisms. First, there is the practical advantage of being able to recognize immediately that a particular syllogism is invalid when it violates one of the rules. Second, studying the six rules and reflecting on them gives one a deeper understanding of the relationship which must exist between premisses and conclusion in order for a syllogism to be valid.

The six rules are given here in a slightly rephrased version in order to promote fuller understanding.

Rule 1: In order for a standard-form categorical syllogism to be valid, it must contain exactly three unequivocal class terms. In order for a syllogism to be valid, what is affirmed by the conclusion must follow necessarily from what is affirmed by the premisses. The conclusion always affirms that a certain relationship holds between its two terms. In order for this to follow validly from the premisses, the premisses must affirm a relationship between each of the conclusion's terms and some common middle term. If there are four terms in the argument or if there are three terms but one of them is used equivocally (that is, with one sense in one of its occurrences and with a different sense in its other occurrence), then the premisses cannot serve to connect the conclusion's terms to some common middle term, and hence the argument must be invalid. Thus, a valid syllogism can have only three terms, each of which is used in the same sense in both of its occurrences. A syllogism which violates Rule 1 is said to commit the fallacy of **Four Terms.**

Rule 2: In order for a standard-form categorical syllogism to be valid, the middle term must be distributed in at least one of its occurrences. If *M* is undistributed in both of its occurrences, then neither premiss says anything about the *whole* of the class *M*. Thus, in the major premiss, class *P* is said to be related to only *part* of class *M;* and in the minor premiss, class *S* is said to be related to only *part* of class *M;* and these two *parts* may be *different* parts, in which case class *P* and class *S* would each be connected with a different part of class *M* and thus not necessarily connected with each other at all. Therefore, no proposition about the connection of *S* and *P* can follow validly from premisses in which *M* is undistributed in both of its occurrences. For a syllogism to be valid, the middle term must serve to connect the major and minor terms, and the middle term cannot do this unless it is distributed at least once. A syllogism that violates Rule 2 is said to commit the fallacy of the **Undistributed Middle.**

Rule 3: In order for a standard-form categorical syllogism to be valid, any term distributed in the conclusion must also be distributed in the premisses. If a term is distributed in the conclusion, then the conclusion affirms something about *all* members of the class designated by that term, and if that term is undistributed in the premisses, then the premisses do not affirm anything about *all* members of the class designated by that term, which means that the conclusion affirms more than what is affirmed by the premisses, which means that the conclusion could be false even though the premisses were true, which means that the syllogism is invalid. If the major term is distributed in the conclusion but undistributed in the major premiss, the syllogism is said to commit the fallacy of **Illicit Major.** If the minor term is distributed in the conclusion but undistributed in the minor premiss, the syllogism is said to commit the fallacy of **Illicit Minor.**

Rule 4: In order for a standard-form categorical syllogism to be valid, it cannot have two negative premisses. If a syllogism has two negative premisses, then the major premiss says that all or part of *P* is *excluded* from all or part of *M*, and the minor premiss says that all or part of *S* is *excluded* from all or part of *M*. But such premisses may be true no matter how *S* and *P* are related, so from two negative premisses no relationship between *S* and *P* can be validly inferred. A syllogism which violates Rule 4 is said to commit the fallacy of **Exclusive Premisses.**

Rule 5: In order for a standard-form categorical syllogism with a negative premiss to be valid, it must also have a negative conclusion. An affirmative conclusion affirms that *S* is either wholly or partially included in *P*. This can follow validly only from two *affirmative* premisses, one of which affirms that *S* is wholly or partially included in *M* and the other of which affirms that *M* is wholly or partially included in *P*. Therefore, if one premiss of a syllogism is negative, only a negative conclusion can be validly inferred. A syllogism which violates Rule 5 is said to commit the fallacy of **Drawing an Affirmative Conclusion from a Negative Premiss.**

*Rule 6: In order for a standard-form categorical syllogism with a particular conclusion (**I** or **O**) to be valid, it must have a particular premiss.* A syllogism with two universal premisses and a particular conclusion cannot be valid, for a particular conclusion (***I*** or ***O***) has existential import and thus affirms the existence of something, whereas two universal premisses have no existential import, so that the conclusion would affirm more than the premisses, which means that the conclusion could be false even though the premisses were both true, which means that the syllogism would be invalid. Notice how this rule reflects the Boolean interpretation of existential import. A syllogism which violates Rule 6 is said to commit the **Existential Fallacy.**

SOLUTIONS
to selected exercises on pages 221–223

Page 221, I, #2: Drawing an Affirmative Conclusion from a Negative Premiss, breaks Rule 5.

Page 221, I, #6: Undistributed Middle, breaks Rule 2.

Page 221, I, #11: Existential Fallacy, breaks Rule 6.

Page 221, II, #2: Fallacy of Four Terms (because there is an equivocation on "criminal actions"), breaks Rule 1.

Page 221, II, #6: Drawing an Affirmative Conclusion from a Negative Premiss, breaks Rule 5.

Page 222, III, #2: Undistributed Middle, breaks Rule 2.

Page 222, III, #6: Exclusive Premisses, breaks Rule 4; and Drawing an Affirmative Conclusion from a Negative Premiss, breaks Rule 5.

Page 223, IV, #2: ***AII*** and ***EIO*** are the only moods in which a first-figure syllogism with a particular conclusion can be valid. Proof: if the conclusion is particular, it must be ***I*** or ***O.*** If the conclusion is ***I,*** neither premiss can be negative (Rule 5), nor can the premisses be ***AA*** (Rule 6), or ***II*** (Rule 2), or ***IA*** (which would violate Rule 2 in the first figure). Hence, the premisses can only be ***AI.*** If the conclusion is ***O,*** then in the first figure the major premiss must be ***E*** or ***O*** (otherwise Illicit Major), and therefore the minor premiss must be ***A*** or ***I*** (Rule 4). The premisses cannot be ***EA*** (Rule 6), or ***OA*** (Rule 2), or ***OI*** (Rule 2). Hence, the premisses can only be ***EI.***

Page 223, IV, #6: There are no moods in which a valid syllogism can have just two terms distributed, each one twice, for one of those distributed terms would have to be the middle term (Rule 2), and some other term would have to be distributed once in the conclusion (making the conclusion either ***A*** or ***O***) and once in a premiss, making a total of three distributed terms in the premisses, which means that one premiss must be ***E,*** which means that the conclusion must be ***O*** rather than ***A*** (Rule 5). But then the other premiss cannot be ***E*** or ***A*** (Rule 6), or ***O*** (Rule 4), or ***I*** (for then the premisses would not have three distributed terms).

Page 223, IV, #11: The conclusion must be either ***A*** or ***E*** or ***I*** or ***O.***
If the conclusion is ***A,*** then neither premiss can be negative (Rule 5), nor can the premisses be ***II*** (Rule 2). Thus, the only possible

premisses are ***AA, AI,*** or ***IA. AI*** and ***IA*** can both be eliminated on the grounds that the premisses of a valid syllogism must distribute at least one more term than is distributed in the conclusion, since the premisses must distribute any term distributed in the conclusion (Rule 3) and the premisses must also distribute the middle term (Rule 2). If the number of terms distributed in the premisses is not at least one more than the number of terms distributed in the conclusion, we shall say that the syllogism violates Rule 2–3. Thus, ***AIA*** and ***IAA*** both violate Rule 2–3, for no matter what figure they are in they must violate either Rule 2 or Rule 3. Hence, the only possible mood is ***AAA,*** which is valid only in the first figure, since ***AAA***-2 violates Rule 2, and ***AAA***-3 and ***AAA***-4 violate Rule 3 (Illicit Minor). Therefore, the only valid form with an ***A*** conclusion is ***AAA***-1.

If the conclusion is ***E,*** then at least three terms must be distributed in the premisses (Rule 2–3), which means that one premiss must be ***E,*** which means that the other premiss cannot be ***E*** or ***O*** (Rule 4) or ***I*** (Rule 2–3), which means that the other premiss must be ***A.*** Thus, the only possible moods are ***EAE*** and ***AEE.*** Now, ***EAE*** is invalid in the third and fourth figures (Rule 3, Illicit Minor), but ***EAE***-1 and ***EAE***-2 are valid. Similarly, ***AEE*** is invalid in the first and third figures (Rule 3, Illicit Major), but ***AEE***-2 and ***AEE***-4 are valid. Therefore, the only valid forms with an ***E*** conclusion are ***EAE***-1, ***EAE***-2, ***AEE***-2, and ***AEE***-4.

If the conclusion is ***I,*** then neither premiss can be negative (Rule 5), nor can the premisses be ***AA*** (Rule 6) or ***II*** (Rule 2). Thus, the only possible premisses are ***AI*** or ***IA.*** Now, ***AII*** is invalid in the second and fourth figures (Rule 2), but ***AII***-1 and ***AII***-3 are valid. Similarly, ***IAI*** is invalid in the first and second figures (Rule 2), but ***IAI***-3 and ***IAI***-4 are valid. Therefore, the only valid forms with an ***I*** conclusion are ***AII***-1, ***AII***-3, ***IAI***-3, and ***IAI***-4.

If the conclusion is ***O,*** then the major premiss cannot be ***I*** (Rule 3, Illicit Major), so the major premiss must be either ***A*** or ***E*** or ***O.*** We shall consider each of these cases separately. If the major premiss is ***A,*** then the minor premiss cannot be ***A*** or ***E*** (Rule 6) or ***I*** (Rule 2–3), but it can be ***O.*** Now, ***AOO*** is invalid in the first and third figures (Rule 3, Illicit Major) and invalid in the fourth figure (Rule 2), but ***AOO***-2 is valid. If the major premiss is ***E,*** then the minor premiss cannot be ***A*** (Rule 6) or ***E*** or ***O*** (Rule 4), but it can be ***I,*** and ***EIO*** is valid in all four figures. If the major premiss is ***O,*** then the minor premiss cannot be ***E*** or ***O*** (Rule 4) or ***I*** (Rule 2–3), but it can be ***A.*** Now, ***OAO*** is invalid in the first figure (Rule 2) and invalid in the second and fourth figures (Rule 3, Illicit Major), but ***OAO***-3 is valid. Therefore, the only valid forms with an ***O*** conclusion are ***AOO***-2, ***EIO***-1, ***EIO***-2, ***EIO***-3, ***EIO***-4, and ***OAO***-3.

Notice that we can now prove that any syllogism which conforms to all six Syllogistic Rules is valid by testing the validity of these fifteen valid forms with Venn Diagrams.

EXAMINATION
on Chapter 6

Write your answers on a separate sheet of paper, then check them against the answers given at the end of the examination. If you miss a question, restudy the appropriate part of the text.

1. Name the mood and figure of *all* the valid standard-form categorical syllogisms whose premisses are represented by the following Venn Diagram. Assume that *P* is the major term, *S* is the minor term, and *M* is the middle term.

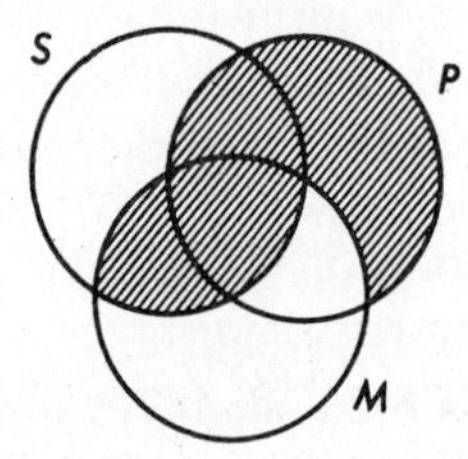

2. Name the mood and figure of *all* the valid standard-form categorical syllogisms whose premisses are represented by the following Venn Diagram. Assume that *P* is the major term, *S* is the minor term, and *M* is the middle term.

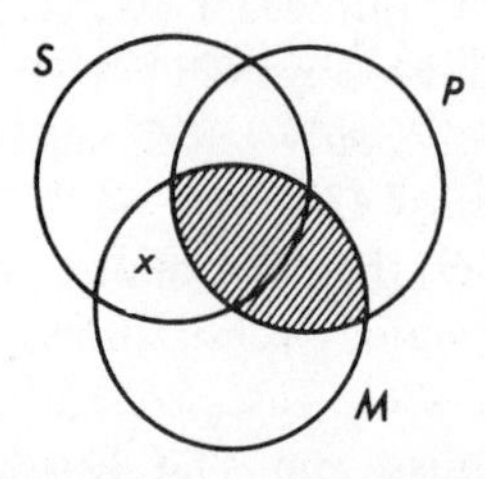

3. One of the methods of refuting a given argument (that is, proving it invalid) is to construct a logical analogy. What two attributes must a logical analogy have in order to refute a given argument successfully?

4. Test the validity of each of the following syllogisms by means of a Venn Diagram. State whether each argument is valid or invalid. If an argument is invalid, state which of the six Syllogistic Rules it violates.
   a. ***AEE*-1.**
   b. ***AOO*-1.**
   c. ***OAO*-3.**

5. Test the validity of each of the following arguments by means of a Venn Diagram. [This can be done even though the arguments are not standard-form categorical syllogisms.]
   a. All household pets are domestic animals.
      No unicorns are domestic animals.
      There are unicorns.
      Therefore, some unicorns are not household pets.
   b. Some M is not P.
      All M is either S or P.
      Therefore, some S is not P.
   c. Everything which is both M and S is also P.
      Some S is either M or P.
      Therefore, some S is P.

6. Answer the following questions by appealing to the six Syllogistic Rules. Make sure you consider all possible cases.
   a. Can a valid standard-form categorical syllogism in the third figure have a universal conclusion?
   b. Can a valid standard-form categorical syllogism in the first figure have a negative minor premiss?
   c. Can a valid standard-form categorical syllogism in the second figure have an affirmative conclusion?
   d. Can a valid standard-form categorical syllogism in the third figure have a universal conclusion?
   e. Can a valid standard-form categorical syllogism have a term which occurs undistributed in the conclusion but distributed in the premisses?
   f. Can a valid standard-form categorical syllogism have a negative conclusion and two affirmative premisses?

ANSWERS

1. ***AEE***-2 and ***AEE***-4.
2. ***EIO***-1, ***EIO***-2, ***EIO***-3, ***EIO***-4.
3. The logical analogy must (1) have the same form as the given argument, and (2) have obviously true premisses and an obviously false conclusion.

4. a.

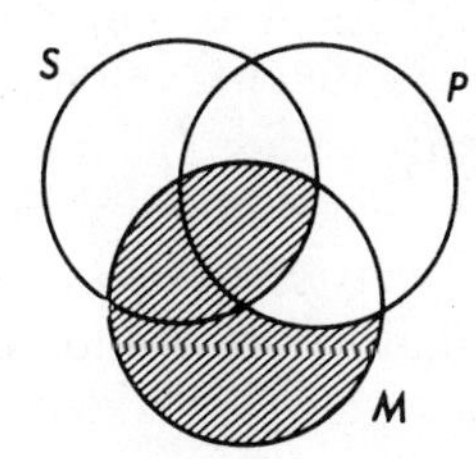

invalid

Rule 3

b.

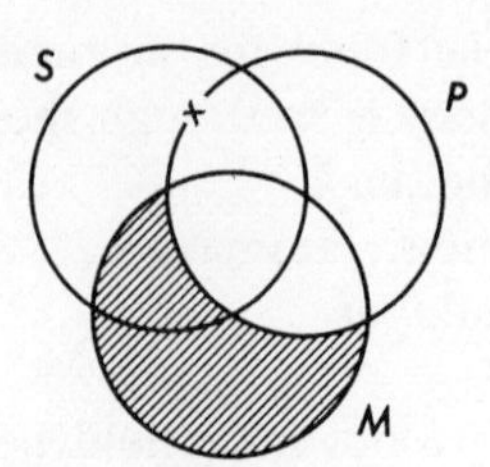

invalid
Rule 3

c.

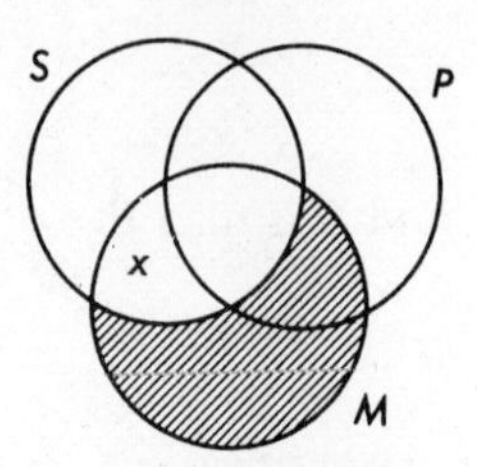

valid

5. a.

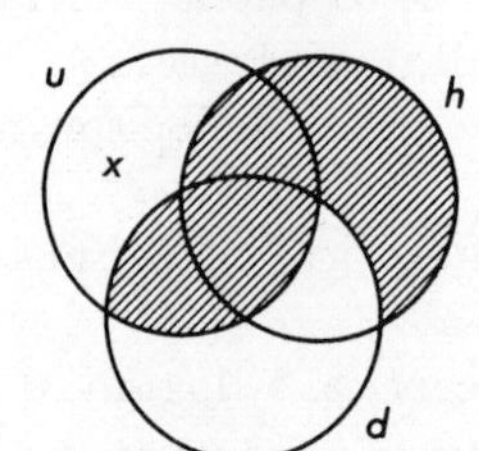

valid

b.

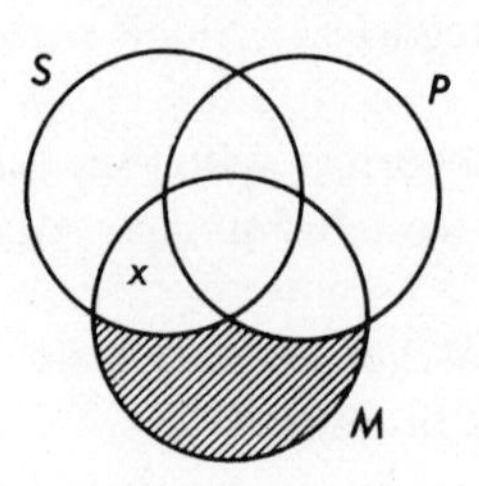

valid

c.

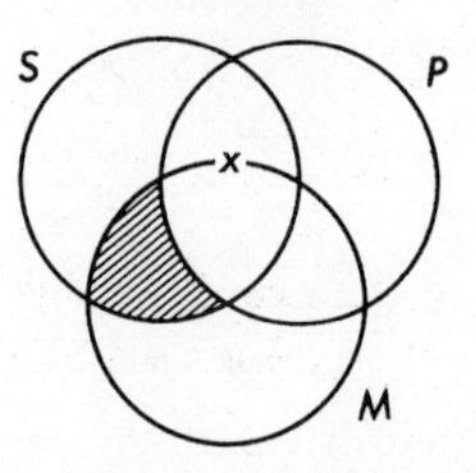

valid

6. a. No. If the conclusion is universal, then the minor term is distributed in the conclusion, which means that the minor term must be distributed in the minor premiss (Rule 3) where in the third figure it occurs as the predicate, which means that the minor premiss must be negative, which means that the conclusion must be negative (Rule 5), which means that the conclusion distributes the major term, which must then also be distributed in the major

premiss (Rule 3) where in the third figure the major term occurs as the predicate, which means that the major premiss must be negative, which means that there would have to be two negative premisses, which is impossible (Rule 4).

b. No. If the minor premiss is negative, then the conclusion must be negative (Rule 5), which means that the major term is distributed in the conclusion, which means that the major term must be distributed in the major premiss (Rule 3) where in the first figure it occurs as the predicate, which means that the major premiss must be negative, which means that there would be two negative premisses, which is impossible (Rule 4).

c. No. In the second figure the middle term occurs as the predicate in each premiss. Since the middle term must be distributed in at least one premiss (Rule 2), at least one premiss must be negative. Therefore, the conclusion must be negative (Rule 5).

d. No. If the conclusion is universal, it must be either ***A*** or ***E***. If the conclusion is ***A***, then the minor term is distributed in the conclusion, which means that the minor term must be distributed in the minor premiss (Rule 3) where in the third figure it occurs as the predicate, which means that the minor premiss must be negative, which violates Rule 5. If the conclusion is ***E***, then both the major and minor terms are distributed in the conclusion, which means that they must both be distributed in the premisses (Rule 3) where in the third figure they both occur as predicates, which means that both premisses must be negative, which violates Rule 4.

e. No. If there is a term distributed in the premisses which is not distributed in the conclusion, then (since the middle term must also be distributed in the premisses) there must be either three terms distributed in the premisses and one in the conclusion, or two terms distributed in the premisses and none in the conclusion. We shall consider these two cases separately. If there are three terms distributed in the premisses and one in the conclusion, then one of the premisses must be ***E*** and thus the conclusion (which distributes one term) must be ***O*** (Rule 5). But the other premiss cannot be ***A*** or ***E*** (Rule 6) or ***O*** (Rule 4) or ***I*** (since then there would not be three terms distributed in the premisses). On the other hand, if there are two terms distributed in the premisses and none in the conclusion, then the conclusion must be ***I*** and thus both premisses must be affirmative (Rule 5). But the premisses cannot be ***AA*** (Rule 6) or ***II*** (Rule 2) or ***AI*** or ***IA*** (since then there would not be two terms distributed in the premisses).

f. No. If the conclusion is negative, then it distributes at least one term, which means that the premisses must distribute at least two terms, the term distributed in the conclusion (Rule 3) and the middle term (Rule 2). But the only pair of affirmative premisses in which two terms are distributed is ***AA,*** and ***AAO*** violates Rule 6 while ***AAE*** violates either Rule 2 or Rule 3, since the premisses cannot distribute the major term, the minor term, and the middle term.

Chapter 7
Arguments in Ordinary Language

READ PAGES 224–227 OF THE TEXT

7.1 Reducing the Number of Terms in a Syllogistic Argument

We shall call an argument a **syllogistic argument** if it either is a standard-form categorical syllogism or can be translated into a standard-form categorical syllogism without any change of meaning. Many syllogistic arguments encountered in ordinary discourse are not standard-form categorical syllogisms, and we want to develop techniques for translating such syllogistic arguments into standard form so that we can apply the tests of validity studied in the preceding chapter of the text (that is, Venn Diagrams and the six Syllogistic Rules).

In this section you learned two techniques for translating syllogistic arguments into standard-form categorical syllogisms:

1. If a syllogistic argument has more than three terms because some terms are synonyms of others, then replace terms by their synonyms in such a way as to reduce the total number of terms to three.
2. If a syllogistic argument has more than three terms because some terms are complements of others, then eliminate complements by using conversion, obversion, or contraposition to replace some propositions by other propositions logically equivalent to them in such a way as to reduce the total number of terms to three.

SOLUTIONS
to selected exercises on pages 227–228

There is, in general, more than one standard-form translation of a given syllogistic argument, so the translations provided below are not necessarily the only correct ones. However, the various standard-form translations of a given syllogistic argument are either all valid or all invalid.

Page 227, #2:

Some metals are rare and costly substances.
All welder's materials are metals. [by obversion]
Therefore, some welder's materials are rare and costly substances.

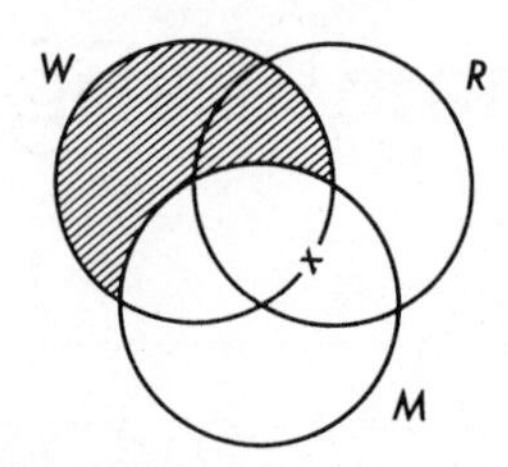

invalid

Undistributed Middle

Page 228, #6:

All material things are changeable things. [by obversion]
All worldly goods are material things. [by obversion]
Therefore, all worldly goods are changeable things.

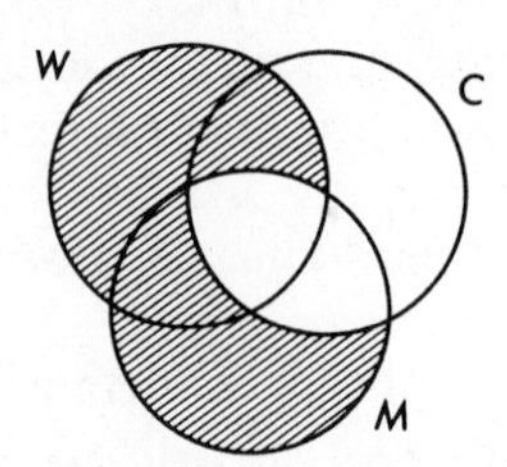

valid

READ PAGES 228–233 OF THE TEXT

7.2 Translating Categorical Propositions into Standard Form

A syllogistic argument may not be in standard form because some of its constituent propositions are not standard-form categorical propositions. In this section you learned techniques for translating propositions into standard form. Listed below on the left are various kinds of propositions which can be translated into standard form. On the right, opposite each item, is a statement of the technique for translating that item into a standard-form categorical proposition. Cover up the right-hand column until you have recalled to your own satisfaction how to translate each item into standard form. Restudy in the text the explanation of any technique which you do not fully understand. You must master these techniques in order to understand and apply the material in the rest of this chapter.

1. A proposition is not in standard form because it is a singular proposition, that is, its subject term is not a class term but a proper name or definite description which refers to a single individual entity.

   No translation is necessary. Singular propositions are to be treated as if they were already in standard form. Affirmative singular propositions are to be treated as ***A*** propositions, and negative singular propositions are to be treated as ***E*** propositions. Thus, "Socrates is a mortal" is already in standard form and is to be treated as if it said "All things that are Socrates are mortals." And "Socrates is not a mortal" is already in standard form and is to be treated as if it said "No things that are Socrates are mortals." Likewise, the name of a single individual can appear as the predicate term of a standard-form categorical proposition. An affirmative proposition of this type is to be treated as an ***A*** proposition, and a negative proposition of this type is to be treated as an ***E*** proposition.

2. A proposition is not in standard form because the predicate is an adjective (or adjectival phrase), rather than a class term.

   Replace the adjective with the corresponding class term, that is, the class term which designates the class of all those entities which have the attribute connoted by the adjective.

3. A proposition is not in standard form because its main verb is not a form of the verb "to be."

   Preserve the quantifier and the subject term of the given proposition but translate the rest into an equivalent expression using some form of the verb "to be" plus a class term.

EXAMPLE:
Some men play chess.

TRANSLATION:
Some men are chess players.

4. A proposition is not in standard form because the words are not arranged in the standard order.

Arrange the words in the standard order.

EXAMPLE:
These bananas are all rotten.

TRANSLATION:
All these bananas are rotten things.

5. A proposition is not in standard form because its quantity is not indicated by one of the standard quantifiers ("all," "no," "some") but is indicated in some other way.

Determine the intended meaning of the proposition. Express this intended meaning in standard form by using the appropriate standard quantifier.

EXAMPLES:	TRANSLATIONS:
Every politician is a realist.	All politicians are realists.
Any stipulation is arbitrary.	All stipulations are arbitrary things.
A man is a rational animal.	All men are rational animals.
A man is waiting.	Some men are those who are waiting.
The Volkswagen is an inexpensive car.	All Volkswagens are inexpensive cars.
Our Volkswagen is an inexpensive car.	[No translation necessary. The proposition is already in standard form as an *A* proposition.]

6. A proposition is not in standard form because it is a so-called **exclusive** proposition, beginning with the words "only" or "none but."

Translate into an *A* proposition with subject and predicate terms interchanged.

EXAMPLES:	TRANSLATIONS:
Only seniors can enroll in that course.	All those who can enroll in that course are seniors.
None but fools would do that.	All those who would do that are fools.

7. A proposition is not in standard form because it contains no word which indicates quantity.

Determine the intended meaning of the proposition and express that intended meaning in standard form.

EXAMPLES:	TRANSLATIONS:
Whales are mammals.	All whales are mammals.
Whales live in these waters.	Some whales are creatures who live in these waters.

8. A proposition is not in standard form even though it does affirm a relationship between two classes.

Determine what relationship between the two classes is being affirmed and express this in standard form.

EXAMPLES:	TRANSLATIONS:
Not all politicians are realists.	Some politicians are not realists.
There are idealistic politicians.	Some politicians are idealists.
There are no idealistic politicians.	No politicians are idealists.
No one is both idealistic and a politician.	No idealists are politicians.

9. A proposition is not in standard form because it is a so-called **exceptive** proposition, which really makes two affirmations at once. For example, "All except *S* are *P*" affirms both that all non-*S* is *P* and that no *S* is *P*. A proposition can also be exceptive because of the occurrence of one of the following quasinumerical quantifiers: "almost all," "not quite all," "all but a few," "only some," "almost no," "almost everyone."

Determine the intended meaning of the proposition and express this intended meaning in two separate standard-form categorical propositions.

EXAMPLES:	TRANSLATIONS:
Almost all *S* are *P*.	Some *S* is *P*. Some *S* is not *P*.
Not quite all *S* are *P*.	Some *S* is *P*. Some *S* is not *P*.
All but a few *S* are *P*.	Some *S* is *P*. Some *S* is not *P*.
Only some *S* are *P*.	Some *S* is *P*. Some *S* is not *P*.
Almost no *S* are *P*.	Some *S* is *P*. Some *S* is not *P*.
Almost everyone is *P*.	Some persons are *P*. Some persons are not *P*.
All except *S* are *P*.	All non-*S* is *P*. No *S* is *P*.
All but *S* are *P*.	All non-*S* is *P*. No *S* is *P*.
S alone are not *P*.	All non-*S* is *P*. No *S* is *P*.

If an argument conforms to all the requirements of a standard-form categorical syllogism except that one of its premisses is an exceptive proposition, then the validity or invalidity of the argument is determined by whether or not the conclusion follows validly from either part of the translation of the exceptive premiss, together with the other premiss.

If an argument conforms to all the requirements of a standard-form categorical syllogism except that both of its premisses are exceptive propositions, then the argument is valid if and only if the conclusion follows validly from some combination of the parts of the premisses.

If an argument conforms to all the requirements of a standard-form categorical syllogism except that its conclusion and one or both of its premisses are exceptive propositions, then the argument is valid if and only if *each* part of the conclusion follows validly from some combination of the parts of the premisses.

Of course, if an argument conforms to all the requirements of a standard-form categorical syllogism except that its conclusion is an exceptive proposition, then the argument cannot be valid, because no pair of standard-form premisses can imply both parts of an exceptive proposition.

SOLUTIONS

to selected exercises on page 234

It is very important for you to develop an ability to translate quickly and confidently into standard form. Otherwise, you will find it difficult to determine the validity or invalidity of many syllogisms in ordinary language.

Page 234, #2: No orchids are fragrant things.

Page 234, #6: All Ropos are real Havanas.

Page 234, #11: All persons who hear her sing are inspired persons.

Page 234, #16: All party regulars are supporters of any candidate of the Old Guard. *Or:* All candidates of the Old Guard are persons supported by the party regulars.

Page 234, #21: Some glittering things are not gold things.

READ PAGES 234–237 OF THE TEXT

7.3 Uniform Translation

In order for a syllogistic argument to be a standard-form categorical syllogism, it must contain exactly three class terms. Some syllogistic arguments can be translated into standard form only with the help of a **parameter,** or auxiliary symbol, by means of which one can formulate three class terms which are such that the propositions in the original argument can be translated into standard-form categorical propositions containing these three class terms. The function of the parameter is to provide the basis for the formulation of the three terms. There are three parameters that are especially useful in translating certain syllogistic arguments into standard form: "times," "places," and "cases." If the propositions in the original syllogistic argument make some reference to the times at which various events occur, then "times" will probably be the easiest parameter to use. If the propositions in the syllogistic argument make some reference to the places at which various events occur, then "places" will probably be the easiest parameter to use. Otherwise, "cases" may be the easiest parameter to use. The parameter serves as the basis for the formulation of three class terms which can be used to translate the original propositions into standard form. In choosing a parameter and in formulating the three class terms, one must consider whether the intended meaning of each original proposition can be expressed in standard form as a relationship between two of those class terms.

The choice of an appropriate parameter and the formulation of three class terms which are suitable for a uniform translation of all three propositions into standard form often involve some trial and error. One usually acquires facility at such translations only after considerable practice, so the following exercises should be dealt with carefully and thoroughly.

SOLUTIONS
to selected exercises on pages 237–241

There is usually more than one standard-form translation of a given proposition, so the translations provided here are not necessarily the only correct ones.

Page 237, I, #2: No times when she goes to work are times when she drives her car.

Page 237, I, #6: All places where she may happen to be are places where she tries to sell life insurance.

Page 237, II, #2:
All predicables are things that come in contradictory pairs.
No names are things that come in contradictory pairs.
Therefore, no names are predicables.

AEE-2

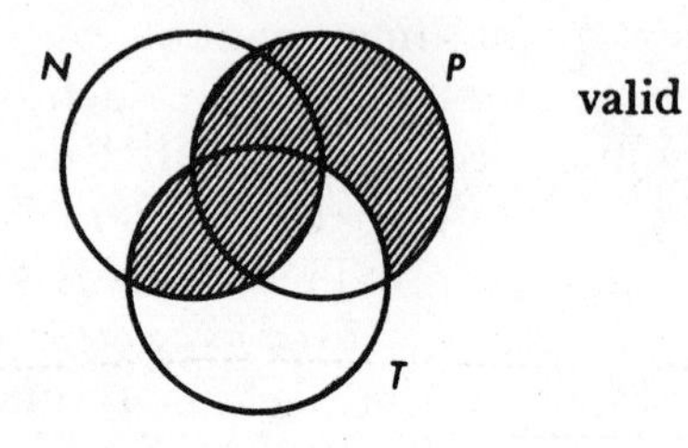

valid

Page 238, II, #6:
All times following rain are times when fish do not bite.
The present time is a time when fish do not bite.
Therefore, the present time is a time following rain.

AAA-2

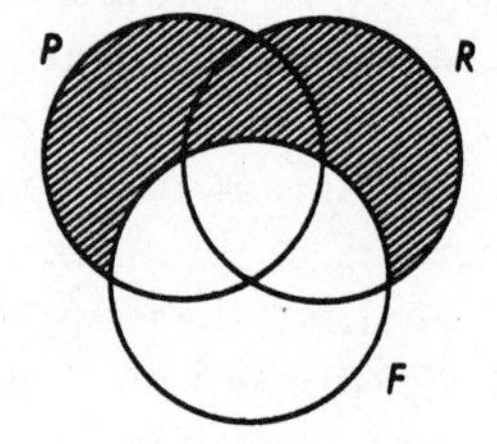

invalid

Undistributed Middle

Page 238, II, #11:
All alcoholics are inebriated people.
No inebriated people are dependable people.
Therefore, no dependable people are alcoholics.

AEE-4

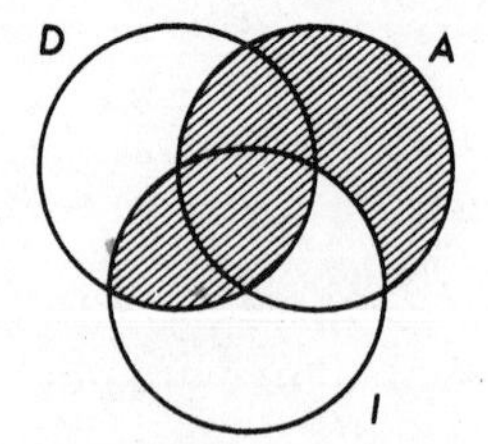

valid

Page 239, II, #16: There are two different plausible interpretations of this argument.

First interpretation:

All people are thinking beings.
All bridge players are people.
Therefore, all bridge players are thinking beings.

***AAA*-1**

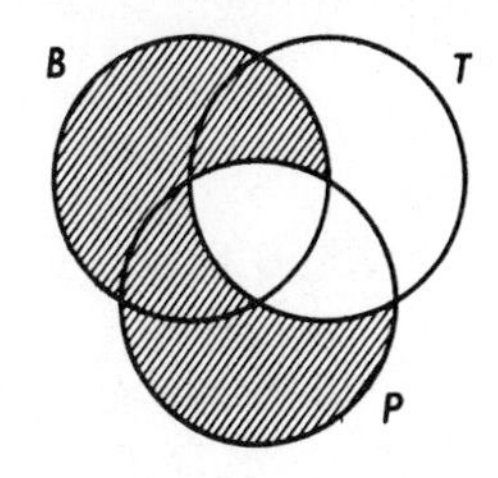

valid

Second interpretation:

All people are beings who think at some time or another.
All bridge players are people.
Therefore, all bridge players are beings who think at all times when they are playing bridge.

Notice that this second interpretation of the argument cannot be reduced to standard form. It has four terms and therefore is invalid because it violates the first syllogistic rule.

Page 239, II, #21:

All practice is theory.
All surgery is practice.
Therefore, all surgery is theory.

***AAA*-1**

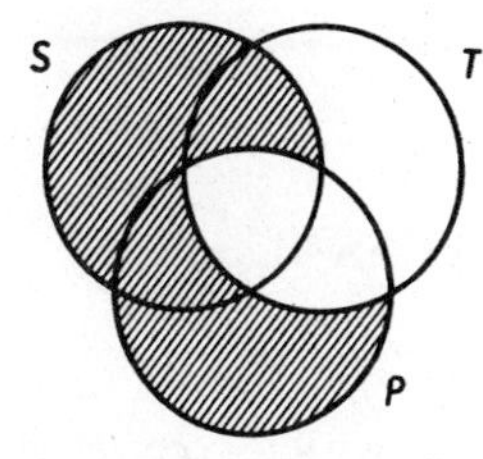

valid

Page 240, II, #26:

All places where there is smoke are places where there is fire.
The basement is not a place where there is smoke.
Therefore, the basement is not a place where there is fire.

***AEE*-1**

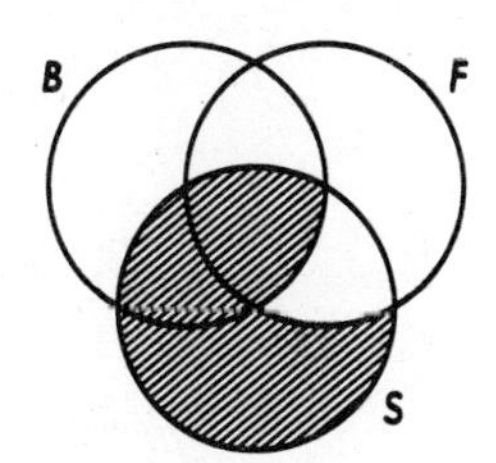

invalid

Illicit Major

Page 240, II, #31:

No persons truly objective in their approach are persons likely to be mistaken.
All persons likely to be mistaken are persons who ignore the facts.
Therefore, no persons who ignore the facts are persons truly objective in their approach.

***EAE*-4**

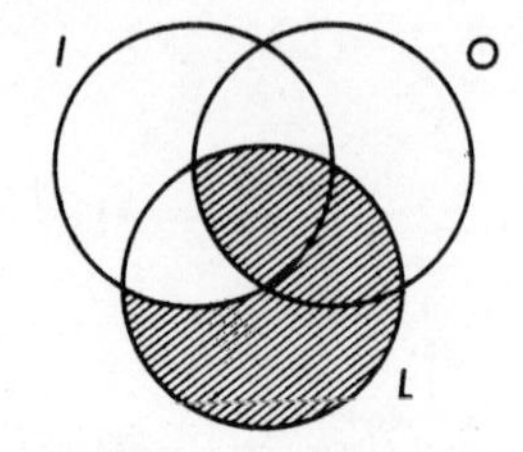

invalid

Illicit Minor

Page 240, II, #36:

All invalid syllogisms are syllogisms that commit an Illicit Major.
This syllogism is not an invalid syllogism.
Therefore, this syllogism is not a syllogism that commits an Illicit Major.

***AEE*-1**

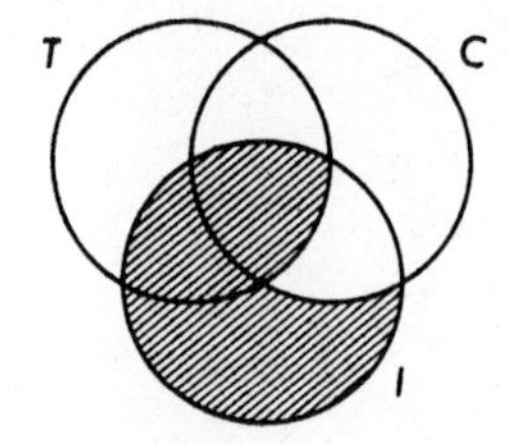

invalid

Illicit Major

Page 241, II, #41:

All situations in which much money is involved are situations in which competition is stiff.
This situation is a situation in which much money is involved.
Therefore, this situation is a situation in which competition is stiff.

***AAA*-1**

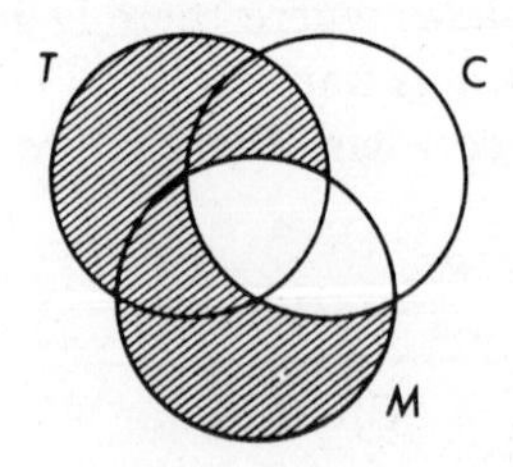

valid

READ PAGES 241–243 OF THE TEXT

7.4 Enthymemes

An **enthymeme** is an argument, part of which is "understood" or implicitly assumed but not explicitly stated. A syllogistic argument whose major premiss is not stated is called a **first-order enthymeme,** and a syllogistic argument whose minor premiss is not stated is called a **second-order enthymeme,** whereas a syllogistic argument whose conclusion is implied but not explicitly stated is called a **third-order enthymeme.** In order to test the validity of an enthymematic syllogistic argument, the missing proposition must be supplied. If the missing proposition is a premiss, it is legitimate to supply only a proposition which can be presumed to be common knowledge. If one supplies an implausible proposition as a premiss, then, although the resulting argument may be valid, it will probably not be sound, and therefore it will not establish the truth of its conclusion. In some cases only the context can determine what proposition should be supplied.

SOLUTIONS
to selected exercises on pages 243–246

Page 243, #2: Second order.

All things which are always in motion are immortal things.
All souls are things which are always in motion.
Therefore, all souls are immortal things.

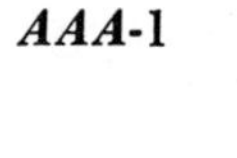

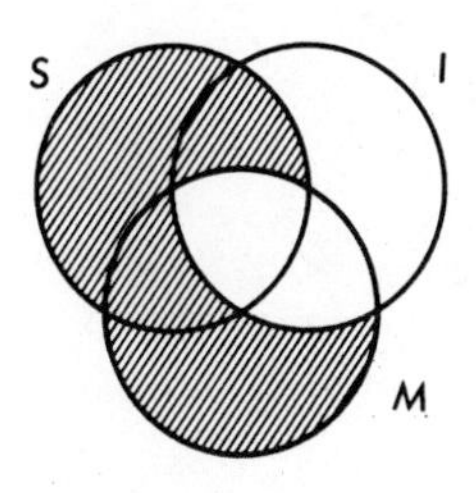

valid

Page 244, #6: Third order.

All successful persons are well-groomed persons.
Leslie Cole is a well-groomed person.
Therefore, Leslie Cole is a successful person.

AAA-2

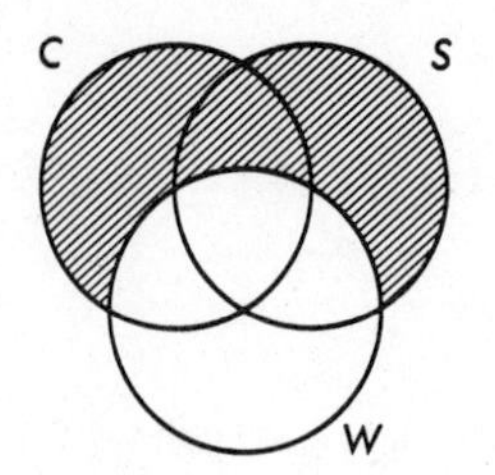

invalid

Undistributed Middle

Page 244, #11: Second order.

All physicians are college graduates.
All members of the A.M.A. are physicians.
Therefore, all members of the A.M.A. are college graduates.

AAA-1

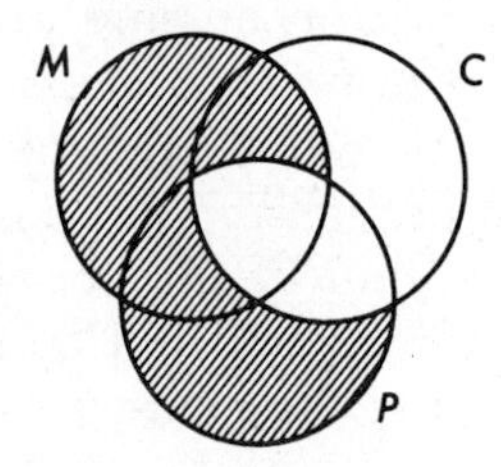

valid

Valid enthymeme with a plausible missing minor premiss.

Page 245, #16: First order.

All persons who have a telephone are persons whose names are listed in the phone book.
The Adamsons are not persons whose names are listed in the phone book.
Therefore, the Adamsons are not persons who have a telephone.

AEE-2

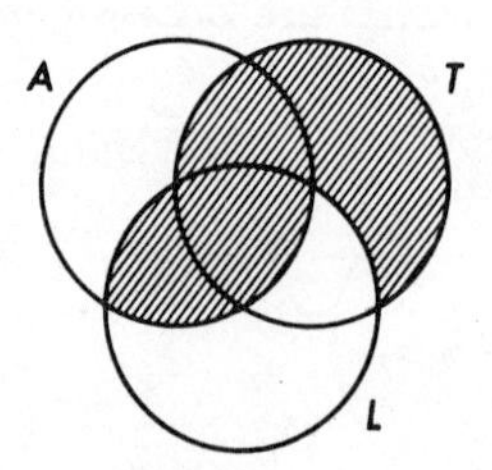

valid

This is a valid enthymeme, but the suppressed major premiss that we have supplied is implausible, since there are many unlisted telephones. On the other hand, if the suppressed major premiss is the converse of the proposition supplied above, then the major premiss will be more plausible but the argument will be invalid:

All persons whose names are listed in the phone book are persons who have a telephone.
The Adamsons are not persons whose names are listed in the phone book.
Therefore, the Adamsons are not persons who have a telephone.

***AEE*-1**

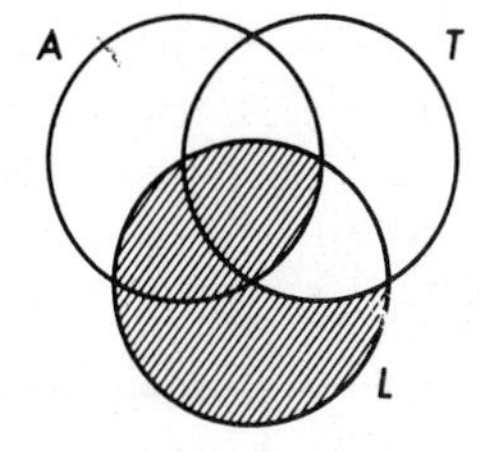

invalid

Illicit Major

Page 245, #21: Third order.

No sense knowledge is immaterial knowledge.
Some knowledge possessed by us is immaterial knowledge.
Therefore, some knowledge possessed by us is not sense knowledge.

***EIO*-2**

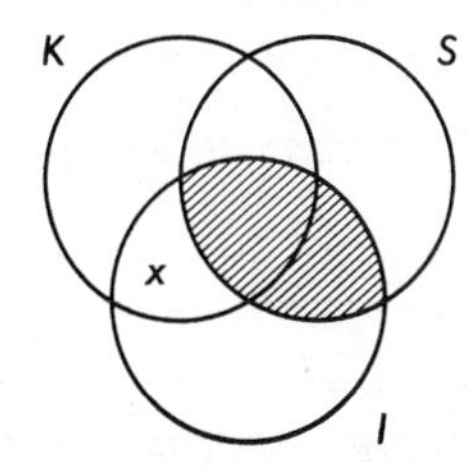

valid

Page 245, #26: First order.

All species which tend to increase at a greater rate than their means of subsistence are species which are occasionally subject to a severe struggle for existence.
Man is a species which tends to increase at a greater rate than his means of subsistence.
Therefore, man is a species which is occasionally subject to a severe struggle for existence.

***AAA*-1**

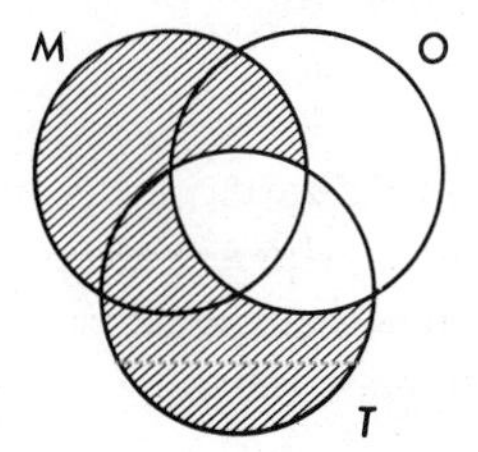

valid

READ PAGES 246–247 OF THE TEXT

7.5 Sorites

Sometimes it is possible to deduce a certain conclusion from a group of more than two premisses by constructing a chain of syllogisms, in which two of the premisses imply an intermediate conclusion, which together with another premiss implies another intermediate conclusion, and so on, until the final conclusion is reached. Of course, the final conclusion follows validly from the original group of premisses if and only if every syllogism in the chain is valid. Where such a chain of syllogisms is stated enthymematically by suppressing all the intermediate conclusions and stating only the original group of premisses and the final conclusion, the resulting argument is called a **sorites.** A sorites is said to be in standard form when it satisfies the following conditions:

1. All of its propositions are standard-form categorical propositions.
2. Each term in the sorites occurs exactly twice.
3. Every proposition (except the last) has a term in common with the proposition which immediately follows it.

You can test the validity of a sorites by the following procedure:

1. Translate the sorites into standard form.
2. Supply the suppressed intermediate conclusions, thus constructing a chain of syllogisms.
3. Test the validity of each syllogism in the chain. The original sorites is valid if and only if every syllogism in the chain is valid.

SOLUTIONS
to selected exercises on pages 247–249

There is, in general, more than one standard-form translation of a given sorites, so the translations provided here are not necessarily the only correct ones. However, the various standard-form translations of a given sorites are either all valid or all invalid.

Page 248, I, #2:

(2′) Jenkins is a person who is always blundering.
(3′) No competent persons are persons who are always blundering.
(1′) All experienced persons are competent persons.
Therefore, Jenkins is not an experienced person.

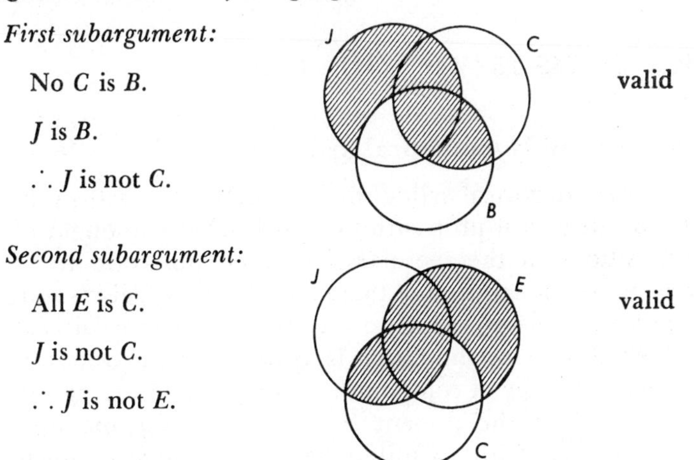

Therefore, the sorites is valid.

Notice that the order of the first two premisses in the sorites has been reversed in the first subargument, so that the subargument will be in standard form.

Page 248, II, #2:

(2′) This dish is a pudding.
(1′) All puddings are nice things.
(3′) No nice things are wholesome things.
Therefore, this dish is not a wholesome thing.

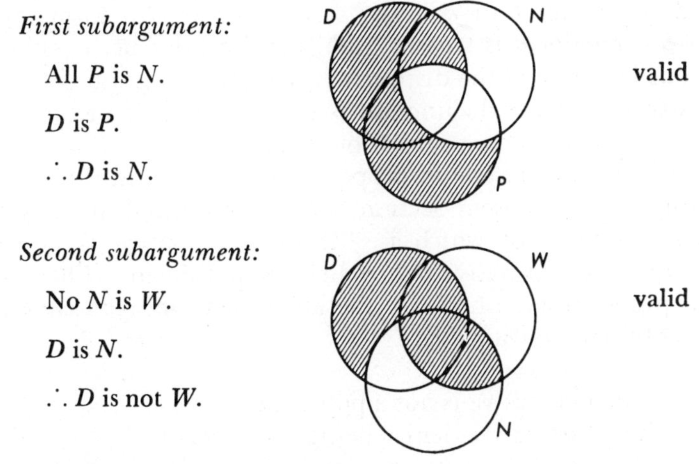

Therefore, the sorites is valid.

Notice that the order of the first two premisses in the sorites has been reversed in the first subargument, so that the subargument will be in standard form.

READ PAGES 249–252 OF THE TEXT

7.6 Disjunctive and Hypothetical Syllogisms

Standard-form categorical syllogisms are composed exclusively of standard-form categorical propositions, which may be thought of as **simple** propositions in the sense that they do not contain other propositions as components. But there are many syllogisms (arguments with two premisses) which are composed of propositions at least one of which is **compound**, that is, contains other propositions as components. One type of compound proposition occurring in the arguments studied in the present section is the **disjunction**, an example of which is: "Either Chubby has been eating too much or Chubby has not been getting enough exercise." The two component propositions which are the **disjuncts** of this disjunction are

Chubby has been eating too much.
Chubby has not been getting enough exercise.

What the disjunction affirms is that at least one of the two propositions above is true, that is, either the first proposition is true or the second proposition is true or both propositions are true. Where the small letters p, q, r, s, and so on, are used to stand for any propositions whatever, the *form* of any disjunction can be schematically represented as "Either p or q." Any disjunction of this form says that either p is true or q is true or both p and q are true, in other words, that at least one of the disjuncts is true. If at least one of the disjuncts is true then the disjunction is true, whereas if neither of the disjuncts is true then the disjunction is false.

The second type of compound proposition occurring in the arguments studied in the present section is the **conditional** (or **hypothetical**), an example of which is, "If the first native is not a politician, then the first native denies being a politician." The two component propositions, which are the **antecedent** and **consequent** respectively of this conditional, are

The first native is not a politician.
The first native denies being a politician.

The *form* of any conditional can be schematically represented as "If p, then q." Any conditional of this form affirms that if p is true then q is true. Such a conditional is false when p is true and q is false.

The *valid* disjunctive and hypothetical syllogisms studied in this section can now be schematically restated as follows:

Disjunctive Syllogism. Valid:

Either p or q.
p is false.
Therefore, q is true.

(If at least one of the two propositions p and q is true, and if p is false, then it follows that q must be true.)

Pure Hypothetical Syllogism. Valid:

If p, then q.
If q, then r.
Therefore, if p, then r.

(If it is true to say that if p is true then q is true and if q is true then r is true, then it follows that it must be true to say that if p is true then r is true.)

Modus Ponens (mixed hypothetical syllogism). Valid:

If p, then q.
p is true.
Therefore, q is true.

(If it is true to say that if p is true then q is true and if p is true, then it follows that q must be true.)

Modus Tollens (mixed hypothetical syllogism). Valid:

If p, then q.
q is false.
Therefore, p is false.

(If it is true to say that if p is true then q is true and if q is false, then it follows that p must be false, for if p were true then q would be true, according to the first premiss, but q is not true, according to the second premiss.)

In the following chapter of the text, techniques will be developed for proving the validity of the preceding four forms of argument.

Each of the following *invalid* forms of argument bears a superficial resemblance to one of the preceding valid forms:

Invalid Disjunctive Syllogism:

Either p or q.
p is true.
Therefore, q is false.

(This argument bears a superficial resemblance to the valid disjunctive syllogism.)

Invalid Pure Hypothetical Syllogism:

If p, then q.
If r, then q.
Therefore, if p, then r.

(This argument bears a superficial resemblance to the valid pure hypothetical syllogism.)

Fallacy of Affirming the Consequent. Invalid:

If p, then q.
q is true.
Therefore, p is true.

(This argument bears a superficial resemblance to *modus ponens.*)

Fallacy of Denying the Antecedent. Invalid:

If p, then q.
p is false.
Therefore, q is false.

(This argument bears a superficial resemblance to *modus tollens.*)

In the following chapter of the text, techniques will be developed for proving the invalidity of the four forms of argument that are listed above.

SOLUTIONS
to selected exercises on pages 252–255

Page 252, #2: Fallacy of Affirming the Consequent. Invalid.

Page 252, #6: *Modus Tollens.* Valid.

Page 253, #11: Fallacy of Denying the Antecedent. Invalid.

Page 253, #16: *Modus Tollens.* Valid.

Page 254, #21: Disjunctive Syllogism. Valid.

Page 254, #26: *Modus Tollens.* Valid.

READ PAGES 255–259 OF THE TEXT

7.7 The Dilemma

A **dilemma** can have two forms, which can be schematically represented by using the symbolism introduced in the preceding section of this book.

COMPLEX DILEMMA: If p then q, and if r then s.
Either p or r.
Therefore, either q or s.

SIMPLE DILEMMA: If p then q, and if r then q.
Either p or r.
Therefore, q.

The difference between these two forms is that in the complex dilemma the two conditionals in the first premiss have two different propositions as consequents, and the conclusion of the complex dilemma is the disjunction of these two propositions; whereas in the simple dilemma the two conditionals in the first premiss have the same proposition as consequent, and the conclusion of the simple dilemma is this proposition. In the following chapter of the text, techniques will be developed for proving the validity of these two forms of argument.

The dilemma occurs in debate when one person argues that his adversary must accept one of two alternative propositions, and that no matter which proposition he accepts, there follows a conclusion which he presumably does not want to accept.

There are three ways of evading the conclusion of such a dilemma:

1. ***Escape Between the Horns.*** That is, reject the disjunctive premiss by showing that it is not necessarily true, that there is some third possibility besides p and r. Where the disjunctive premiss is necessarily true (i.e., where r is the contradictory of p), then it is not possible to escape between the horns.

2. ***Grasp the Dilemma by the Horns.*** That is, reject the premiss which is a conjunction of two conditionals. This can be done by rejecting either of the conditionals, since a conjunction is false if one of its conjuncts is false. To reject one of the conditionals, show that its antecedent can be true while its consequent is false.

3. ***Rebut the Dilemma by Means of a Counterdilemma.*** That is, construct another dilemma with similar premisses (preferably constructed out of the ingredients of the premisses of the original dilemma) but with a different conclusion (preferably the opposite conclusion).

Notice that these three techniques are not ways of proving the original dilemma invalid. They are merely ways of evading the conclusion of the original dilemma.

SOLUTIONS
to selected exercises on pages 259–262

One can always try to refute a given dilemma by escaping between the horns, unless the disjunctive premiss is necessarily true. One can always try to refute a given dilemma by grasping it by the horns, that is, by rejecting one of the conditionals by showing that its antecedent can be true while its consequent is false. The kind of counterdilemma which can be constructed will depend upon the ingredients of the original dilemma.

Page 259, #2: This argument is of the following form, which is slightly different from the forms studied in the preceding section of the text:

> If p is true then q is false, and if r is true then q is true.
> Either q is true or q is false.
> Therefore, either p is false or r is false.

This form of argument is valid. The second premiss states that q is either true or false. If q is true, then p must be false (by *modus tollens* applied to the first conditional in the first premiss), whereas if q is false, then r must be false (by *modus tollens* applied to the second conditional in the first premiss). Therefore, either p or r must be false.

It is impossible to escape between the horns, since the disjunctive premiss is necessarily true. But it would be plausible to grasp the dilemma by either horn, arguing either (a) that we can have peace even though we encourage the competitive spirit, so long as we have stable and just economic and political institutions, or (b) that we can make progress through altruistic cooperation even though we do not encourage the competitive spirit.

One could also rebut the given dilemma by means of the following (nonrefuting) counterdilemma:

If we encourage the competitive spirit, we shall make progress; whereas if we do not encourage the competitive spirit we shall have peace.
We must either encourage or not encourage the competitive spirit.
Therefore, we shall either make progress or have peace.

Page 260, #6: Since the disjunctive premiss of this dilemma is the same proposition as the conclusion of the preceding dilemma, we can escape between the horns for the same reasons as are presented at the end of the text in the solution to the preceding dilemma. It would also be plausible to grasp the present dilemma by the second horn, since a deductive argument which brings nothing new to light may still be of some value. It is not possible to construct a plausible rebutting counterdilemma out of the original dilemma's ingredients, but other rebutting counterdilemmas could be constructed.

Page 261, #11: It is perhaps possible to go between the horns, arguing that there is a mode of living between extravagant and modest. It is possible to grasp the dilemma by either horn, arguing that one who lives extravagantly has no money left to contribute, and that one who lives modestly does so because he has no extra money for extravagances and therefore no extra money for contributions. A plausible but nonrefuting rebuttal can be constructed out of the original dilemma's ingredients.

Page 261, #16: The argument is of the following valid form:

If p, then either q or r.
q is false and r is false.
Therefore, p is false.

It is possible to go between the horns, arguing that a thing can move *from* the place where it is *to* a place where it is not (yet). It is possible to grasp the dilemma by the first horn, arguing that a rotating object moves in the place where it is while remaining therein.

EXAMINATION
on Chapter 7

Write your answers on a separate sheet of paper, then check them against the answers given at the end of the examination. If you miss a question, restudy the appropriate part of the text.

Part I. Translate the following into standard-form categorical propositions. Remember that the standard-form translation of an "exceptive" proposition contains two separate sentences.

1. A student can pass this exam only if he can translate correctly.
2. Only some students will fail this exam.
3. Except when Jane is very tired, she always works after dinner.
4. Smoking is not permitted in this room.
5. A snowstorm is coming.
6. All students, except the lazy ones, are deserving.
7. None but the prejudiced are intolerant.
8. No one is both a liberal and a conservative.
9. Only students who have passed their language requirements are admitted to candidacy.
10. Not quite all students will pass this exam.
11. This exam is not difficult.
12. Only freshmen are not eligible for fraternities.
13. Any action is right if it maximizes human welfare.
14. Students are all altruistic.
15. No children under sixteen will be admitted unless accompanied by an adult.
16. Only six-month residents can register to vote.
17. Smith complains whenever things don't go his way.
18. Any contribution will be helpful.
19. Smith botches whatever he undertakes.
20. There are children present.

Part II. Each of the following five arguments can be translated either into a standard-form categorical syllogism or into a standard-form sorites. Translate each argument into standard form.

If you translate an argument into a standard-form categorical syllogism, then name the mood and figure of its standard-form translation, test its validity by a Venn Diagram, and, if it is invalid, state which of the six Syllogistic Rules it violates.

If an argument is an enthymeme, supply the missing proposition.

If an argument is a sorites, first put it into standard form, then (using an abbreviation for each class term), state explicitly each subargument, test its validity by a Venn Diagram, and, if it is invalid, state which of the six Syllogistic Rules it violates.

Some arguments may be enthymematic sorites.

21. The people are dissatisfied.
    The people are always dissatisfied when things are going badly.
    Therefore, things are going badly.
22. All my children are blonds.
    The bank robber's hair was not at all blond.
    Therefore, my son Junior can't have robbed the bank.
23. The disliked are not welcome, but friends are never disliked; therefore, all friends must be welcome.
24. There is apathy in a university community only when society's values are no longer universally appealing.
    There is apathy at the present time at Ivy Tower University.
    Therefore, society's values are no longer universally appealing.
25. All students who studied this chapter diligently will pass this exam.
    Almost all students will pass this exam.
    Therefore, some students did not study this chapter diligently.

Part III. Answer the following questions:

26. Is a syllogistic argument that is not a standard-form categorical syllogism necessarily invalid if it has two negative premisses?
27. Is it true of any syllogistic argument that if one standard-form translation of it is valid then any other standard-form translation of it must be valid also?
28. Write down the two standard-form categorical propositions which together say that *S* and *P* are complementary classes.
29. A sorites is in standard form when all its propositions are standard-form categorical propositions, and when each term in the sorites occurs exactly twice, and when ______.
30. There are three different ways of refuting a dilemma: going (or escaping) between the horns; rebutting the dilemma by means of a counterdilemma; and ______.
31. State the conditions under which it is *impossible* to refute a dilemma by going (or escaping) between the horns.
32. State the difference between a simple dilemma and a complex dilemma.
33. If you are able to escape between the horns of a dilemma, have you thereby proved the conclusion of the dilemma to be false?

34. Applying everything you have learned in the first seven chapters of the text, decide whether the following argument is valid or invalid, and justify your decision.

    Dogs are common.
    Japanese Spaniels are dogs.
    Therefore, Japanese Spaniels are common.

Part IV. Identify the form of each of the following arguments. The various possible forms are

Valid: *Modus ponens*
Modus tollens
Valid pure hypothetical syllogism
Valid disjunctive syllogism
Invalid: Fallacy of affirming the consequent
Fallacy of denying the antecedent
Invalid pure hypothetical syllogism
Invalid disjunctive syllogism

35. If the President's foreign policies are correct, then we can achieve all of our objectives around the world.
    We cannot achieve all of our objectives around the world.
    Therefore, the President's foreign policies are not correct.
36. If the President's foreign policies are not correct, then we should elect a President from the other party next election.
    The President's foreign policies are correct.
    Therefore, we should not elect a President from the other party next election.
37. Either all S is P or no S is P.
    Some S is not P.
    Therefore, no S is P.
38. Either the President's foreign policies are correct or we should elect a President from the other party next election.
    We should elect a President from the other party next election.
    Therefore, the President's foreign policies are not correct.
39. If the President's foreign policies are not correct, then we should elect a President from the other party next election.
    We should elect a President from the other party next election.
    Therefore, the President's foreign policies are not correct.

ANSWERS

1. All students who can pass this exam are students who can translate correctly. (If your answer is the *converse* of the answer given here, then you are probably uncertain about the meaning of "only if."

Consider an obvious example: "A person can vote only if he is a citizen" translates into "All persons who can vote are citizens," but it does not correctly translate into "All citizens are persons who can vote" [since citizens under the minimum voting age cannot vote]. Thus, in general, "Something is an *S* only if it is a *P*" translates into "All *S* is *P*." This is the converse of "Something is an *S* if it is a *P*," which translates into "All *P* is *S*." Do not confuse "only if" with "if.")

2. Some students are those who will fail this exam. *And:* Some students are not those who will fail this exam.
3. All times after dinner when Jane is not very tired are times when Jane works. *And:* No times after dinner when Jane is very tired are times when Jane works.
4. No acts of smoking are acts permitted in this room. *Or:* This room is not a place where smoking is permitted.
5. Some snowstorms are things which are coming.
6. All nonlazy students are deserving beings. *And:* No lazy students are deserving beings.
7. All intolerant beings are prejudiced beings.
8. No liberals are conservatives.
9. All those who are admitted to candidacy are students who have passed their language requirements.
10. Some students are those who will pass this exam. *And:* Some students are not those who will pass this exam.
11. This exam is not a difficult thing.
12. All nonfreshmen are those who are eligible for fraternities. *And:* No freshmen are those who are eligible for fraternities.
13. All actions which maximize human welfare are right actions.
14. All students are altruistic beings.
15. No children under 16 who are unaccompanied by an adult are those who will be admitted. (Notice that the original proposition is not an "exceptive" proposition, since it does not say that all children under sixteen who are accompanied by an adult will be admitted, because the tickets may be all sold out or the management may refuse admission on some other grounds.)
16. All those who can register to vote are six-month residents.
17. All times when things don't go Smith's way are times when Smith complains.
18. All contributions are helpful things.
19. All things which Smith undertakes are things which he botches.
20. Some children are those who are present.
21. All times when things are going badly are times when the people are dissatisfied.

    The present time is a time when the people are dissatisfied.

    Therefore, the present time is a time when things are going badly.

***AAA*-2**

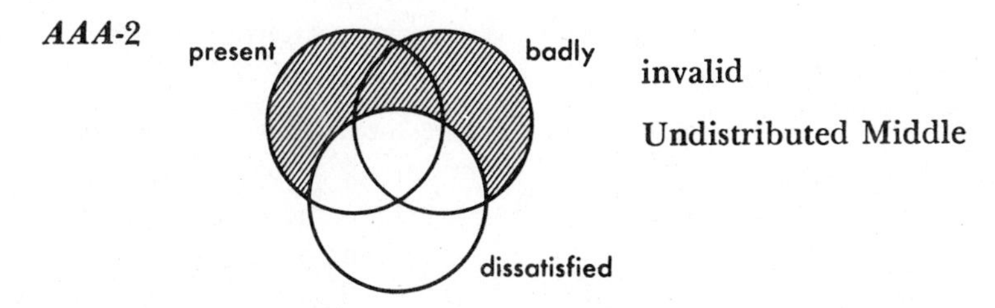

invalid

Undistributed Middle

22. (This argument is an enthymematic sorites. Alternative translations can also be correct.)

    The bank robber is not a blond.
    All children of mine are blonds.
    My son Junior is a child of mine. (suppressed premiss)
    Therefore, my son Junior is not the bank robber.

First subargument:

All *C* is *B*.

R is not *B*.

∴ *R* is not *C*.

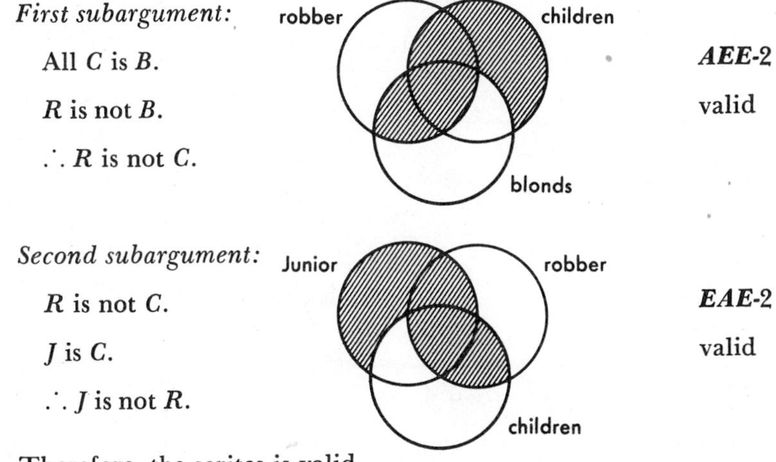

***AEE*-2**

valid

Second subargument:

R is not *C*.

J is *C*.

∴ *J* is not *R*.

***EAE*-2**

valid

Therefore, the sorites is valid.

Notice that the order of the first two premisses in the sorites has been reversed in the first subargument, so that the subargument will be in standard form.

23. (Alternative translations can also be correct.)

    No disliked persons are welcome persons.
    No friends are disliked persons.
    Therefore, all friends are welcome persons.

***EEA*-1**

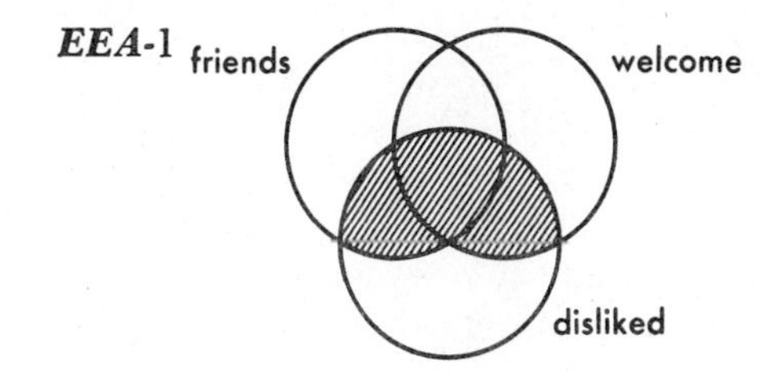

invalid
Exclusive Premisses,
Drawing an Affirmative
Conclusion from a
Negative Premiss

24. (This argument is an enthymematic sorites. Alternative translations can also be correct.)

    All times when there is apathy in a university community are times when society's values are no longer universally appealing.
    All times when there is apathy at Ivy Tower University are times when there is apathy in a university community. (suppressed premiss)
    The present time is a time when there is apathy at Ivy Tower University.
    Therefore, the present time is a time when society's values are no longer universally appealing.

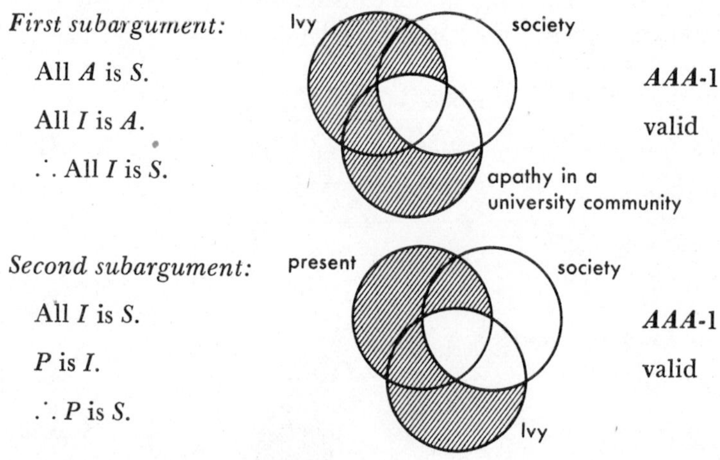

First subargument:

All A is S.

All I is A.

∴ All I is S.

***AAA*-1** valid

Second subargument:

All I is S.

P is I.

∴ P is S.

***AAA*-1** valid

Therefore, the sorites is valid.

25. The second premiss of the given argument is an "exceptive" proposition, which translates into two separate sentences, one of which is the second premiss in the following argument, whose validity establishes the validity of the given argument.

    All students who studied this chapter diligently are those who will pass this exam.
    Some students are not those who will pass this exam.
    Therefore, some students are not students who studied this chapter diligently.

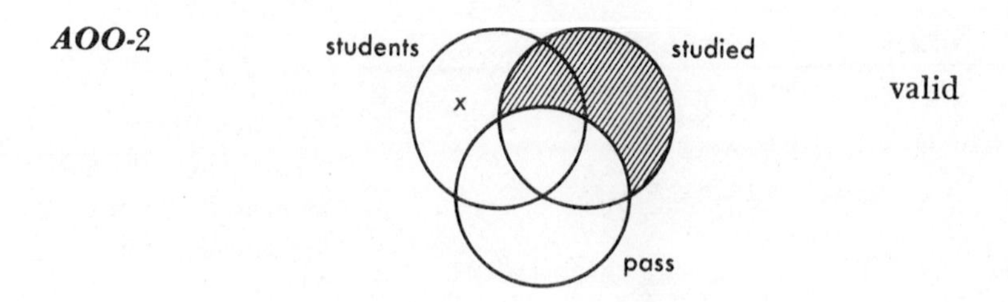

***AOO*-2** valid

26. No.
27. Yes.
28. No *S* is *P*. All non-*S* is *P*.
29. Every proposition (except the last) has a term in common with the proposition which immediately follows it.
30. Taking (or grasping) the dilemma by the horns.
31. If the disjunctive premiss is necessarily true.
32. In a complex dilemma the two conditionals in the premisses have two different propositions as consequents and the conclusion is the disjunction of these two propositions, whereas in a simple dilemma the two conditionals have the same proposition as consequent and the conclusion is this proposition.
33. No.
34. The argument is invalid because it commits the fallacy of division.
35. *Modus tollens.*
36. Fallacy of denying the antecedent.
37. Valid disjunctive syllogism.
38. Invalid disjunctive syllogism.
39. Fallacy of affirming the consequent.

Chapter 8
Symbolic Logic

READ PAGES 263–273 OF THE TEXT

8.1 The Value of Special Symbols

8.2 The Symbols for Conjunction, Negation, and Disjunction

In the next three chapters of the text you will be studying various types of deductive arguments whose logical structure can be clearly represented with the help of a new set of special symbols. In the section of the text that you have just read, you learned to symbolize three types of compound statements: conjunctions, negations, and disjunctions. A **compound statement** contains at least one other statement as a component part, whereas a **simple statement** does not contain any other statement as a component part. In representing the forms of various types of compound statements, the letters p, q, r, s, and so on, can be used to stand for any statement whatever.

Conjunction. Any compound statement composed of two statements connected by the word "and" is of the form $p \cdot q$, where the **dot** ("•") is the symbol for conjunction and p and q are the **conjuncts** of the conjunction. Since $p \cdot q$ is a compound statement which says that both p is true and q is true, the compound statement $p \cdot q$ is true when p is true and q is true, but it is false otherwise; that is, $p \cdot q$ is false when p is true and q is false, when p is false and q is true, and when p is false and q is false. Thus, the truth value of the compound statement $p \cdot q$ is a function of (is determined by) the truth values of its two components, p and q. A **truth table** can be used to display the truth values of $p \cdot q$ for every possible combination of truth values of p and q:

p	q	$p \cdot q$
T	**T**	**T**
T	**F**	**F**
F	**T**	**F**
F	**F**	**F**

This truth table states the truth value (truth or falsity) of $p \cdot q$ for each of the four possible combinations of truth values of p and q. Thus, the first **row** (horizontal line of truth values) of the truth table indicates that when p is true and q is true, then $p \cdot q$ is true. And the second row of the truth table indicates that when p is true and q is false, then $p \cdot q$ is false; whereas the third row indicates that when p is false and q is true, then $p \cdot q$ is false; and the fourth row indicates that when p is false and q is false, then $p \cdot q$ is false.

The truth values of p are listed in the **column** (vertical line of truth values) under p, and the truth values of q are listed in the column under q. In setting up the truth table, these two columns are filled in first in such a way that every possible combination of truth values of p and q is listed, and no combination is listed twice. Thus, since each of the two component statements can have either of two truth values, there are four rows in this truth table, one row for each of the four possible combinations of truth values of p and q. And for each of these possible combinations of truth values of p and q, the appropriate truth value of $p \cdot q$ is then entered in the column headed by $p \cdot q$. Thus, the truth value of $p \cdot q$ in each row is determined by the truth values of p and q in that row.

The preceding truth table may be said to define the dot symbol in the sense of stating how it functions. The dot symbol is used to produce a compound statement that is true when both of its components are true, but false otherwise.

It should be remembered that the word "and" is not the only word in ordinary English that can be symbolized by the dot symbol. The words "but," "yet," "although," "whereas," etc., can also be used to conjoin two statements (i.e., to produce a compound statement in which the truth of both components is affirmed), and when these words are used in this conjunctive sense, they can be represented by the dot symbol. For example, the following statements can all be symbolized as conjunctions:

Our ends may be desirable, *but* our means are questionable.
We must be firm, *yet* we should not be uncompromising.

Although we have generally done the right thing in the past, we may be making a mistake now.
If I move my Pawn I shall lose my Rook, *whereas* if I move my Knight I shall lose my Queen.

Negation. Where p is any statement whatever in ordinary English, the negation (or contradictory or denial) of p can often be formulated in ordinary English by inserting the word "not" in the appropriate place in p. The negation of p can also be formulated by saying "it is false that p" or "it is not the case that p." These last two phrasings make it clear that the negation of p is a compound statement which has p as a component part. Where p is any statement whatever, the negation of p is symbolized as $\sim p$. The negation symbol ("$\sim$") is called the **curl** (or sometimes the tilde). Since the compound statement $\sim p$ states that p is false, $\sim p$ is true when p is false and false when p is true. The way in which the truth value of $\sim p$ is a function of the truth value of p can be most easily displayed in a truth table:

p	$\sim p$
T	**F**
F	**T**

This truth table states the truth value of $\sim p$ for each of the two possible truth values of p. Thus, the first row indicates that when p is true, then $\sim p$ is false, and the second row indicates that when p is false, then $\sim p$ is true. This truth table has only two rows because there is only one component statement, which can have either of two truth values. The two possible truth values of p are first listed in the column under p. Then for each of these possible truth values, the appropriate truth value of $\sim p$ is entered in the column headed by $\sim p$. Thus, the truth value of $\sim p$ in each row is determined by the truth value of p in that row.

The preceding truth table for negation may be said to define the curl symbol in the sense of stating how it functions. The curl symbol is used to produce a compound statement which is false when its component statement is true, and true when its component statement is false.

Disjunction. The compound statement "Fido ran away or Fido got hit by a car" is composed of two component statements connected by the word "or." This compound statement is clearly intended to state that *at least one* (and perhaps both) of the component statements is true. When the word "or" is used to make such a compound statement, "or" is being used in its **inclusive** sense, according to which *p or q* is to be understood as affirming that either p is true or q is true or both p and q are true. Any compound statement composed of two statements connected by the word "or" used in the inclusive sense is of the form $p \vee q$, where the **wedge** ("v") is the symbol for disjunction in the inclusive sense, and p and q are the **disjuncts** of the disjunction. Since $p \vee q$ is a compound statement which affirms that *at least one* of the component statements is true, the compound statement $p \vee q$ is false when p is false and q is false, but it is true otherwise; that is, $p \vee q$ is true when p is true and q is true, when p is true and q is false, and when p is false and q is true.

The way in which the truth value of $p \vee q$ is a function of the truth value of p and the truth value of q can be most easily displayed in a truth table:

p	q	$p \vee q$
T	**T**	**T**
T	**F**	**T**
F	**T**	**T**
F	**F**	**F**

This truth table states the truth value of $p \vee q$ for each of the four possible combinations of truth values of p and q. Since the wedge symbol represents the word "or" in its inclusive sense, $p \vee q$ is false only for the truth values of p and q listed in the fourth row above. You should by now be familiar enough with the construction and meaning of truth tables so that you can review for yourself the reason for each entry in the preceding truth table for disjunction.

The three types of compound statements studied so far (conjunctions, negations, and disjunctions) are called **truth-functional compound statements** because in each case the truth value of the compound statement is a function of (is determined by) the truth values of the component statements. The special symbols used in representing the truth-functional compound statements that we are studying (the dot, curl, wedge, and other symbols to be introduced later) are called **truth-functional connectives** or **truth-functional operators** because they connect or operate on statements in such a way as to produce truth-functional compound statements.

It should be mentioned in this connection that not all compound statements are truth-functional compound statements. There are some compound statements (that is, statements which contain at least one other statement as a component part) whose truth or falsity is *not* a function of the truth or falsity of the component statement (or statements). For example, the truth or falsity of the compound statement "Jones believes that Smith is dishonest" is not determined simply by the truth or falsity of the component statement ("Smith is dishonest"), but is determined by Jones's beliefs.

Punctuation. Just as punctuation is required to avoid ambiguity in compound statements in ordinary English, so punctuation is required to avoid ambiguity in the symbolic translations of compound statements. Thus, a formula of the form $p \vee q \cdot r$ is ambiguous unless it is punctuated either as $p \vee (q \cdot r)$ or as $(p \vee q) \cdot r$. To show that these last two formulas are different, it suffices to point out that where p is true and q and r are both false, the first formula is true whereas the second formula is false. Punctuation must be used wherever necessary to avoid ambiguity.

In order to avoid unnecessary punctuation, we shall follow the convention that the curl symbol applies to the *smallest* statement which the punctuation permits. Thus, a formula of the form $\sim p \vee q$ is to be understood as meaning $(\sim p) \vee q$ rather than $\sim (p \vee q)$. Since p is the *smallest* statement to which the curl symbol in the original expression can apply, the convention stipulates that the curl symbol therefore does apply to p alone. On the other hand, in the formula $\sim (p \vee q) \cdot r$ the curl symbol applies to $(p \vee q)$, since the punctuation does not permit the curl symbol to apply to p alone.

Exclusive Disjunction. The wedge symbol ("v") has already been introduced to represent the *inclusive* sense of the word "or," according to which the compound statement p *or* q is to be understood as affirming that at least one of the component statements is true. Thus, $p \vee q$ is false only when p and q are both false.

But there is another sense in which the word "or" is sometimes used. For example, when the waiter, in explaining the *table d'hôte* menu, says, "You may have salad or you may have dessert," he means that you may have one or the other *but not both.* His compound statement is of the form p *or* q, but he is using the *exclusive* sense of the word "or," according to which he intends to affirm that either p is true or q is true, and also that they are *not* both true. This kind of statement can be represented quite easily with the symbolism which has already been introduced, without the need for a special symbol for exclusive disjunction (that is, the exclusive sense of the word "or"). Any compound statement of the form p *or* q (where "or" is intended in the exclusive sense) can be represented as $(p \vee q) \cdot \sim (p \cdot q)$. In other words, one of the two component statements is true but they are not both true.

It is very important in your study of symbolic logic to master the material as it is presented; otherwise a misunderstanding at some point is likely to create serious difficulties later. For this reason several brief self-quizzes (with answers) will be offered within each chapter to give you an opportunity to ensure that you have mastered the material.

SELF-QUIZ
(covering pages 263–273 of the text)

Make sure that you can answer each of the following questions correctly and with a complete understanding of the reasons for your answer. The correct answer is given to the right of each question, but the answer should be covered up until you have thoroughly thought through the question and formulated your own answer. If you miss a question, restudy the appropriate part of the text.

QUESTIONS	ANSWERS
1. All statements can be divided into two types: simple and ________.	1. Compound.
2. Which of the following statements are simple and which are compound?	
a. I think it's going to rain.	a. Compound.
b. It isn't going to rain.	b. Compound.
c. Castor and Pollux are twins.	c. Simple.
d. "Even though there may be a deceiver of some sort, very powerful and very tricky, who bends all his efforts to keep me perpetually deceived, there cannot be the slightest doubt of my existence." (Descartes, *Meditations*)	d. Compound.
e. "Inquiry is the controlled or directed transformation of an indeterminate situation into one that is so determinate in its constituent distinctions and relations as to convert the elements of the original situation into a unified whole." (Dewey, *Logic: The Theory of Inquiry*)	e. Simple.

f. A choice of salad or dessert is included on the *table d'hôte* menu.

f. Simple.

3. In each of the following truth tables there is one mistake in the right-hand column of truth values. In which row does the mistake occur?

p	q	$p \vee \sim q$
T	**T**	**T**
T	**F**	**T**
F	**T**	**F**
F	**F**	**F**

The mistake is in the fourth row.

p	q	$p \cdot \sim q$
T	**T**	**F**
T	**F**	**T**
F	**T**	**F**
F	**F**	**T**

The mistake is in the fourth row.

p	q	$\sim (p \cdot q)$
T	**T**	**F**
T	**F**	**T**
F	**T**	**T**
F	**F**	**F**

The mistake is in the fourth row.

4. What does "p" represent in the following formula? $p \cdot q$

4. "p" represents any statement whatever.

5. The component statements p and q in the disjunction $p \vee q$ are called ______.

5. Disjuncts.

6. Explain the difference between a truth-functional compound statement and a compound statement that is not truth-functionally compound.

6. The truth value of a truth-functional compound statement is determined by the truth value (s) of its component statement (s), whereas this is not the case for a compound statement that is not truth-functionally compound.

7. Which of the following statements are truth-functional compound statements and which are not truth-functional compound statements?
   a. I think it's going to rain.
   b. It isn't going to rain.
   c. Either war must be eliminated or the human race will be eliminated.
   d. I believe that either war must be eliminated or the human race will be eliminated.

   a. Not a truth-functional compound statement.
   b. A truth-functional compound statement.
   c. A truth-functional compound statement.
   d. Not a truth-functional compound statement.

8. What does a truth table display?

8. A truth table displays the truth values of a compound statement for all possible combinations of truth values of its component statements.

9. Why are there exactly four rows in the truth table which displays the truth values of $p \cdot q$ for the various possible combinations of truth values of p and q?

9. Because there are exactly four different combinations of truth values of p and q.

10. What does the third row of the truth table for conjunction indicate?

10. It indicates that when p is false and q is true, then $p \cdot q$ is false.

11. "p or q" (where "or" is intended in the inclusive sense) affirms that ______.

11. At least one of the component statements is true.

12. "p or q" (where "or" is intended in the exclusive sense) affirms that ______.

12. One or the other (but not both) of the component statements is true.

13. Where "+" is the symbol for exclusive disjunction (for "or" in the exclusive sense), determine the truth values in the right-hand column of the following truth table.

p	q	$p+q$
T	T	
T	F	
F	T	
F	F	

13. $p+q$
F
T
T
F

14. You know that the exclusive disjunction of p with q can be represented by $(p \vee q) \cdot \sim (p \cdot q)$. Can it also be represented by $(p \vee q) \cdot (\sim p \vee \sim q)$?

14. Yes.

SOLUTIONS

to selected exercises on pages 274–277

In working on these exercises you will probably find it helpful to adopt a systematic procedure for determining the truth value of a compound statement on the basis of the truth values of its component statements. The following procedure, if followed carefully, should enable you to avoid careless mistakes.

Given the following formula, for example,

$$\sim[\sim (A \cdot X) \cdot (Y \vee \sim B)]$$

where A and B are true statements and X and Y are false statements, you can determine the truth or falsity of the formula by replacing "A" and "B" by "**T**," indicating a true statement, and replacing "X" and "Y" by "**F**," indicating a false statement. This will result in the following formula:

$$\sim[\sim (\mathbf{T} \cdot \mathbf{F}) \cdot (\mathbf{F} \vee \sim \mathbf{T})]$$

We can now simplify this formula, starting with the innermost parts and working outward. In the left-hand set of parentheses we have the conjunction of a true statement and a false statement, which means that we have a false statement within the left-hand set of parentheses (according to the truth table for conjunction). When we next rewrite the whole formula, we shall replace the symbols within the left-hand set of parentheses with "**F**," since we know that the compound statement within those parentheses is false. Looking at the rightmost occurrence of the curl symbol, we find that it occurs in a formula "**∼T**," and since any statement which is not true is false, we can replace "**∼T**" by "**F**" when we next rewrite the whole formula. Let us now rewrite the formula, making the two replacements indicated:

$$\sim[\sim \mathbf{F} \cdot (\mathbf{F} \vee \mathbf{F})]$$

Note first that we have dropped the leftmost set of parentheses in the original formula because they are now unnecessary for clear punctuation. We can further simplify the preceding formula in the following way. The second occurrence of the curl symbol is in a formula "**~F**," which can be replaced by "**T**" according to the truth table for negation. Also, within the set of parentheses on the right we have a disjunction of a false statement with a false statement, which means that we have a false statement within that set of parentheses. When we next rewrite the whole formula, we shall replace the symbols within that set of parentheses with "**F**," since we know that the compound statement within those parentheses is false. Let us now rewrite the formula again, making the two replacements indicated:

$$\sim[\mathbf{T} \cdot \mathbf{F}]$$

Note first that we have dropped the parentheses in the previous formula because they are now unnecessary. Within the brackets above we have the conjunction of a true and a false statement, which means that we have a false statement within the brackets. So we can rewrite

$$\sim\mathbf{F}$$

which is, in turn,

$$\mathbf{T}$$

In this way we have determined that the original compound statement is true. A similar procedure will be used in providing the following answers to the exercises, including complete solutions for those exercises for which only the final answers are given in the back of the text.

Page 274, I, #1:

$$\mathbf{T} \vee \mathbf{F}$$
$$\mathbf{T}$$

Page 274, I, #2:

$$\sim(\mathbf{T} \cdot \mathbf{F})$$
$$\sim\mathbf{F}$$
$$\mathbf{T}$$

Page 274, I, #5:

$$\sim\mathbf{F} \vee \sim\mathbf{T}$$
$$\mathbf{T} \vee \mathbf{F}$$
$$\mathbf{T}$$

Page 274, I, #6:

$$\mathbf{T} \vee \sim\mathbf{T}$$
$$\mathbf{T} \vee \mathbf{F}$$
$$\mathbf{T}$$

Notice that the statement in the text is a disjunction one of whose disjuncts is the negation of the other. Therefore, one disjunct must be true and the other false, which automatically makes the whole disjunction true.

Page 274, I, #10:

$$\begin{array}{l} F \vee \sim(T \cdot F) \\ F \vee \sim F \\ F \vee T \\ \quad T \end{array}$$

Page 274, I, #11:

$$\begin{array}{l} T \cdot \sim(T \vee F) \\ T \cdot \sim T \\ T \cdot F \\ \quad F \end{array}$$

Page 274, I, #15:

$$\begin{array}{l} \sim[\sim(F \vee T) \vee \sim(\sim T \cdot \sim F)] \\ \sim[\sim T \vee \sim(F \cdot T)] \\ \sim[F \vee \sim F] \\ \sim[F \vee T] \\ \sim T \\ \quad F \end{array}$$

Page 274, I, #16:

$$\begin{array}{l} F \vee (\sim T \vee T) \\ F \vee (F \vee T) \\ F \vee T \\ \quad T \end{array}$$

Page 275, I, #20:

$$\begin{array}{c} (T \vee \sim F) \vee \sim(\sim T \cdot \sim F) \\ (T \vee T) \vee \sim(F \cdot T) \\ T \vee \sim F \\ T \vee T \\ T \end{array}$$

Page 275, I, #21:

$$\begin{array}{l} \sim[\sim(F \cdot F) \vee \sim(\sim T \vee \sim F)] \\ \sim[\sim F \vee \sim(F \vee T)] \\ \sim[T \vee \sim T] \\ \sim[T \vee F] \\ \sim T \\ \quad F \end{array}$$

Page 275, II, #1:

$$\sim A \vee B$$
$$\sim \mathbf{T} \vee \mathbf{T}$$
$$\mathbf{F} \vee \mathbf{T}$$
$$\mathbf{T}$$

Notice that you could have skipped from line 2 to line 4 because the right-hand disjunct in line 2 is true, which automatically makes the whole disjunction true.

Page 275, II, #2:

$$\sim B \vee X$$
$$\sim \mathbf{T} \vee \mathbf{F}$$
$$\mathbf{F} \vee \mathbf{F}$$
$$\mathbf{F}$$

Page 275, II, #5:

$$(A \cdot X) \vee (B \cdot Y)$$
$$(\mathbf{T} \cdot \mathbf{F}) \vee (\mathbf{T} \cdot \mathbf{F})$$
$$\mathbf{F} \vee \mathbf{F}$$
$$\mathbf{F}$$

Page 275, II, #6:

$$(B \cdot C) \vee (Y \cdot Z)$$
$$(\mathbf{T} \cdot \mathbf{T}) \vee (\mathbf{F} \cdot \mathbf{F})$$
$$\mathbf{T} \vee \mathbf{F}$$
$$\mathbf{T}$$

Page 275, II, #10:

$$\sim (X \cdot \sim Y) \vee (B \cdot \sim C)$$
$$\sim (\mathbf{F} \cdot \sim \mathbf{F}) \vee (\mathbf{T} \cdot \sim \mathbf{T})$$
$$\sim (\mathbf{F} \cdot \mathbf{T}) \vee (\mathbf{T} \cdot \mathbf{F})$$
$$\sim \mathbf{F} \vee \mathbf{F}$$
$$\mathbf{T} \vee \mathbf{F}$$
$$\mathbf{T}$$

Page 275, II, #11:

$$(A \vee X) \cdot (Y \vee B)$$
$$(\mathbf{T} \vee \mathbf{F}) \cdot (\mathbf{F} \vee \mathbf{T})$$
$$\mathbf{T} \cdot \mathbf{T}$$
$$\mathbf{T}$$

Page 275, II, #15:

$$\sim (X \vee Z) \cdot (\sim X \vee Z)$$
$$\sim (\mathbf{F} \vee \mathbf{F}) \cdot (\sim \mathbf{F} \vee \mathbf{F})$$
$$\sim \mathbf{F} \cdot (\mathbf{T} \vee \mathbf{F})$$
$$\mathbf{T} \cdot \mathbf{T}$$
$$\mathbf{T}$$

Page 275, II, #16:

$$\sim(A \vee C) \vee \sim(X \cdot \sim Y)$$
$$\sim(\mathbf{T} \vee \mathbf{T}) \vee \sim(\mathbf{F} \cdot \sim\mathbf{F})$$
$$\sim\mathbf{T} \vee \sim(\mathbf{F} \cdot \mathbf{T})$$
$$\mathbf{F} \vee \sim\mathbf{F}$$
$$\mathbf{F} \vee \mathbf{T}$$
$$\mathbf{T}$$

Page 275, II, #20:

$$\sim[(A \cdot B) \vee \sim(B \cdot A)]$$
$$\sim[(\mathbf{T} \cdot \mathbf{T}) \vee \sim(\mathbf{T} \cdot \mathbf{T})]$$
$$\sim[\mathbf{T} \vee \sim\mathbf{T}]$$
$$\sim[\mathbf{T} \vee \mathbf{F}]$$
$$\sim\mathbf{T}$$
$$\mathbf{F}$$

Page 275, II, #21:

$$[A \vee (B \vee C)] \cdot \sim[(A \vee B) \vee C]$$
$$[\mathbf{T} \vee (\mathbf{T} \vee \mathbf{T})] \cdot \sim[(\mathbf{T} \vee \mathbf{T}) \vee \mathbf{T}]$$
$$[\mathbf{T} \vee \mathbf{T}] \cdot \sim[\mathbf{T} \vee \mathbf{T}]$$
$$\mathbf{T} \cdot \sim\mathbf{T}$$
$$\mathbf{T} \cdot \mathbf{F}$$
$$\mathbf{F}$$

Page 276, III, #1:

$$A \vee P$$
$$\mathbf{T} \vee P$$
$$\mathbf{T}$$

Page 276, III, #2:

$$Q \cdot X$$
$$Q \cdot \mathbf{F}$$
$$\mathbf{F}$$

Page 276, III, #5:

$$P \vee \sim P$$

The statement is necessarily *true*. Although the truth value of P is not known, we do know that P is either true or false, since we assume in the system of logic which we are developing here that there are only two truth values. Now, if P is true then the left-hand disjunct is true and thus the whole disjunction is true; whereas if P is false then the right-hand disjunct is true and thus the whole disjunction is true. Thus, the disjunction is true no matter what the truth value of P. Thus, the disjunction is *necessarily* true.

Page 276, III, #6:

$$\sim P \vee (Q \vee P)$$

The statement is necessarily *true*. We can apply the same kind of reasoning as in the preceding exercise #5. If P is true then the right-hand disjunct is true and thus the whole disjunction is true; whereas if P is false then the left-hand disjunct is true and thus the whole disjunction is true.

Page 276, III, #10:

$$\sim Q \cdot [(P \vee Q) \cdot \sim P]$$

The statement is necessarily *false*. We can apply the same kind of reasoning as above. If Q is true then the left-hand conjunct is false and thus the whole conjunction is false; whereas if Q is false then the right-hand conjunct is false (because if P is true then its right-hand conjunct is false; whereas if P is false then its left-hand conjunct is false) and thus the whole conjunction is false.

Page 276, III, #11:

$$(P \vee Q) \cdot \sim (Q \vee P)$$

The statement is necessarily *false*. What is within the left set of parentheses has the same truth value as what is within the right set of parentheses since $P \vee Q$ is equivalent in truth value to $Q \vee P$. Thus, $P \vee Q$ and $\sim (Q \vee P)$ must have *different* truth values. Thus, one of them must be false. Thus, their conjunction must be false.

Page 276, III, #15:

$$P \cdot [\sim (P \vee Q) \vee \sim P]$$

The statement is necessarily *false*. If P is false then the left-hand conjunct is false and thus the whole conjunction is false; whereas if P is true then the right-hand conjunct is false (because both of its disjuncts are false) and thus the whole conjunction is false.

Page 276, III, #16:

$$\sim (P \cdot Q) \vee (Q \cdot P)$$

The statement is necessarily *true*. What is within the left set of parentheses has the same truth value as what is within the right set of parentheses since $P \cdot Q$ is equivalent in truth value to $Q \cdot P$. Thus, $\sim (P \cdot Q)$ and $Q \cdot P$ must have *different* truth values. Thus, one of them must be true. Thus, their disjunction must be true.

Page 276, III, #20:

$$\sim[P \vee (B \cdot Y)] \vee [(P \vee B) \cdot (P \vee Y)]$$
$$\sim[P \vee (\mathbf{T} \cdot \mathbf{F})] \vee [(P \vee \mathbf{T}) \cdot (P \vee \mathbf{F})]$$
$$\sim[P \vee \mathbf{F}] \vee [\mathbf{T} \cdot P]$$
$$\sim P \vee P$$

Therefore, the statement is necessarily *true*. The reasoning is straightforward. We know that B is true and Y is false. This gives us line 2. Now, $\mathbf{T} \cdot \mathbf{F}$ is false; $P \vee \mathbf{T}$ is true; and $P \vee \mathbf{F}$ has the same truth value as P and thus can be replaced by P (because we are concerned here only with determining the truth value of a truth-functionally compound statement). Making these three replacements, we obtain line 3. But now $P \vee \mathbf{F}$ has the same truth value as P; and $\mathbf{T} \cdot P$ has the same truth value as P. Thus, we obtain line 4, which is necessarily true.

Page 276, III, #21:

$$[P \vee (Q \cdot A)] \cdot \sim[(P \vee Q) \cdot (P \vee A)]$$
$$[P \vee (Q \cdot \mathbf{T})] \cdot \sim[(P \vee Q) \cdot (P \vee \mathbf{T})]$$
$$[P \vee Q] \cdot \sim[(P \vee Q) \cdot \mathbf{T}]$$
$$[P \vee Q] \cdot \sim[P \vee Q]$$

Therefore, the statement is necessarily *false*. The reasoning is straightforward. We know that A is true. This gives us line 2. Now, $Q \cdot \mathbf{T}$ has the same truth value as Q and thus can be replaced by Q (because we are concerned only with determining the truth value of a truth-functionally compound statement), and $P \vee \mathbf{T}$ is true. Making these replacements, we obtain line 3. But now $(P \vee Q) \cdot \mathbf{T}$ has the same truth value as $P \vee Q$ and thus can be replaced by $P \vee Q$. Thus, we obtain line 4, which is necessarily false (because $P \vee Q$ and $\sim (P \vee Q)$ must have different truth values, and thus one of them must be false, and thus their conjunction must be false).

Page 276, IV, #2: $I \vee L$

Page 276, IV, #6: $(I \vee L) \cdot \sim (I \cdot L)$

Page 277, IV, #11: $\sim E \vee J$

Page 277, IV, #16: $(\sim I \cdot \sim L) \vee (I \cdot L)$

Notice that the sentence means that *either* both Iran and Libya do not raise the price of oil *or* they both do raise the price of oil. In general, p unless q means $p \vee q$. This will become more obvious in the next section of the text.

Page 277, IV, #21: $(E \cdot S) \vee (J \vee L)$

READ PAGES 277–285 OF THE TEXT

8.3 Conditional Statements and Material Implication

In this section you studied another type of compound statement, which is composed of two component statements, usually with the word "if" before the first component statement and the word "then" between the two component statements. Compound statements of this type are called **conditionals** (or hypotheticals, or implications), and they are of the form "If p then q," where the first component statement is called the **antecedent** and the second component statement is called the **consequent.**

There are several different types of conditionals, four of which are listed in the text on page 278. The first of these conditionals is a statement whose truth or falsity is determined by the principles of logic; the second is a statement whose truth or falsity is determined by definition; the third is a statement whose truth or falsity is determined by the facts of the universe (and the causal laws which are true of these facts); and the fourth is a statement whose truth or falsity is determined by a decision.

Although the words "if—then" are used in a different way in each of these four types of conditionals, each conditional is nevertheless of the form "If p then q," and in each conditional a *part* of what is being affirmed is that if p is true then q is true, in other words, that it is not the case that p is true and q is false, or $\sim(p \cdot \sim q)$. Now we shall use a special symbol to represent this part of the meaning of the words "if—then" which all four types of conditionals have in common. Our special symbol is the **horseshoe** ("$\supset$"), and we define $p \supset q$ to mean the same thing as $\sim(p \cdot \sim q)$. In other words, $p \supset q$ says that if p is true then q is true, which means that it is not the case that p is true and q is false, which means that $\sim(p \cdot \sim q)$. Since $p \supset q$ is defined in such a way that it means the same thing as $\sim(p \cdot \sim q)$, both formulas must (by definition) have the same truth values for the various possible combinations of truth values of p and q. Thus, in the following truth table, where the four possible combinations of truth values for p and q are listed in columns (1) and (2), the truth values of $\sim(p \cdot \sim q)$ are calculated and listed in column (5), and the truth values of "$p \supset q$," which are by definition the same as those of $\sim(p \cdot \sim q)$, are listed in column (6). In columns (3) and (4) are listed truth values which are useful for calculating the truth values in column (5).

(1) p	(2) q	(3) $\sim q$	(4) $p \cdot \sim q$	(5) $\sim(p \cdot \sim q)$	(6) $p \supset q$
T	**T**	**F**	**F**	**T**	**T**
T	**F**	**T**	**T**	**F**	**F**
F	**T**	**F**	**F**	**T**	**T**
F	**F**	**T**	**F**	**T**	**T**

Columns (1) and (2) are the **guide columns,** in which are listed all possible combinations of truth values for p and q. Column (3) is filled in by referring to column (2) and applying the information contained in the truth table for negation. Column (4) is filled in by referring to columns (1) and (3) and applying the information contained in the truth table for conjunction. Column (5) is filled in by referring to column (4) and applying the information contained in the truth table for negation. And column (6) is filled in so as to *duplicate* column (5) because $p \supset q$ is *defined* to mean the same thing as $\sim (p \cdot \sim q)$, and the two formulas must therefore have the same truth values, since they are equivalent by definition.

The horseshoe symbol ("$\supset$") is thus seen to be a truth-functional connective because the truth value of a compound statement of the form $p \supset q$ is a function of the truth values of the component statements p and q.

The phrase "if—then" can be used in ordinary English in stating any of the four types of conditionals listed in the text on page 278. The horseshoe symbol represents a *part* of the meaning of the phrase "if—then" that is common to all four of its uses. This common partial meaning that is present in each of the four types of conditionals but is not identical with any one of them is called **material implication.** Thus, the horseshoe is the symbol for material implication, and "p materially implies q" means that it is not the case that p is true and q is false, which means that $\sim (p \cdot \sim q)$.

Conditional statements occur in many of the arguments that you are about to study in the text. These conditionals may be of any one of the four types listed in the text. No matter which type of conditional is present, however, a part of the meaning of the conditional can be represented with the horseshoe symbol, and in the arguments with which you will be dealing in the text, it is only this part of the meaning of each conditional that is relevant in determining the validity or invalidity of the argument in which the conditional occurs. Thus, if you use the horseshoe symbol to represent any conditional statement which you encounter in the text, you will not be ignoring, or abstracting from, or losing anything relevant to the validity or invalidity of the argument. Therefore, for the purposes of determining the validity or invalidity of the arguments with which you will be dealing here, all conditionals (that is, all statements of the form "If p then q") may be symbolized by means of the horseshoe.

SOLUTIONS
to selected exercises on pages 285–288

Use the same general procedure that you used in the preceding exercises. Work from the innermost parts outward, applying the information contained in the truth table for material implication.

Page 285, I, #1:

$$\begin{array}{c} A \supset B \\ \mathbf{T} \supset \mathbf{T} \\ \mathbf{T} \end{array}$$

Page 285, I, #2:

$$\begin{array}{c} A \supset X \\ \mathbf{T} \supset \mathbf{F} \\ \mathbf{F} \end{array}$$

Page 285, I, #5:

$$\begin{array}{l} (A \supset B) \supset Z \\ (\mathbf{T} \supset \mathbf{T}) \supset \mathbf{F} \\ \qquad\quad \mathbf{T} \supset \mathbf{F} \\ \qquad\qquad\ \mathbf{F} \end{array}$$

Page 285, I, #6:

$$\begin{array}{l} (X \supset Y) \supset Z \\ (\mathbf{F} \supset \mathbf{F}) \supset \mathbf{F} \\ \qquad\quad \mathbf{T} \supset \mathbf{F} \\ \qquad\qquad\ \mathbf{F} \end{array}$$

Page 285, I, #10:

$$\begin{array}{l} X \supset (Y \supset Z) \\ \mathbf{F} \supset (\mathbf{F} \supset \mathbf{F}) \\ \mathbf{F} \supset \mathbf{T} \\ \quad \mathbf{T} \end{array}$$

Notice that here you could skip from line 2 to line 4 because the antecedent of the main conditional in line 2 is false, which automatically makes the whole conditional true, according to the truth table for material implication.

Page 285, I, #11:

$$\begin{array}{l} [(A \supset B) \supset C] \supset Z \\ [(\mathbf{T} \supset \mathbf{T}) \supset \mathbf{T}] \supset \mathbf{F} \\ \qquad\quad [\mathbf{T} \supset \mathbf{T}] \supset \mathbf{F} \\ \qquad\qquad\quad \mathbf{T} \supset \mathbf{F} \\ \qquad\qquad\qquad \mathbf{F} \end{array}$$

Page 286, I, #15:

$$\begin{array}{l} [(X \supset Z) \supset C] \supset Y \\ [(\mathbf{F} \supset \mathbf{F}) \supset \mathbf{T}] \supset \mathbf{F} \\ \qquad\quad [\mathbf{T} \supset \mathbf{T}] \supset \mathbf{F} \\ \qquad\qquad\quad \mathbf{T} \supset \mathbf{F} \\ \qquad\qquad\qquad \mathbf{F} \end{array}$$

Page 286, I, #16:

$$[(Y \supset B) \supset Y] \supset Y$$
$$[(\mathbf{F} \supset \mathbf{T}) \supset \mathbf{F}] \supset \mathbf{F}$$
$$[\mathbf{T} \supset \mathbf{F}] \supset \mathbf{F}$$
$$\mathbf{F} \supset \mathbf{F}$$
$$\mathbf{T}$$

Page 286, I, #20:

$$[(A \cdot X) \supset Y] \supset [(X \supset A) \supset (A \supset Y)]$$
$$[(\mathbf{T} \cdot \mathbf{F}) \supset \mathbf{F}] \supset [(\mathbf{F} \supset \mathbf{T}) \supset (\mathbf{T} \supset \mathbf{F})]$$
$$[\mathbf{F} \supset \mathbf{F}] \supset [\mathbf{T} \supset \mathbf{F}]$$
$$\mathbf{T} \supset \mathbf{F}$$
$$\mathbf{F}$$

Page 286, I, #21:

$$[(A \cdot X) \vee (\sim A \cdot \sim X)] \supset [(A \supset X) \cdot (X \supset A)]$$
$$[(\mathbf{T} \cdot \mathbf{F}) \vee (\sim \mathbf{T} \cdot \sim \mathbf{F})] \supset [(\mathbf{T} \supset \mathbf{F}) \cdot (\mathbf{F} \supset \mathbf{T})]$$
$$[\mathbf{F} \vee (\mathbf{F} \cdot \mathbf{T})] \supset [\mathbf{F} \cdot \mathbf{T}]$$
$$[\mathbf{F} \vee \mathbf{F}] \supset \mathbf{F}$$
$$\mathbf{F} \supset \mathbf{F}$$
$$\mathbf{T}$$

Page 286, II, #1:

$$P \supset A$$
$$P \supset \mathbf{T}$$
$$\mathbf{T}$$

Notice that the consequent in line 2 is true, which automatically makes the conditional true, according to the truth table for material implication.

Page 286, II, #2:

$$X \supset Q$$
$$\mathbf{F} \supset Q$$
$$\mathbf{T}$$

Notice that the antecedent in line 2 is false, which automatically makes the conditional true, according to the truth table for material implication.

Page 286, II, #5:

$$(P \supset P) \supset X$$
$$\mathbf{T} \supset \mathbf{F}$$
$$\mathbf{F}$$

Notice that $P \supset P$ is necessarily true, because it is true where P is true and it is also true where P is false.

Page 286, II, #6:

$$(X \supset Q) \supset X$$
$$(\mathbf{F} \supset Q) \supset \mathbf{F}$$
$$\mathbf{T} \supset \mathbf{F}$$
$$\mathbf{F}$$

Page 286, II, #10:

$$(Q \supset Q) \supset (A \supset X)$$
$$\mathbf{T} \supset (\mathbf{T} \supset \mathbf{F})$$
$$\mathbf{T} \supset \mathbf{F}$$
$$\mathbf{F}$$

Page 286, II, #11:

$$(P \supset X) \supset (X \supset P)$$
$$(P \supset \mathbf{F}) \supset (\mathbf{F} \supset P)$$
$$(P \supset \mathbf{F}) \supset \mathbf{T}$$
$$\mathbf{T}$$

Notice that the consequent of the main conditional in line 3 is true, which automatically makes the whole conditional true, according to the truth table for material implication.

Page 286, II, #15:

$$[(X \supset Q) \supset Q] \supset Q$$
$$[(\mathbf{F} \supset Q) \supset Q] \supset Q$$
$$[\mathbf{T} \supset Q] \supset Q$$
$$\mathbf{T}$$

Notice first that in line 2 $\mathbf{F} \supset Q$ is necessarily true (because where the antecedent of a conditional is false, the whole conditional is automatically true, according to the truth table for material implication). Notice also that line 3 is necessarily true, because where Q is true the consequent of the main conditional is true, which makes the main conditional automatically true; whereas if Q is false the antecedent of the main conditional is false, which makes the main conditional automatically true.

Page 286, II, #16:

$$(P \supset X) \supset (\sim X \supset \sim P)$$
$$(P \supset \mathbf{F}) \supset (\sim \mathbf{F} \supset \sim P)$$
$$(P \supset \mathbf{F}) \supset (\mathbf{T} \supset \sim P)$$
$$\mathbf{T}$$

Line 3 is necessarily true, because where P is true the antecedent of the main conditional is false, which makes the main conditional automatically true; whereas if P is false the consequent of the main conditional is true, which makes the main conditional automatically true.

Page 286, II, #20:

$$(P \supset \sim\sim P) \supset (A \supset \sim B)$$
$$(\mathbf{P} \supset \mathbf{P}) \supset (\mathbf{T} \supset \sim\mathbf{T})$$
$$\mathbf{T} \supset (\mathbf{T} \supset \mathbf{F})$$
$$\mathbf{T} \supset \mathbf{F}$$
$$\mathbf{F}$$

Notice that $\sim\sim P$ in line 1 can be replaced by P because they have the same truth value.

Page 286, II, #21:

$$\sim(A \cdot P) \supset (\sim A \vee \sim P)$$
$$\sim(\mathbf{T} \cdot P) \supset (\sim\mathbf{T} \vee \sim P)$$
$$\sim P \supset (\mathbf{F} \vee \sim P)$$
$$\sim P \supset \sim P$$
$$\mathbf{T}$$

Notice in line 2 that $\mathbf{T} \cdot P$ has the same truth value as P and thus can be replaced by P (because we are concerned here only with determining the truth value of a truth-functionally compound statement). Notice also in line 3 that $\mathbf{F} \vee \sim P$ has the same truth value as $\sim P$ and thus can be replaced by $\sim P$. And finally notice that $\sim P \supset \sim P$ is necessarily true, because it is true where P is true and it is also true where P is false.

Page 287, III, #2:

$$A \supset (B \vee C)$$

Page 287, III, #6:

$$(A \vee B) \supset C$$

Page 287, III, #11:

$$(\sim A \supset \sim B) \cdot C$$

Page 287, III, #16:

$$(B \vee C) \supset A$$

Page 288, III, #21:

$$A \supset B$$

Notice that "A is a sufficient condition for B" is represented as $A \supset B$; whereas "A is a necessary condition for B" is represented as $B \supset A$.

READ PAGES 288–296 OF THE TEXT

8.4 Argument Forms and Arguments

In this section you learned how to use a truth table to determine the validity or invalidity of an argument composed of simple statements and truth-functional compound statements. Consider, for example, the following argument:

(1) If Jones plays, then State will win.
State will not win.
Therefore, Jones will not play.

This argument can be stated schematically by letting J stand for "Jones plays" and letting S stand for "State will win." Then argument (1) can be rewritten as follows:

$$
\begin{aligned}
(2)\quad & J \supset S \\
& \sim S \\
& \therefore \sim J
\end{aligned}
$$

Arguments (1) and (2) are merely different ways of stating the same argument. In (2), J and S are used to stand for the component statements of (1). The capital letters J and S are called **statement constants** because they are used to stand for specific (constant) statements.

The preceding argument has a certain *form,* which can be described as follows: the first premiss is a conditional; the second premiss is the negation of the consequent of the first premiss; and the conclusion is the negation of the antecedent of the first premiss. We can represent this *form* of argument by using p, q, r, s, and so on, to stand for any statements whatever. Then the form of the preceding argument can be written as follows:

$$
\begin{aligned}
(3)\quad & p \supset q \\
& \sim q \\
& \therefore \sim p
\end{aligned}
$$

Argument form (3) is not itself an argument; it is an **argument form** or schematic representation of a form that many different arguments can have. The small letters p, q, and so on, are called **statement variables** because they stand for any statements whatever, just as x and y in algebra are (number) variables because they stand for any numbers whatever. Argument (1) is a **substitution instance** of argument form (3), because (1) results from (3) by replacing p and q by statements (the same statement replacing the same statement variable throughout).

You will recall from the first chapter of the text that an argument is valid if and only if it is impossible for all the premisses to be true and the conclusion false. Similarly, an argument form may be said to be valid if and only if it is impossible for an argument of that form to have all true premisses and a false conclusion. Thus, to prove that argument (1) is valid, it suffices to prove that argument form (3) is valid, which can be done by using a truth table to show that it is impossible for a substitution instance of argument form (3) to have all true premisses and a false conclusion:

		(premiss)	(premiss)	(conclusion)
p	q	$p \supset q$	$\sim q$	$\sim p$
T	**T**	**T**	**F**	**F**
T	**F**	**F**	**T**	**F**
F	**T**	**T**	**F**	**T**
F	**F**	**T**	**T**	**T**

How does this truth table show that it is impossible for a substitution instance of argument form (3) to have all true premisses and a false conclusion? First, we note that, although there are an infinite number of substitution instances of argument form (3), each substitution instance must be of one of the following four types:

1. A substitution instance in which the statement substituted for p is true and the statement substituted for q is true.
2. A substitution instance in which the statement substituted for p is true and the statement substituted for q is false.
3. A substitution instance in which the statement substituted for p is false and the statement substituted for q is true.
4. A substitution instance in which the statement substituted for p is false and the statement substituted for q is false.

Since any one of the infinite number of substitution instances of argument form (3) must be of one of these four types, if we can prove that it is impossible for a substitution instance of any one of these four types to have true premisses and a false conclusion, we will have proved that it is impossible for any one of the infinite number of substitution instances of argument form (3) to have true premisses and a false conclusion.

Examining the preceding truth table we find that in the two guide columns on the left are listed the four possible combinations of truth values for p and q. Each of these four combinations represents one of the four types of substitution instances of argument form (3). Thus, row (1) of the truth table represents the class of substitution instances in which a true statement is substituted for p and a true statement is substituted for q. Row (2) represents the class of substitution instances in which a true statement is substituted for p and a false statement is substituted for q. And so on for rows (3) and (4).

Now an inspection of the truth table shows that it is impossible for a substitution instance of argument form (3) to have all true premisses and a false conclusion. The two premisses of the argument form head columns (3) and (4). The only row in which both premisses are true is row (4), and in that row the conclusion is true also. Thus, it is impossible for any substitution instance of argument form (3) to have true premisses and a false conclusion, and so all such substitution instances are valid. If any substitution instance has true premisses it must also have a true conclusion. Another way of explaining the reasoning is this: We can see from row (4) of the truth table that the only substitution instances which have all true premisses are those in which a false statement is substituted for p and a false statement is substituted for q, and all such substitution instances have a true conclusion also, as is indicated in row (4). Hence, it is impossible for a substitution instance of argument form (3) to have all true premisses and a false conclusion, and so all such substitution instances are valid.

In this way we have proved the validity of argument (1). Notice that we have also proved the validity of *all* other substitution instances of argument form (3), even those substitution instances which result by replacing p or q by a compound statement rather than a simple statement. For example, where J stands for "Jones plays," S stands for "State will win," and K stands for "Kelly plays," then the following argument is also proved valid

$$(J \vee K) \supset S$$
$$\sim S$$
$$\therefore \sim (J \vee K)$$

because it is also a substitution instance of argument form (3), where the *compound* statement "$J \vee K$" is substituted for p. Thus, if an argument form is valid, then *all* substitution instances of that form are valid, even those substitution instances in which a *compound* statement is substituted for a statement variable. Be sure to remember this point, especially in light of the fact that an invalid argument form can have a valid substitution instance (as will be explained shortly).

Let us now consider how a truth table can be used to prove the invalidity of an invalid argument, such as the following:

If Jones plays, then State will win.
Jones will not play.
Therefore, State will not win.

By using standard symbols, we can represent this argument as follows:

$$J \supset S$$
$$\sim J$$
$$\therefore \sim S$$

To determine the validity or invalidity of this argument, we must determine whether or not it is impossible for the premisses to be true and the conclusion false. First, we note that the specific *form* of the argument can be described as follows: the first premiss is a conditional; the second premiss is the negation of the antecedent of the first premiss; and the conclusion is the negation of the consequent of the first premiss. We can represent this *form* as follows:

$$p \supset q$$
$$\sim p$$
$$\therefore \sim q$$

The following truth table can now be used to determine whether it is possible for a substitution instance of this argument form to have all true premisses and a false conclusion:

		(premiss)	(premiss)	(conclusion)
p	q	$p \supset q$	$\sim p$	$\sim q$
T	**T**	**T**	**F**	**F**
T	**F**	**F**	**F**	**T**
F	**T**	**T**	**T**	**F**
F	**F**	**T**	**T**	**T**

In the third row of this truth table, we see that it is possible for the premisses of an argument of this form to be true while the conclusion is false. Therefore, the argument form is invalid, and so the original argument is invalid also. It should be carefully noted, however, that we are justified in making this inference from the invalidity of the argument form to the invalidity of the substitution instance only if the substitution instance conforms to the conditions listed in the following paragraph.

First, the substitution instance must conform to the conditions stated in the footnote on page 289 of the text. In particular, the conclusion of the substitution instance cannot be necessarily true, for if it were then the argument would automatically be valid regardless of the nature of the premisses, since it would be impossible for the premisses to be true and the conclusion false because it would be impossible for the conclusion to be false. Moreover, the premisses of the substitution instance cannot be necessarily false, for if they were then the argument would automatically be valid regardless of the nature of the conclusion, since it would be impossible for the premisses to be true and the conclusion false because it would be impossible for the premisses to be true. Second, in order to make an inference from the invalidity of an argument form to the invalidity of a substitution instance of that form, the argument form in question must be *the specific form* of the substitution instance, where **the specific form** of a given argument is defined to be that argument form from which the given argument results by substituting a different *simple* statement for each different statement variable. Where argument form (*F*) is *the specific form* of argument (*A*), then it is correct to make an inference from the invalidity of (*F*) to the invalidity of (*A*). But if the above conditions are not satisfied, then it is not necessarily correct to make an inference from the invalidity of an argument form to the invalidity of a substitution instance of that form. For example, the following argument form is obviously invalid:

$$p$$
$$q$$
$$\therefore r$$

But if we substitute the *compound* statement $J \supset S$ for p and if we substitute J for q and S for r, then we get the following valid substitution instance:

$$J \supset S$$
$$J$$
$$\therefore S$$

Here we have a valid substitution instance of an invalid argument form only because we have substituted a *compound* statement for one of the statement variables in the argument form. If we had substituted only *simple* statements for the statement variables in the argument form, then we could be certain that any substitution instance which we produced would be invalid if the argument form were invalid. It should be clear from the preceding example that we must add the qualification that it is correct to make an inference from the invalidity of a particular argument form to the invalidity of a substitution instance of that form only if the form in question is *the specific form* of the substitution instance.

Subject to the conditions discussed in the preceding paragraph, we can now say in general that to determine the validity or invalidity of an argument it suffices to use a truth table to determine the validity or invalidity of *the specific form* of the argument. Thus, the validity or invalidity of an argument is dependent only on its form

and not on its specific content. For example, any argument of the form *modus ponens* is valid, no matter what statements are substituted for p and q; and any argument *the specific form* of which is

$$\begin{array}{l} p \supset q \\ q \\ \therefore p \end{array}$$

is invalid, no matter what *simple* statements are substituted for p and q (so long as the conditions stated in the footnote on page 289 of the text are satisfied).

Let us now apply the principles developed in this section to one more example:

> If Jones plays then State will win, and if Kelly plays then State will win.
> Either Jones plays or Kelly plays.
> Therefore, State will win.

The specific form of this argument is as follows:

$$\begin{array}{l} (p \supset q) \cdot (r \supset q) \\ p \vee r \\ \therefore q \end{array}$$

To determine the validity or invalidity of the preceding argument we can use a truth table to determine the validity or invalidity of *the specific form.* Our truth table will require three guide columns because there are three different statement variables in the form, and the truth table will require eight rows because there are eight different combinations of truth values for three statement variables. In general, where an argument form has n different statement variables its truth table requires n guide columns and 2^n rows. Thus, a truth table with four guide columns would have sixteen rows, and a truth table with five guide columns would have thirty-two rows, and so on. The truth values in the guide columns can be filled in systematically as follows: In the left-hand guide column fill in the top half of the rows with **T**'s and the bottom half wih **F**'s. In the next guide column fill in the first quarter of the rows with **T**'s, the second quarter with **F**'s, the third quarter with **T**'s, and the fourth quarter with **F**'s. In the third guide column (if there is one), alternate **T**'s and **F**'s every one eighth of the rows. In the fourth guide column (if there is one) alternate **T**'s and **F**'s every one sixteenth of the rows, and so on. The truth table for the argument form above is then as follows:

					(premiss)	(premiss)	(conclusion)
p	q	r	$p \supset q$	$r \supset q$	$(p \supset q) \cdot (r \supset q)$	$p \vee r$	q
T	T	T	T	T	T	T	T
T	T	F	T	T	T	T	T
T	F	T	F	F	F	T	F
T	F	F	F	T	F	T	F
F	T	T	T	T	T	T	T
F	T	F	T	T	T	F	T
F	F	T	T	F	F	T	F
F	F	F	T	T	T	F	F

Is there any row in which the premisses are both true and the conclusion is false? No. The premisses are both true in rows (1), (2), and (5), but in each of these rows the conclusion is also true. Therefore, the argument form is valid, and so any argument of that form is valid also, because it is impossible for any substitution instance of the argument form to have true premisses and a false conclusion.

Let us review briefly the procedure for using a truth table to test the validity of an argument:

1. Represent *the specific form* of the argument, using p, q, and so on.
2. Set up a truth table with a guide column for each different statement variable in the argument form whose validity is to be tested, and with a column for each premiss and a column for the conclusion, and with any additional columns that may be helpful in determining the truth values of the premisses and the conclusion.
3. Fill in systematically all possible combinations of truth values for the individual statement variables heading the guide columns. A truth table with n guide columns requires 2^n rows. In the left-hand guide column fill in the top half of the rows with **T**'s, the bottom half with **F**'s. In the next guide column alternate **T**'s and **F**'s every quarter of the rows, and so on.
4. Referring to the truth values in the guide columns, fill in the appropriate truth values in the other columns.
5. Inspect the truth table. If there is a row in which the premisses are all true and the conclusion is false, then the argument form is invalid. If there is no such row then the argument form is valid. If an argument form is valid then any substitution instance of it is valid. If an argument form is invalid then any substitution instance of it is invalid so long as (1) the argument form in ques-

tion is *the specific form* of the substitution instance and (2) the substitution instance conforms to the conditions stated in the footnote on page 289 of the text.

SELF-QUIZ

(covering pages 288–296 of the text)

Make sure that you cover up the answers in the right-hand column until you have thoroughly thought through each question and formulated your own answer. If you miss a question, restudy the appropriate part of the text.

QUESTIONS	ANSWERS
1. Any statement of the form "If p then q" is called a ______.	1. Conditional (or hypothetical, or implication).
2. Where "If p then q" represents the form of a conditional statement, p is called the ______ of the conditional, and q is called the ______ of the conditional.	2. Antecedent; consequent.
3. In any statement of the form "If p then q" it is being asserted that if p is true then q is true, which means that it is not the case that p is true and q is false, which can be symbolized as ______.	3. $\sim (p \cdot \sim q)$
4. Using the horseshoe symbol for material implication, a statement of the form "If p then q" can be symbolized as ______.	4. $p \supset q$
5. Since $p \supset q$ asserts that if p is true than q is true, which means that it is not the case that p is true and q is false, which can be symbolized as "$\sim (p \cdot \sim q)$," the two expressions "$p \supset q$" and "$\sim (p \cdot \sim q)$" mean the same thing and therefore have the same truth values. In the following truth table there is one mistake in assigning truth values. Where is the mistake?	5. The mistake is in the third column in the third row.

p	q	$\sim(p \cdot \sim q)$	$p \supset q$
T	T	T	T
T	F	F	F
F	T	F	T
F	F	T	T

6. The horseshoe symbol is a ______ connective because the truth value of a compound statement of the form $p \supset q$ is a function of the truth values of the component statements p and q.

6. Truth-functional.

7. An argument is valid if and only if it is impossible for the premisses to be ______ and the conclusion ______.

7. True; false.

8. In representing the form of an argument, we use p, q, etc., which are called ______.

8. Statement variables.

9. If (F) is the form of argument (A), then (A) is a ______ of (F).

9. Substitution instance.

10. An argument form is invalid if it is possible for ______.

10. A substitution instance of that argument form to have true premisses and a false conclusion.

11. One can determine the validity or invalidity of an argument by examining ______ to see whether it is possible for any substitution instance of that argument form to have true premisses and a false conclusion.

11. *The specific form* of the argument.

12. *The specific form* of a given argument is that argument form from which the given argument results by substituting a different ______ statement for each different statement variable in the argument form.

12. Simple.

13. In order to test the validity of

13. Sixteen.

an argument form which contains four statement variables one requires a truth table with ______ rows.

14. Pair each of the following argument forms with its name:

1. $p \vee q$
   $\sim p$
   $\therefore q$
2. $p \supset q$
   p
   $\therefore q$
3. $p \supset q$
   $\sim q$
   $\therefore \sim p$
4. $p \supset q$
   $q \supset r$
   $\therefore p \supset r$
5. $p \supset q$
   q
   $\therefore p$
6. $p \supset q$
   $\sim p$
   $\therefore \sim q$
7. $(p \supset q) \cdot (r \supset s)$
   $p \vee r$
   $\therefore q \vee s$

(a) *Modus Ponens.*
(b) Constructive Dilemma.
(c) Hypothetical Syllogism.
(d) Disjunctive Syllogism.
(e) Fallacy of Denying the Antecedent.
(f) Fallacy of Affirming the Consequent.
(g) *Modus Tollens.*

14. (1) – (d)
(2) – (a)
(3) – (g)
(4) – (c)
(5) – (f)
(6) – (e)
(7) – (b)

SOLUTIONS

to selected exercises on pages 297–300

Page 297, I, #b: 6 is the specific form of b.

Page 297, I, #f: 16 is the specific form of f.

Page 297, I, #k: 4 has k as a substitution instance.

Page 297, II:

Refer to page 177 of this book for an explanation of the general procedure to follow in solving these problems.

Page 297, II, #2:

p	q	$p \supset q$	$\sim p$	$\sim q$	$\sim p \supset \sim q$
T	T	T	F	F	T
T	F	F	F	T	T
F	T	T	T	F	F
F	F	T	T	T	T

invalid. (Shown by the third row.)

Page 297, II, #6:

p	q	$p \supset q$	$p \cdot q$	$p \supset (p \cdot q)$
T	T	T	T	T
T	F	F	F	F
F	T	T	F	T
F	F	T	F	T

valid.

Page 297, II, #11:

p	q	r	$p \supset q$	$p \supset r$	$q \vee r$
T	T	T	T	T	T
T	T	F	T	F	T
T	F	T	F	T	T
T	F	F	F	F	F
F	T	T	T	T	T
F	T	F	T	T	T
F	F	T	T	T	T
F	F	F	T	T	F

invalid. (Shown by the eighth row.)

Page 298, II, #16: You should recognize this argument form as the Constructive Dilemma. Notice the way in which all possible combinations of truth values for the four statement variables are listed systematically in the guide columns.

p	q	r	s	$p \supset q$	$r \supset s$	$(p \supset q) \cdot (r \supset s)$	$p \vee r$	$q \vee s$
T	T	T	T	T	T	T	T	T
T	T	T	F	T	F	F	T	T
T	T	F	T	T	T	T	T	T
T	T	F	F	T	T	T	T	T
T	F	T	T	F	T	F	T	T
T	F	T	F	F	F	F	T	F
T	F	F	T	F	T	F	T	T
T	F	F	F	F	T	F	T	F
F	T	T	T	T	T	T	T	T
F	T	T	F	T	F	F	T	T
F	T	F	T	T	T	T	F	T
F	T	F	F	T	T	T	F	T
F	F	T	T	T	T	T	T	T
F	F	T	F	T	F	F	T	F
F	F	F	T	T	T	T	F	T
F	F	F	F	T	T	T	F	F

valid.

Page 298, II, #21:

p	q	$p \vee q$	$p \cdot q$	$(p \vee q) \supset (p \cdot q)$	$\sim(p \vee q)$	$\sim(p \cdot q)$
T	**T**	**T**	**T**	**T**	**F**	**F**
T	**F**	**T**	**F**	**F**	**F**	**T**
F	**T**	**T**	**F**	**F**	**F**	**T**
F	**F**	**F**	**F**	**T**	**T**	**T**

valid.

Page 298, III, #2:

$(C \vee D) \supset (C \cdot D)$ | | $(p \vee q) \supset (p \cdot q)$
$C \cdot D$ has the specific form $p \cdot q$
$\therefore C \vee D$ | | $\therefore p \vee q$

p	q	$p \vee q$	$p \cdot q$	$(p \vee q) \supset (p \cdot q)$
T	**T**	**T**	**T**	**T**
T	**F**	**T**	**F**	**F**
F	**T**	**T**	**F**	**F**
F	**F**	**F**	**F**	**T**

valid.

Page 298, III, #6:

$K \vee L$ | | $p \vee q$
K has the specific form p
$\therefore \sim L$ | | $\therefore \sim q$

p	q	$p \vee q$	$\sim q$
T	**T**	**T**	**F**
T	**F**	**T**	**T**
F	**T**	**T**	**F**
F	**F**	**F**	**T**

invalid. (Shown by first row.)

Page 299, IV, #2: To determine the validity or invalidity of the arguments in this set of exercises, first determine *the specific form* of each argument, then use a truth table to determine the validity or invalidity of that form. The solution to this problem will be explained in detail. Let D stand for "Denmark drifts further to the left." Let E stand for "Esthonia continues to be a puppet of Soviet Russia." And let F stand for "Finland must become increasingly subservient to Soviet Russia." The argument can then be written as

$D \supset (E \supset F)$
E
$\therefore D \supset F$

This argument has *the specific form*

$p \supset (q \supset r)$
q
$\therefore p \supset r$

whose validity or invalidity can be determined by the following truth table:

p	q	r	$q \supset r$	$p \supset (q \supset r)$	$p \supset r$
T	T	T	T	T	T
T	T	F	F	F	F
T	F	T	T	T	T
T	F	F	T	T	F
F	T	T	T	T	T
F	T	F	F	T	T
F	F	T	T	T	T
F	F	F	T	T	T

valid.

Page 299, IV, #6:

$E \supset P$
$P \supset S$
$S \supset \sim E$
$\therefore \sim E$

has the specific form

$p \supset q$
$q \supset r$
$r \supset \sim p$
$\therefore \sim p$

p	q	r	$p \supset q$	$q \supset r$	$\sim p$	$r \supset \sim p$
T	T	T	T	T	F	F
T	T	F	T	F	F	T
T	F	T	F	T	F	F
T	F	F	F	T	F	T
F	T	T	T	T	T	T
F	T	F	T	F	T	T
F	F	T	T	T	T	T
F	F	F	T	T	T	T

valid.

READ PAGES 300–304 OF THE TEXT

8.5 Statement Forms and Statements

A **statement form** is a formula containing statement variables but no statements, such that when statements are substituted for the statement variables (the same statement being substituted for the same statement variable throughout) the result is a statement. Statement forms are either tautologous, self-contradictory, or contingent.

A **tautologous statement form** has only true substitution instances. The most obvious example of a tautologous statement form is $p \vee {\sim}p$. To determine whether or not a given statement form is tautologous, construct a truth table showing the truth values of that statement form for all possible combinations of truth values for the individual statement variables in the statement form. If the column headed by the statement form in question has only **T**'s, this shows that the statement form has only true substitution instances and is therefore tautologous. For example, the following truth table shows that $[(p \supset q) \supset p] \supset p$ is a tautologous statement form because there are only **T**'s in the right-hand column:

p	q	$p \supset q$	$(p \supset q) \supset p$	$[(p \supset q) \supset p] \supset p$
T	**T**	**T**	**T**	**T**
T	**F**	**F**	**T**	**T**
F	**T**	**T**	**F**	**T**
F	**F**	**T**	**F**	**T**

This truth table shows that any substitution instance of the given statement form is necessarily true in virtue of its form alone, regardless of its specific content. Any statement which is a substitution instance of a tautologous statement form is itself a **tautologous statement** or a **tautology,** that is, a statement which is necessarily true in virtue of its form alone.

A **self-contradictory statement form** (for example, $p \cdot {\sim}p$) has only false substitution instances, as can be shown by a truth table. Any statement which is a substitution instance of a self-contradictory statement form is itself a **self-contradictory statement** or a **contradiction,** that is, a statement which is necessarily false in virtue of its form alone.

A statement form which has some true substitution instances and some false substitution instances is called a **contingent statement form,** because the truth value of a particular substitution instance is *contingent* on the truth values of the statements which are substituted for the statement variables in the given statement form. For example, the following truth table shows that $p \vee q$ is a contingent statement form because there are some **T**'s and some **F**'s in the right-hand column:

p	q	$p \vee q$
T	**T**	**T**
T	**F**	**T**
F	**T**	**T**
F	**F**	**F**

A statement which is a substitution instance of a contingent statement form is itself a **contingent statement,** so long as the following conditions are satisfied. First, the statements substituted for the statement variables cannot be either necessarily true or necessarily false. For example, although $p \vee q$ is a contingent statement form, if we substitute a necessarily true statement for p the result will be a necessarily true substitution instance rather than a contingent substitution instance. Second, we can legitimately infer that a given statement is contingent on the grounds that it is a substitution instance of a certain contingent statement form only if the statement form in question is *the specific form* of the given statement, where **the specific form** of a given statement is defined to be that statement form from which the given statement results by substituting a different *simple* statement for each different statement variable. For example, although $p \vee q$ is a contingent statement form, it can have a noncontingent substitution instance (for example, Jones plays or Jones does not play) if a *compound* statement (Jones does not play) is substituted for one of the statement variables.

In order to study certain very useful tautologies it is necessary to introduce another truth-functional connective (the last that we shall need). Two statements are said to be **materially equivalent,** or equivalent in truth value, when they have the same truth value, that is, when they are either both true or both false. For example, "London is in France" and "Paris is in Italy" are materially equivalent, because they are both false. Using obvious abbreviations, we can represent the affirmation that these two statements are materially equivalent as $L \equiv P$, where "$\equiv$" is the symbol for material equivalence. In general, $p \equiv q$ (which is called a **biconditional**) is true when p and q have the same truth value and false when they have different truth values. This is displayed clearly in the following truth table, which can be considered as a definition of the symbol for material equivalence:

p	q	$p \equiv q$
T	T	T
T	F	F
F	T	F
F	F	T

You can see from this truth table that the biconditional $p \equiv q$ is a contingent statement form. Similarly, the biconditional $L \equiv P$ (mentioned above) is a contingent statement, because its truth is not determined by its form alone but is contingent on the facts of geography and history. There are, however, certain biconditional statement forms which are tautologous, that is, which have only true substitution instances. The following three tautologous biconditionals were examined in the text and should be remembered:

$$p \equiv \sim\sim p$$
$$\sim(p \vee q) \equiv (\sim p \cdot \sim q)$$
$$\sim(p \cdot q) \equiv (\sim p \vee \sim q)$$

The first biconditional is the principle of double negation. The second and third are known as De Morgan's Theorems.

There are, of course, also self-contradictory biconditional statement forms, for example, $p \equiv \sim p$. To determine whether a given biconditional statement form is tautologous, self-contradictory, or contingent, set up a truth table and examine the truth values in the column headed by the biconditional. If the truth values in that column are all **T**'s then the biconditional is tautologous; if they are all **F**'s, the biconditional is self-contradictory; and if there are some **T**'s and some **F**'s, the biconditional is contingent. Any substitution instance of a tautologous biconditional statement form is itself a tautologous statement, and any substitution instance of a self-contradictory biconditional statement form is itself a self-contradictory statement. With respect to contingent biconditional statement forms we must introduce the usual qualifications, so that we can say that a substitution instance of a contingent biconditional statement form is a contingent statement if the substitution instance results by substituting a different *simple* statement for each different statement variable in the statement form (where it is explicitly assumed, as explained in footnote 8 on page 289 of Copi's text, that all simple statements are contingent).

If a biconditional statement is a tautology, the two statements on either side of the biconditional symbol are said to be **logically equivalent,** that is, equivalent in virtue of their logical form alone. Similarly, if a biconditional statement form is tautologous, the two statement forms on either side of the biconditional symbol are said to be logically equivalent. Thus, two statements (or statement forms) are logically equivalent when the affirmation of their material equivalence is a tautology. Be sure not to confuse the concepts of *material equivalence* and *logical equivalence.* "London is in France" and "Paris is in Italy" are materially equivalent because they have the same truth value, but they are not logically equivalent because $L \equiv P$ is not a tautology, that is, not a statement which is *necessarily* true by virtue of its *logical form* alone.

The affirmation that $p \equiv q$ says, of course, that if p is true then q is true and if q is true then p is true, which is the same as saying that p is true if and only if q is true. Thus, $p \equiv q$ can be read as "p if and only if q" where "p if and only if q" can also be symbolized as $(p \supset q) \cdot (q \supset p)$ which is logically equivalent to $p \equiv q$, as can be checked by a truth table.

Corresponding to every argument (whether valid or invalid) there is a conditional statement whose antecedent is the conjunction of the premisses of the argument and whose consequent is the conclusion of the argument. For example, corresponding to any argument of the form

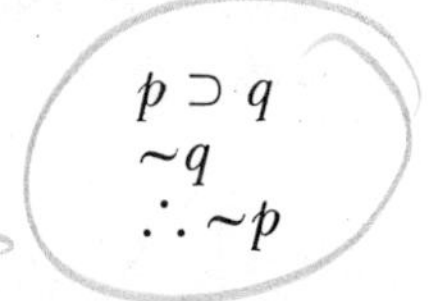

$$p \supset q$$
$$\sim q$$
$$\therefore \sim p$$

there is a corresponding conditional statement of the form $[(p \supset q) \cdot \sim q] \supset \sim p$. Now an argument is valid if and only if it is impossible for all the premisses to be true and the conclusion false. And a conditional statement is tautologous if and only if it is impossible for the antecedent to be true and the consequent false. From this it follows that an argument is valid if and only if its corresponding conditional statement is tautologous, because the conditions that would make the argument invalid (all true premisses and a false conclusion) are exactly the same conditions that would make the corresponding conditional statement nontautologous (true antecedent and false consequent). Thus, we can determine whether or not an argument is valid by determining whether or not its corresponding conditional statement is a tautology.

SELF-QUIZ

(covering pages 300–304 of the text)

QUESTIONS	ANSWERS
1. In the preceding section we studied statement forms and	1. Tautologous.

statements which were either contingent, self-contradictory or ______.	
2. A formula which contains statement variables but no statements and which is such that a statement results when statements are substituted for the statement variables in the formula is called a ______.	2. Statement form.
3. Any statement of a certain form is said to be a ______ of that statement form.	3. Substitution instance.
4. Is $A \supset (B \vee C)$ a substitution instance of $p \supset q$?	4. Yes.
5. Is $p \supset q$ *the specific form* of $A \supset (B \vee C)$?	5. No.
6. What is *the specific form* of $A \supset (B \vee C)$?	6. $p \supset (q \vee r)$
7. A statement form which has only true substitution instances is said to be a ______ statement form.	7. Tautologous.
8. A statement form is self-contradictory if its truth table has ______ in the column headed by the statement form.	8. All **F**'s.
9. Is it true that *any* statement which is a substitution instance of a contingent statement form is itself a contingent statement?	9. No.
10. Two statements are materially equivalent if and only if they have ______.	10. The same truth value.
11. In the following table there is one mistake in assigning truth values. Where is the mistake?	11. The mistake is in the third column in the third row.

p	q	$(p \supset q) \cdot (q \supset p)$	$p \equiv q$
T	**T**	**T**	**T**
T	**F**	**F**	**F**
F	**T**	**T**	**F**
F	**F**	**T**	**T**

12. Two statements are logically equivalent if the affirmation of their material equivalence is a ________.	12. Tautology.
13. According to De Morgan's Theorems, $\sim(p \vee q)$ is logically equivalent to ________; and $\sim(p \cdot q)$ is logically equivalent to ________.	13. $\sim p \cdot \sim q$; $\sim p \vee \sim q$.
14. Using the curl and the wedge, write a formula which is logically equivalent to $\sim(p \cdot \sim q)$.	14. $\sim p \vee q$.
15. Using the curl and the dot, write a formula which is logically equivalent to $p \vee \sim q$.	15. $\sim(\sim p \cdot q)$.
16. Is the following statement form tautologous: $(p \equiv q) \equiv [(p \supset q) \cdot (q \supset p)]$?	16. Yes.
17. Is the following statement form tautologous: $(p \supset q) \equiv (\sim p \vee q)$?	17. Yes.
18. Corresponding to every argument there is a conditional statement whose antecedent is ________ and whose consequent is ________.	18. The conjunction of the premisses of the argument; the conclusion of the argument.
19. Write the corresponding conditional of the following argument: $A \supset (B \supset C)$ $\sim B$ $\therefore A \supset \sim C$	19. $\{[A \supset (B \supset C)] \cdot \sim B\} \supset (A \supset \sim C)$.
20. An argument is valid if and only if its corresponding conditional is a ________.	20. Tautology.

SOLUTIONS
to selected exercises on pages 304–305

Page 304, I, #2: d is the specific form of 2, and a has 2 as a substitution instance.

Page 304, I, #6: b has 6 as a substitution instance.

Page 304, II, #2:

p	q	$p \supset q$	$(p \supset q) \supset q$	$p \supset [(p \supset q) \supset q]$
T	T	T	T	T
T	F	F	T	T
F	T	T	T	T
F	F	T	F	T

tautologous.

Page 304, II, #6:

p	q	$p \supset p$	$\sim q$	$q \cdot \sim q$	$(p \supset p) \supset (q \cdot \sim q)$
T	T	T	F	F	F
T	F	T	T	F	F
F	T	T	F	F	F
F	F	T	T	F	F

self-contradictory.

Page 305, III, #2:

p	q	$p \supset q$	$\sim p$	$\sim q$	$\sim p \supset \sim q$	$(p \supset q) \equiv (\sim p \supset \sim q)$
T	T	T	F	F	T	T
T	F	F	F	T	T	F
F	T	T	T	F	F	F
F	F	T	T	T	T	T

not a tautology.

Page 305, III, #6:

p	q	$p \cdot q$	$p \vee (p \cdot q)$	$p \equiv [p \vee (p \cdot q)]$
T	T	T	T	T
T	F	F	T	T
F	T	F	F	T
F	F	F	F	T

tautology.

Page 305, III, #11:

p	q	$\sim q$	$q \cdot \sim q$	$p \vee (q \cdot \sim q)$	$p \equiv [p \vee (q \cdot \sim q)]$
T	T	F	F	T	T
T	F	T	F	T	T
F	T	F	F	F	T
F	F	T	F	F	T

tautology.

Page 305, III, #16:

p	q	r	$q \vee r$	$p \cdot (q \vee r)$	$p \vee q$	$p \vee r$	$(p \vee q) \cdot (p \vee r)$	$[p \cdot (q \vee r)] \equiv [(p \vee q) \cdot (p \vee r)]$
T	T	T	T	T	T	T	T	T
T	T	F	T	T	T	T	T	T
T	F	T	T	T	T	T	T	T
T	F	F	F	F	T	T	T	F
F	T	T	T	F	T	T	T	F
F	T	F	T	F	T	F	F	T
F	F	T	T	F	F	T	F	T
F	F	F	F	F	F	F	F	T

not a tautology.

READ PAGES 305–308 OF THE TEXT

8.6 The Paradoxes of Material Implication

8.7 The Three "Laws of Thought"

These two sections require no additional review or further explanation.

EXAMINATION on Chapter 8

Write your answers on a separate sheet of paper, then check them against the answers given at the end of the examination. If you miss a question, restudy the appropriate part of the text.

1. State why the following is not a truth-functional compound statement:

   Smith has said that if the United Nations is not strengthened, then there will be another world war.

2. Using the dot and the curl (but *none* of the other truth-functional connectives) write a formula logically equivalent to the formula $p \equiv q$.
3. Using the dot and the curl (but *none* of the other truth-functional connectives) write an expression which is logically equivalent to $p + q$ (where "+" is thc symbol for "or" in the *exclusive* sense).
4. Copi lists four different types of implications: logical, definitional,

causal, and decisional. What is the relationship of material implication to these four?

5. According to the principle of Refutation by Logical Analogy, to prove the invalidity of any argument it suffices to formulate another argument which (a) has the same form as the first, and (b) ______.
6. How, *in general,* does one prove the invalidity of a certain argument form?
7. Is the following argument valid?

   Argument (A) is a substitution instance of argument form (F).
   Argument form (F) is an invalid argument form.
   Therefore, argument (A) is an invalid argument.
8. Although the following argument is a substitution instance of *modus ponens, modus ponens* is not *the specific form* of the following argument. What is *the specific form* of the following argument?

$$(A \cdot B) \supset C$$
$$A \cdot B$$
$$\therefore C$$

9. Is it true that if two statement forms are logically equivalent then either (a) they *each* have only true substitution instances, or (b) they *each* have only false substitution instances.
10. Under what conditions are two *statements* logically equivalent?
11. A statement form which has only ______ is a self-contradictory statement form.
12. Is it true that *whenever* two statements are logically equivalent they materially imply each other?
13. Can the principles and techniques of logic be used to determine the truth or falsity of a contingent statement?
14. Is the following argument valid?

    Statement (S) is a substitution instance of statement form (F).
    Statement form (F) is not tautologous.
    Therefore, statement (S) is not a tautology.
15. Is it true that two statements are not materially equivalent whenever they are not both true?
16. Which of the following statements are true and which are false?
    a. All invalid argument forms have only invalid substitution instances.
    b. There are some valid argument forms some of whose substitution instances are valid and some of whose substitution instances are invalid.
    c. An argument is invalid only if *the specific form* of the argument is invalid.
    d. An argument is valid only if *the specific form* of the argument is valid.

e. An argument form is valid if any substitution instance of it is valid.

f. An argument form is invalid if any substitution instance of it is invalid.

17. The three so-called laws of thought are the principle of identity, the principle of noncontradiction, and the principle of excluded middle. Express each of these three principles in symbolic form by using a statement variable and truth-functional connectives.
18. Where A, B, and C are true statements, and X, Y, and Z are false statements, what is the truth value of the following compound statement?

$$\sim[\sim A \equiv (\sim B \supset X)] \supset \sim[(\sim A \vee \sim Y) \cdot (Z \vee \sim C)]$$

19. Use a truth table to determine the validity or invalidity of the following argument form:

$$p \supset q$$
$$\sim p \supset r$$
$$\therefore q \vee r$$

20. Use a truth table to determine whether the following statement form is tautologous, self-contradictory, or contingent:

$$p \equiv [p \cdot (\sim p \supset q)]$$

ANSWERS

1. The statement is not truth-functionally compound because its truth value is not a function of the truth values of its component statements.
2. $\sim(p \cdot \sim q) \cdot \sim(q \cdot \sim p)$. There are other equally correct answers, for example, $\sim[\sim(p \cdot q) \cdot \sim(\sim p \cdot \sim q)]$.
3. $\sim(p \cdot q) \cdot \sim(\sim p \cdot \sim q)$. There are other equally correct answers.
4. Material implication is a common partial meaning of the four different types of implications listed.
5. Has true premisses and a false conclusion.
6. One proves the invalidity of an argument form by showing that it is possible for a substitution instance of that form to have true premisses and a false conclusion.
7. No.
8. $(p \cdot q) \supset r$
   $p \cdot q$
   $\therefore r$
9. No.
10. Two statements are logically equivalent when the affirmation of their material equivalence is a tautology.
11. False substitution instances.

12. Yes.
13. No.
14. No.
15. No.
16. a. False.
    b. False.
    c. True.
    d. True.
    e. False.
    f. True.
17. $p \supset p$
    $\sim(p \cdot \sim p)$
    $p \vee \sim p$
18. True.
19.

p	q	r	$p \supset q$	$\sim p$	$\sim p \supset r$	$q \vee r$
T	T	T	T	F	T	T
T	T	F	T	F	T	T
T	F	T	F	F	T	T
T	F	F	F	F	T	F
F	T	T	T	T	T	T
F	T	F	T	T	F	T
F	F	T	T	T	T	T
F	F	F	T	T	F	F

valid.

20.

p	q	$\sim p$	$\sim p \supset q$	$p \cdot (\sim p \supset q)$	$p \equiv [p \cdot (\sim p \supset q)]$
T	T	F	T	T	T
T	F	F	T	T	T
F	T	T	T	F	T
F	F	T	F	F	T

tautologous.

Chapter 9
The Method of Deduction

READ PAGES 309–312 OF THE TEXT

9.1 Formal Proof of Validity

The validity of an argument can be proved by deducing the conclusion from the premisses by means of a sequence of elementary valid arguments. Each elementary valid argument in the sequence must be a substitution instance of an elementary valid argument form, and the elementary valid argument forms that are here permitted as justification for the lines in a proof are listed on page 312 of the text and should be learned so thoroughly that you can use them in the exercises without referring back to the list.

A **formal proof of validity** for an argument consists of a sequence of statements, in which the premisses of the argument are listed first, and each statement after the premisses follows from preceding statements in the sequence by virtue of an elementary valid argument form, and the last statement in the sequence is the conclusion of the argument whose validity is being proved.

In writing out a formal proof of validity you should

1. Number the lines.
2. Just to the right of the last premiss, place a diagonal line, then three dots (indicating "therefore"), and then the conclusion to be deduced.
3. To the right of each line which is not a premiss, write the numbers of the lines from which the line in question follows and the abbreviation of the elementary valid argument form by virtue of which the line follows.

The validity of the elementary valid argument forms, or rules of inference, listed on page 312 of the text can be established by using truth tables. Rules 6 and 9 are probably the only rules listed whose validity may not be immediately apparent.

Remember that a line in a proof is justified only if that line follows from preceding lines by virtue of one of the rules of inference. In other words, the preceding lines and the line in question must together constitute a substitution instance of one of the elementary valid argument forms listed as rules of inference. And remember that a substitution instance can be produced by substituting a *compound* statement (as well as a simple statement) for a statement variable. Thus, the following argument is a substitution instance of *modus tollens,* where the compound statement $A \cdot B$ is substituted for p:

$$(A \cdot B) \supset C$$
$$\sim C$$
$$\therefore \sim (A \cdot B)$$

SOLUTIONS
to selected exercises on pages 312–315

You can achieve mastery of the material in this chapter only by working out answers to the exercises by yourself. Use the following answers *only* to check on the correctness of your own answers.

Page 313, I, #2: *Simplification* (Simp.)

Page 313, I, #6: *Disjunctive Syllogism* (D.S.)

Page 313, I, #11: *Conjunction* (Conj.)

Page 313, I, #16: *Disjunctive Syllogism* (D.S.)

Page 314, II, #2:
4. 1, Simp.
5. 2, 4, C.D.
6. 5, 3, D.S.*

Page 314, II, #6:
5. 1, Abs.
6. 5, 3, H.S.*
7. 2, 6, M.P.
8. 7, 4, D.S.*

* Note that the numbers referring to previous lines are listed in the order which corresponds to the order of the premisses in the argument form which is appealed to as justification.

SOLUTIONS
to selected exercises on pages 315–318

In the second set of exercises you were given a formal proof of validity. All you had to do was to supply a justification for each line after the premisses. In this third set of exercises you must discover a formal proof of validity; that is, you must construct a sequence of lines by means of which the conclusion can be deduced from the premisses. There are no fixed procedures which can be followed in constructing formal proofs of validity. Insight and ingenuity and perhaps some trial and error are required. Nevertheless, the more familiar you are with the rules of inference, the easier it will be for you to construct a sequence of lines that will lead validly from the premisses to the conclusion. And the more of these exercises that you conscientiously work out *on your own,* the more familiar you will become with the rules and with the various ways in which they can be used to construct proofs of validity.

The following formal proofs of validity are not the only possible formal proofs. There may be other alternative sequences of lines which work equally well.

Page 315, III, #2:

1. $D \supset E$	
2. $\sim (D \cdot E)$	$/ \therefore \sim D$
3. $D \supset (D \cdot E)$	1, Abs.
4. $\sim D$	3, 2, M.T.

Page 315, III, #6:

1. $(O \vee P) \supset Q$	
2. $\sim Q \cdot \sim O$	$/ \therefore \sim (O \vee P)$
3. $\sim Q$	2, Simp.
4. $\sim (O \vee P)$	1, 3, M.T.

Page 315, IV, #2:

1. $D \supset E$	
2. $F \vee \sim E$	
3. $\sim F \cdot \sim D$	$/ \therefore \sim D$
4. $\sim F$	3, Simp.
5. $\sim E$	2, 4, D.S.
6. $\sim D$	1, 5, M.T.

Notice that $\sim D$ cannot be deduced directly from line 3, because the rule of inference *Simplification* is of the form

$$\begin{array}{l} p \cdot q \\ \therefore p \end{array}$$

which permits the deduction of the left-hand conjunct (p) but *not* the right-hand conjunct (q).

Page 315, IV, #6:

1.	$W \supset X$	
2.	$(W \cdot X) \supset Y$	
3.	$(W \cdot Y) \supset Z$	$/ \therefore W \supset Z$
4.	$W \supset (W \cdot X)$	1, Abs.
5.	$W \supset Y$	4, 2, H.S.
6.	$W \supset (W \cdot Y)$	5, Abs.
7.	$W \supset Z$	6, 3, H.S.

Page 316, V, #2:

1.	$(A \supset S) \cdot (B \supset F)$	
2.	$A \vee B$	
3.	$(S \supset B) \cdot (F \supset W)$	$/ \therefore B \vee W$
4.	$S \vee F$	1, 2, C.D.
5.	$B \vee W$	3, 4, C.D.

Page 317, V, #6: Notice that the word "but" is used in its conjunctive sense in the first premiss and is therefore to be symbolized by the dot symbol. Notice that the word "implies" in the third premiss is symbolized by the horseshoe symbol.

1.	$(J \supset R) \cdot (\sim J \supset E)$	
2.	$R \supset I$	
3.	$[(J \supset R) \cdot (R \supset I)] \supset [(J \cdot I) \vee (\sim J \cdot \sim I)]$	
4.	$(J \cdot I) \supset T$	
5.	$(\sim J \cdot \sim I) \supset D$	$/ \therefore T \vee D$
6.	$J \supset R$	1, Simp.
7.	$(J \supset R) \cdot (R \supset I)$	6, 2, Conj.
8.	$(J \cdot I) \vee (\sim J \cdot \sim I)$	3, 7, M.P.
9.	$[(J \cdot I) \supset T] \cdot [(\sim J \cdot \sim I) \supset D]$	4, 5, Conj.
10.	$T \vee D$	9, 8, C.D.

Notice that lines 4 and 5 must first be conjoined to produce line 9 before C.D. can be used to produce line 10. Line 9 is necessary because lines 4, 5, 8, and 10 are not a substitution instance of the elementary valid argument form C.D. as it appears on page 312 of the text, whereas lines 9, 8, and 10 are a substitution instance of C.D. In order for an argument to be a substitution instance of C.D., the first premiss of the argument must be a *conjunction* of two conditionals. If the two conditionals originally occur as separate lines in the proof, they must first be conjoined before C.D. can be used.

READ PAGES 318–323 OF THE TEXT

9.2 The Rule of Replacement

Where we are dealing only with simple statements and truth-functional compound statements (as in the present chapter), the **Rule of Replacement** permits us to infer from any statement the result of replacing any component of that statement by any other statement *logically* equivalent to the component replaced, where the component replaced can be either a *part* of the original statement or the *whole* of the original statement. In order to understand what kinds of inferences the Rule of Replacement permits and why these inferences are valid, let S^* be the statement inferred from S by the Rule of Replacement, and let Q be the statement which is replaced by R, where Q is logically equivalent to R. In other words, Q is either a part of S or else the whole of S; the Rule of Replacement is used to justify replacing Q with R, where Q and R are logically equivalent; and the statement which is inferred, S^*, differs from S only in having R where S has Q.

Now there are two separate cases to be considered. First, where Q is the whole of S, and R replaces Q, it follows that R will be the whole of S^*; and since Q and R are logically equivalent, it follows that S and S^* will be logically equivalent and hence have the same truth value, so that if S is true then S^* must be true also, which means that the inference from S to S^* is valid.

On the other hand, where Q is only a part of S, the truth value of S (which is a truth-functional compound statement) will be a function of the truth value of Q. Now we know that in any truth-functional compound statement, if a part of the statement is replaced by another statement having the same truth value, then the truth value of the new compound statement will be the same as the truth value of the original compound statement. Hence, if Q is replaced by R (where R is logically equivalent to Q and thus has the same truth value as Q), then the truth value of the new compound statement S^* will be the same as the truth value of the original compound statement S, so that if S is true then S^* must be true also, which means that the inference from S to S^* is valid.

Thus, it is valid to infer from any simple statement or from any truth-functional compound statement the result of replacing any component of that statement by any other statement logically equivalent to the component replaced, where the component replaced can be either a *part* of the original statement or the *whole* of the original statement. In constructing a formal proof of validity, you are permitted to appeal to any of the logical equivalences listed on page 319 of the text as a justification for replacing a statement with a logically equivalent statement. These logical equivalences thus constitute ten additional rules of inference, according to which one statement may replace another statement so long as the affirmation of the material equivalence of these two statements is a substitution instance of one of the logical equivalences listed.

Notice that the statement that is replaced by a logically equivalent statement may constitute either the *whole* of a line of a proof or *only part* of a line of a proof. In this respect, the last ten rules of inference are different from the first nine rules of inference. The first nine rules can be used only with *whole* lines of a proof serving as premisses. In other words, in order for a line of a proof to follow from preceding lines by virtue of one of the first nine rules, those *whole* preceding lines must be a substitution instance of the premisses of the rule of inference being used.

The proper use of the rules should become almost automatic after you have completed the exercises which follow this section, but in working on those exercises you may find the following hints helpful.

In constructing a formal proof of validity, you must be careful not to omit a necessary line. Each inference must be *exactly* of one of the forms listed as rules of inference. For example, in the following proof

1. $(A \supset B) \cdot (C \supset D)$	
2. $C \vee A$	$/\therefore B \vee D$
3. $A \vee C$	2, Com.
4. $B \vee D$	1, 3, C.D.

line 3 is necessary because line 4 cannot be inferred directly from lines 1 and 2, since lines 1 and 2 are not *exactly* of the form of the premisses of C.D. as listed in the nineteen rules of inference.

You must be especially careful not to omit a necessary line when you are using a rule of inference in which a negation sign appears. For example, the following proof would be incorrect if line 2 were omitted:

1. $E \vee F$	$/\therefore \sim E \supset F$
2. $\sim \sim E \vee F$	1, D.N.
3. $\sim E \supset F$	2, Impl.

Line 3 cannot be inferred directly from line 1 because the rule of Material Implication justifies replacing a statement of the form $\sim p \vee q$ by a statement of the form $p \supset q$, where the statement replaced *must* have a negation sign in front of the left-hand disjunct (and there is no negation sign in front of the left-hand disjunct in line 1). Hence, line 2 is necessary in order to infer line 3.

The same principle applies when you are using any other rule of inference in which a negation sign occurs. Thus, the following proof would be incorrect if we inferred line 3 directly from line 1 by Transposition:

1. $G \supset \sim H$ $\quad /\therefore H \supset \sim G$
2. $\sim\sim H \supset \sim G$ $\quad$ 1, Trans.
3. $H \supset \sim G$ $\quad$ 2, D.N.

Transposition justifies replacing a statement of the form $p \supset q$ by a statement of the form $\sim q \supset \sim p$, so that if $\sim H$ is the consequent of the first statement, then $\sim\sim H$ will be the antecedent of the second statement, as in line 2.

Similarly, it would be incorrect to omit line 3 in the following proof:

1. $\sim I \vee J$
2. I $\quad /\therefore J$
3. $\sim\sim I$ $\quad$ 2, D.N.
4. J $\quad$ 1, 3, D.S.

You cannot infer line 4 directly from lines 1 and 2 because of the form in which the rule D.S. is stated.

There are other situations in which you may be tempted to omit necessary lines. For example, the following proof is incorrect

1. $(K \supset L) \cdot (L \supset M)$ $\quad /\therefore K \supset M$
2. $K \supset M$ $\quad$ 1, H.S.

because the rule H.S. can be used only where the two conditionals occur in *separate* lines. Thus, to infer line 2 from line 1 you would have to introduce three intermediate lines:

1. $(K \supset L) \cdot (L \supset M)$ $\quad /\therefore K \supset M$
2. $K \supset L$ $\quad$ 1, Simp.
3. $(L \supset M) \cdot (K \supset L)$ $\quad$ 1, Com.
4. $L \supset M$ $\quad$ 3, Simp.
5. $K \supset M$ $\quad$ 2, 4, H.S.

You may, of course, use only one rule at a time. The following proof is incorrect because two rules are used at once in the justification of line 2:

1. $N \cdot O$ $\quad /\therefore O$
2. O $\quad$ 1, Com., Simp.

A correct proof would be

1.	$N \cdot O$	$/\therefore O$
2.	$O \cdot N$	1, Com.
3.	O	2, Simp.

In the exercises which follow the present section, you will again be required to translate from ordinary English into symbols. You may find the following hints useful.

Any statement of the form "p only if q" means that p can be true only if q is also true, which means that if p is true then q must also be true, which means that $p \supset q$. In other words, "p only if q" is to be translated as $p \supset q$, not as $q \supset p$.

On the other hand, "p if q" is just an inverted way of saying "if q then p," which is translated as $q \supset p$. Hence, "p if and only if q" is translated literally as $(q \supset p) \cdot (p \supset q)$, which means the same as $q \equiv p$, which means the same as $p \equiv q$.

"p provided that q" means the same as "p if q," which is symbolized as $q \supset p$.

"Neither p nor q" can be symbolized either as $\sim p \cdot \sim q$ or as $\sim (p \vee q)$, which are equivalent by De Morgan's Theorem.

Sometimes a compound statement can be translated into a conditional even though it does not contain the words "if–then" or "implies." For example, a sentence like "the continuation of the thaw in the mountains will flood the valley" is one way of affirming a causal implication and can be symbolized as $T \supset V$, where T stands for "the thaw continues in the mountains" and V stands for "the valley floods."

If a sentence is a conjunction of three statements and thus of the form "p and q and r," it can be symbolized either as $(p \cdot q) \cdot r$ or as $p \cdot (q \cdot r)$, but it cannot be symbolized as $p \cdot q \cdot r$, which is not well formed unless parentheses are added. Because of the way in which the dot symbol is defined, a conjunction must be composed of *two* conjuncts (which may themselves be compound).

Remember that two statements in ordinary English may be *conjoined* not only by the word "and" but also by the words "but," "although," "whereas," "while," and so on.

Before going on to the exercises you should become familiar enough with rules 10 through 19 so that you can not only recognize instances of their use but also apply them in constructing formal proofs of validity. Rules 13 and 18 are probably the least obvious. You may even want to use truth tables to convince yourself that they really do state logical equivalences.

In working out solutions to the exercises which follow the present section of the text, you should be careful to avoid the mistakes which are reviewed in the following self-quiz.

SELF-QUIZ

(covering pages 309–323 of the text)

QUESTIONS / ANSWERS

Explain the error in each of the following proofs:

1. $A \cdot B$ $\quad /\therefore \sim(\sim A \vee \sim B)$
2. $\sim(\sim A \vee \sim B)$ 1, De M.

Because of the form in which De Morgan's Theorem is stated, line 2 cannot be inferred directly from line 1. The proof should be

1. $A \cdot B$ $\quad /\therefore \sim(\sim A \vee \sim B)$
2. $\sim\sim(A \cdot B)$ 1, D.N.
3. $\sim(\sim A \vee \sim B)$ 2, De M.

---

1. $(C \supset D) \cdot (\sim C \supset E)$ $/\therefore D \vee E$
2. $C \vee \sim C$ Tautology
3. $D \vee E$ 1, 2, C.D.

In spite of the fact that line 2 is a tautology and therefore necessarily true, the presence of line 2 prevents the sequence of statements from being a proof. A formal proof of validity consists (by definition) only of premisses and lines which follow from preceding lines by virtue of the rules of inference listed in the text. But line 2 is not a premiss and does not follow from preceding lines by virtue of a rule of inference.

---

1. $(F \cdot G) \supset H$ $\quad /\therefore F \supset H$
2. $F \supset H$ 1, Simp.

Although F follows from $F \cdot G$ by the rule of Simplification where $F \cdot G$ is a *whole* line of a proof, the rule of Simplification cannot be used on only *part* of a line of a proof.

---

1. $\sim K \supset L$ $\quad /\therefore K \vee L$
2. $K \vee L$ 1, Impl.

The proof should be

1. $\sim K \supset L$ $\quad /\therefore K \vee L$
2. $\sim\sim K \vee L$ 1, Impl.
3. $K \vee L$ 2, D.N.

---

1. $\sim M \supset N$
2. $\sim N$ $\quad /\therefore M$
3. M 1, 2, M.T.

The proof should be

1. $\sim M \supset N$
2. $\sim N$ $\quad /\therefore M$
3. $\sim\sim M$ 1, 2, M.T.
4. M 3, D.N.

1. $O \vee P$
2. $\sim P \quad /\therefore O$
3. $O \quad$ 1, 2, D.S.

The proof should be
1. $O \vee P$
2. $\sim P \quad /\therefore O$
3. $P \vee O \quad$ 1, Com.
4. $O \quad$ 3, 2, D.S.

1. $(Q \supset R) \cdot (S \supset T)$
2. $S \vee Q \quad /\therefore T \vee R$
3. $T \vee R \quad$ 1, 2, C.D.

The proof should be
1. $(Q \supset R) \cdot (S \supset T)$
2. $S \vee Q \quad /\therefore T \vee R$
3. $(S \supset T) \cdot (Q \supset R) \quad$ 1, Com.
4. $T \vee R \quad$ 3, 2, C.D.

1. $U \supset \sim V$
2. $V \quad /\therefore \sim U$
3. $\sim U \quad$ 1, 2, M.T.

The proof should be
1. $U \supset \sim V$
2. $V \quad /\therefore \sim U$
3. $\sim \sim V \quad$ 2, D.N.
4. $\sim U \quad$ 1, 3, M.T.

1. $W \supset (\sim X \supset Y) \quad /\therefore W \supset (\sim Y \supset X)$
2. $W \supset (\sim Y \supset X) \quad$ 1, Trans.

The proof should be
1. $W \supset (\sim X \supset Y) \quad /\therefore W \supset (\sim Y \supset X)$
2. $W \supset (\sim Y \supset \sim \sim X) \quad$ 1, Trans.
3. $W \supset (\sim Y \supset X) \quad$ 2, D.N.

SOLUTIONS
to selected exercises on pages 323–327

Page 323, I, #2: Material Implication (Impl.)

Page 324, I, #6: De Morgan's Theorems (De M.)

Page 324, I, #11: Material Implication (Impl.)

Page 324, I, #16: Tautology (Taut.)

Page 324, II, #2:
3. 1, Com.
4. 3, Exp.
5. 4, 2, H.S.

Page 325, II, #6:
4. 2, Exp.
5. 3, De M.
6. 4, 5, Conj.
7. 1, Dist.
8. 6, 7, C.D.
9. 8, Equiv.

Page 326, III, #2:

1.	C	$/\therefore D \supset C$
2.	$C \vee \sim D$	1, Add.
3.	$\sim D \vee C$	2, Com.
4.	$D \supset C$	3, Impl.

Page 326, III, #6:

1.	$N \supset O$	$/\therefore (N \cdot P) \supset O$
2.	$\sim N \vee O$	1, Impl.
3.	$(\sim N \vee O) \vee \sim P$	2, Add.
4.	$\sim P \vee (\sim N \vee O)$	3, Com.
5.	$(\sim P \vee \sim N) \vee O$	4, Assoc.
6.	$\sim (P \cdot N) \vee O$	5, De M.
7.	$(P \cdot N) \supset O$	6, Impl.
8.	$(N \cdot P) \supset O$	7, Com.

Page 326, IV, #2:

1.	$D \supset (E \vee F)$	
2.	$\sim E \cdot \sim F$	$/\therefore \sim D$
3.	$\sim (E \vee F)$	2, De M.
4.	$\sim D$	1, 3, M.T.

Page 326, IV, #6:

1.	$R \vee (S \cdot \sim T)$	
2.	$(R \vee S) \supset (U \vee \sim T)$	$/\therefore T \supset U$
3.	$(R \vee S) \cdot (R \vee \sim T)$	1, Dist.
4.	$R \vee S$	3, Simp.
5.	$U \vee \sim T$	2, 4, M.P.
6.	$\sim T \vee U$	5, Com.
7.	$T \supset U$	6, Impl.

Page 326, IV, #11:

1.	$M \supset N$	
2.	$M \supset (N \supset O)$	$/\therefore M \supset O$
3.	$M \supset (M \cdot N)$	1, Abs.
4.	$(M \cdot N) \supset O$	2, Exp.
5.	$M \supset O$	3, 4, H.S.

Page 326, IV, #16:

1.	$\sim B \vee [(C \supset D) \cdot (E \supset D)]$	
2.	$B \cdot (C \vee E)$	$/\therefore D$
3.	B	2, Simp.
4.	$\sim \sim B$	3, D.N.
5.	$(C \supset D) \cdot (E \supset D)$	1, 4, D.S.
6.	$(C \vee E) \cdot B$	2, Com.
7.	$C \vee E$	6, Simp.
8.	$D \vee D$	5, 7, C.D.
9.	D	8, Taut.

SOLUTIONS

to selected exercises on pages 327–330

In these exercises in part V you must translate from ordinary English into symbols, and also you must construct your own formal proofs of validity. It might be wise to check your translation of an argument against the following translation before looking for a proof of validity. Otherwise, if you happened to mistranslate, you would run the risk of searching for a proof that did not even exist.

It is very important that you try to work out translations and proofs for these arguments *on your own*. Only intensive practice with the rules will enable you to develop the kind of facility that will make it relatively easy to construct formal proofs of validity for arguments that you have never before seen. Of course there may come a time in working on a problem when you are so hopelessly stuck that nothing more can be gained by continued struggle. When this time comes (after perhaps fifteen minutes) nothing is lost (except pride) by turning to the proof below.

Remember that the formal proofs of validity given here are not necessarily the only possible proofs. There may be other alternative sequences of lines which work equally well.

Page 327, V, #2:

1. $C \vee V$	
2. $\sim V$	$/ \therefore C$
3. $V \vee C$	1, Com.
4. C	3, 2, D.S.

Notice here that line 3 is necessary because of the form in which the rule D.S. is stated.

Page 327, V, #6:

1. $F \supset R$	
2. $R \supset \sim E$	
3. F	$/ \therefore \sim E$
4. R	1, 3, M.P.
5. $\sim E$	2, 4, M.P.

Notice here that in the first premiss "p only if q" is symbolized as $p \supset q$.

Page 328, V, #11:

1. $G \supset F$	
2. $F \supset \sim P$	
3. P	$/ \therefore \sim G$
4. $G \supset \sim P$	1, 2, H.S.
5. $\sim \sim P$	3, D.N.
6. $\sim G$	4, 5, M.T.

Notice here that line 5 is necessary because of the form in which the rule M.T. is stated.

Page 328, V, #16:

1.	$(T \vee C) \supset (V \cdot P)$	
2.	$P \supset O$	
3.	$\sim O$	$/ \therefore \sim T$
4.	$\sim P$	2, 3, M.T.
5.	$\sim P \vee \sim V$	4, Add.
6.	$\sim V \vee \sim P$	5, Com.
7.	$\sim (V \cdot P)$	6, De M.
8.	$\sim (T \vee C)$	1, 7, M.T.
9.	$\sim T \cdot \sim C$	8, De M.
10.	$\sim T$	9, Simp.

Page 329, V, #21:

1.	$(H \supset P) \cdot (S \supset W)$	$/ \therefore (H \vee S) \supset (P \vee W)$
2.	$H \supset P$	1, Simp.
3.	$\sim H \vee P$	2, Impl.
4.	$(\sim H \vee P) \vee W$	3, Add.
5.	$\sim H \vee (P \vee W)$	4, Assoc.
6.	$(P \vee W) \vee \sim H$	5, Com.
7.	$(S \supset W) \cdot (H \supset P)$	1, Com.
8.	$S \supset W$	7, Simp.
9.	$\sim S \vee W$	8, Impl.
10.	$(\sim S \vee W) \vee P$	9, Add.
11.	$\sim S \vee (W \vee P)$	10, Assoc.
12.	$\sim S \vee (P \vee W)$	11, Com.
13.	$(P \vee W) \vee \sim S$	12, Com.
14.	$[(P \vee W) \vee \sim H] \cdot [(P \vee W) \vee \sim S]$	6, 13, Conj.
15.	$(P \vee W) \vee (\sim H \cdot \sim S)$	14, Dist.
16.	$(\sim H \cdot \sim S) \vee (P \vee W)$	15, Com.
17.	$\sim (H \vee S) \vee (P \vee W)$	16, De M.
18.	$(H \vee S) \supset (P \vee W)$	17, Impl.

READ PAGES 330–332 OF THE TEXT

9.3 Proof of Invalidity

An argument is invalid if it is possible for the premisses to be true and the conclusion false. Therefore, to prove the invalidity of a given truth-functional argument, it suffices to discover a set of truth values (for the simple statements contained in the argument) which will make the premisses true and the conclusion false.

Such a set of truth values corresponds to an assignment of truth values in the guide columns of a truth table in a row in which the premisses are true and the conclusion false. The method of proving invalidity explained in this section simply enables you to avoid setting up the whole truth table. In effect, you merely show that there is a row of the truth table in which the premisses are true and the conclusion false, and which therefore proves the invalidity of the argument.

SOLUTIONS

to selected exercises on page 332

The invalidity of an argument is proved by finding an assignment of truth values for the simple statements in the argument which will make the premisses true and the conclusion false. There may be more than one such assignment, but only one is required to prove invalidity.

In looking for a set of truth values which will prove invalidity, you may discover that certain truth values are required in order to make the conclusion false or to make one or another of the premisses true. If so, these truth values will be included within the set for which you are looking. But some insight and ingenuity and trial and error may be necessary in order to find the remaining truth values.

Page 332, #2:

	E	F	G	H
	t	f	f	f
or	f	t	f	f

In order for the conclusion to be false, G must be false. If G is false, then, in order for the third premiss to be true, H must be false. If G and H are false, then, in order for the second premiss to be true, either E or F must be true. But in order for the first premiss to be true, either E or F must be false. Thus, one of the statements E or F must be true and the other must be false, but it does not matter which is which, so that there are two truth value assignments, either one of which proves invalidity.

Page 332, #6:

A	B	C
f	f	f

In order for the conclusion to be false, B and C must both be false. In order for the fourth premiss to be true, A must be false. These truth values also make the first three premisses true.

READ PAGES 332–335 OF THE TEXT

9.4 Inconsistency

An argument is valid if it is impossible for its premisses to be true and its conclusion false. Now the premisses of an argument are said to be **inconsistent** if they cannot all be true, from which it follows that an argument with inconsistent premisses is necessarily valid no matter what its conclusion, since it is impossible for the premisses to be true and the conclusion false because it is impossible for the premisses to be true.

The premisses of a truth-functional argument are inconsistent if and only if there is no set of truth values for the component simple statements of the argument which makes all of the premisses true. Thus, if an argument has inconsistent premisses, then the conjunction of the premisses is self-contradictory; and from inconsistent premisses it is always possible with the nineteen rules of inference to deduce an explicit contradiction, that is, to deduce two lines of the form p and $\sim p$. And from these two lines it is possible to deduce any conclusion whatever, as can be seen from the following form of proof

1. p	
2. $\sim p$	$/ \therefore q$
3. $p \vee q$	1, Add.
4. q	3, 2, D.S.

where q can be any conclusion whatever.

There is no reason to be upset over the fact that any conclusion, however absurd, follows validly from inconsistent premisses, since the truth of the conclusion can never be established in this way, because in order to prove the truth of a conclusion you must argue validly from *true* premisses, and an argument with inconsistent premisses cannot have all true premisses.

To construct a formal proof of validity for an argument with inconsistent premisses, first deduce an explicit contradiction, then use the form of proof just outlined to deduce the conclusion of the argument from the two contradictory lines.

SOLUTIONS
to selected exercises on page 336

Aside from constructing a truth table, there is no simple method for determining immediately whether an argument is valid or invalid.

You must study the symbolic translation of an argument in order to discover either a formal proof of validity or a set of truth values which will prove invalidity. With very complicated arguments you may save some time by looking first for a set of truth values which will prove invalidity, and then if you fail to find such a set and are convinced that there is no such set, you can turn your attention resolutely toward constructing a formal proof of validity.

Page 336, I, #2:

	E	F	G	H
	t	t	f	f
or	f	f	t	t

Page 336, I, #6:

1.	$[(D \vee E) \cdot F] \supset G$	
2.	$(F \supset G) \supset (H \supset I)$	
3.	H	$/ \therefore D \supset I$
4.	$(D \vee E) \supset (F \supset G)$	1, Exp.
5.	$(D \vee E) \supset (H \supset I)$	4, 2, H.S.
6.	$[(D \vee E) \cdot H] \supset I$	5, Exp.
7.	$[H \cdot (D \vee E)] \supset I$	6, Com.
8.	$H \supset [(D \vee E) \supset I]$	7, Exp.
9.	$(D \vee E) \supset I$	8, 3, M.P.
10.	$\sim (D \vee E) \vee I$	9, Impl.
11.	$I \vee \sim (D \vee E)$	10, Com.
12.	$I \vee (\sim D \cdot \sim E)$	11, De M.
13.	$(I \vee \sim D) \cdot (I \vee \sim E)$	12, Dist.
14.	$I \vee \sim D$	13, Simp.
15.	$\sim D \vee I$	14, Com.
16.	$D \supset I$	15, Impl.

SOLUTIONS
to selected exercises on pages 336–339

Try conscientiously to work out solutions to the problems in part II *on your own*. Compare your translation with that given here before looking for a proof of validity or invalidity.

Pages 336, II, #2:

1.	$(O \cdot T) \supset (S \supset M)$	
2.	$R \supset \sim M$	
3.	$T \cdot R$	
4.	$O \cdot S$	$/ \therefore V$
5.	O	4, Simp.
6.	T	3, Simp

7.	$O \cdot T$	5, 6, Conj.
8.	$S \supset M$	1, 7, M.P.
9.	$S \cdot O$	4, Com.
10.	S	9, Simp.
11.	M	8, 10, M.P.
12.	$R \cdot T$	3, Com.
13.	R	12, Simp.
14.	$\sim M$	2, 13, M.P.
15.	$M \vee V$	11, Add.
16.	V	15, 14, D.S.

The premisses of the preceding argument are inconsistent. The contradiction is made explicit in lines 11 and 14.

Page 337, II, #6:

1.	$N \supset \sim (M \cdot G)$	
2.	$[(P \vee D) \supset \sim W] \cdot [\sim W \supset \sim (K \vee S)]$	
3.	$\sim G \cdot (D \cdot K)$	$/ \therefore \sim N$
4.	$(D \cdot K) \cdot \sim G$	3, Com.
5.	$D \cdot K$	4, Simp.
6.	D	5, Simp.
7.	$D \vee P$	6, Add.
8.	$P \vee D$	7, Com.
9.	$(P \vee D) \supset \sim W$	2, Simp.
10.	$\sim W$	9, 8, M.P.
11.	$[\sim W \supset \sim (K \vee S)] \cdot [(P \vee D) \supset \sim W]$	2, Com.
12.	$\sim W \supset \sim (K \vee S)$	11, Simp.
13.	$\sim (K \vee S)$	12, 10, M.P.
14.	$\sim K \cdot \sim S$	13, De M.
15.	$\sim K$	14, Simp.
16.	$K \cdot D$	5, Com.
17.	K	16, Simp.
18.	$K \vee \sim N$	17, Add.
19.	$\sim N$	18, 15, D.S.

The premisses of the preceding argument are inconsistent. The contradiction is made explicit in lines 15 and 17.

Page 338, II, #11:

1.	$L \supset H$	
2.	$L \supset (H \supset F)$	
3.	$H \supset (F \supset D)$	$/ \therefore L \supset D$
4.	$L \supset (L \cdot H)$	1, Abs.
5.	$(L \cdot H) \supset F$	2, Exp.
6.	$L \supset F$	4, 5, H.S.
7.	$L \supset (F \supset D)$	1, 3, H.S.

8.	$L \supset (L \cdot F)$	6, Abs.
9.	$(L \cdot F) \supset D$	7, Exp.
10.	$L \supset D$	8, 9, H.S.

EXAMINATION
on Chapter 9

Write your answers on a separate sheet of paper, then check them against the answers given at the end of the examination. If you miss a question, restudy the appropriate part of the text.

Part I. Construct a formal proof of validity for each of the following arguments. No proof requires more than three additional lines, and each proof has already appeared in the exercises of this chapter.

1. 1. $A \supset B$
   2. $A \supset (B \supset C)$ $/\therefore A \supset C$
2. 1. $D \supset E$
   2. $F \supset \sim E$ $/\therefore D \supset \sim F$
3. 1. $\sim G \supset G$ $/\therefore G$
4. 1. $(H \cdot I) \supset J$
   2. $\sim J$ $/\therefore H \supset \sim I$
5. 1. $(K \cdot L) \supset M$
   2. $(K \supset M) \supset N$ $/\therefore L \supset N$

Part II. Symbolize each of the following statements, using the abbreviations suggested:

6. Even though labor costs have risen, neither the cost of electricity nor the cost of telephone service has risen. (*L*—Labor costs have risen; *E*—The cost of electricity has risen; *T*—The cost of telephone service has risen.)
7. The continuation of rain will break the dam, unless the flood gates are opened. (*R*—Rain continues; *D*—The dam breaks; *F*—The flood gates are opened.)
8. There can be a lasting settlement only if both sides are willing to compromise. (*L*—There is a lasting settlement; *B*—Both sides are willing to compromise.)
9. Had the dam not broken, the valley would not have been flooded. (*D*—The dam broke; *V*—The valley was flooded.)
10. God is neither impotent nor malevolent, provided that he exists. (*I*—God is impotent; *M*—God is malevolent; *E*—God exists.)
11. The dam won't break if the rain stops. (*D*—The dam breaks; *S*—The rain stops.)
12. It is not the case that if the moon were made of green cheese then space vehicles would not be able to land on it. (*M*—The moon is made of green cheese; *S*—Space vehicles are able to land on the moon.)

Part III. Answer the following questions:

13. The nineteen rules of inference are used to establish the validity of various arguments. But suppose that someone questioned the validity of one of the nineteen rules. How could you establish its validity?
14. Is it true of any truth-functional argument with inconsistent premisses that the conjunction of its premisses is a substitution instance of a self-contradictory statement form?
15. Construct a formal proof of validity for the following argument without using the rule of Transposition:

$$1.\ A \supset B \qquad /\therefore \sim B \supset \sim A$$

Part IV. For each of the following arguments, if the argument is valid construct a formal proof of validity for it, and if the argument is invalid prove its invalidity by the method of assigning truth values.

16. 1. $A \supset B$
    2. $A \supset \sim B \quad /\therefore \sim A$
17. 1. $C \supset D \quad /\therefore (E \cdot C) \supset D$
18. 1. $F \vee (G \cdot H)$
    2. $(F \vee G) \supset (I \equiv \sim J)$
    3. $(I \supset \sim J) \supset (J \cdot \sim K)$
    4. $(K \supset L) \cdot (L \supset J)$
    5. $(G \supset H) \supset L \quad /\therefore L$
19. 1. $M \supset N \quad /\therefore M \supset (N \vee O)$
20. 1. $P \supset Q$
    2. $\sim P \supset Q \quad /\therefore Q$
21. 1. $(R \cdot S) \supset (T \supset U)$
    2. $V \supset \sim U$
    3. $\sim (S \supset \sim V)$
    4. $\sim (R \supset \sim T) \quad /\therefore \sim R$

ANSWERS

1. 3. $A \supset (A \cdot B)$ — 1, Abs.
   4. $(A \cdot B) \supset C$ — 2, Exp.
   5. $A \supset C$ — 3, 4, H.S.
2. 3. $\sim \sim E \supset \sim F$ — 2, Trans.
   4. $E \supset \sim F$ — 3, D.N.
   5. $D \supset \sim F$ — 1, 4, H.S.
3. 2. $\sim \sim G \vee G$ — 1, Impl.
   3. $G \vee G$ — 2, D.N.
   4. G — 3, Taut.
4. 3. $\sim (H \cdot I)$ — 1, 2, M.T.
   4. $\sim H \vee \sim I$ — 3, De M.
   5. $H \supset \sim I$ — 4, Impl.

5. 3. $(L \cdot K) \supset M$ 1, Com.
   4. $L \supset (K \supset M)$ 3, Exp.
   5. $L \supset N$ 4, 2, H.S.
6. $L \cdot ({\sim}E \cdot {\sim}T)$
7. ${\sim}F \supset (R \supset D)$
8. $L \supset B$
9. ${\sim}D \supset {\sim}V$
10. $E \supset ({\sim}I \cdot {\sim}M)$
11. $S \supset {\sim}D$
12. ${\sim}(M \supset {\sim}S)$ (Notice that from this seemingly true statement, one can deduce that the moon is made of green cheese.)
13. By a truth table.
14. Yes.
15. 2. ${\sim}A \vee B$ 1, Impl.
    3. $B \vee {\sim}A$ 2, Com.
    4. ${\sim}{\sim}B \vee {\sim}A$ 3, D.N.
    5. ${\sim}B \supset {\sim}A$ 4, Impl.
16. 3. ${\sim}B \supset {\sim}A$ 1, Trans.
    4. $A \supset {\sim}A$ 2, 3, H.S.
    5. ${\sim}A \vee {\sim}A$ 4, Impl.
    6. ${\sim}A$ 5, Taut.
17. 2. $(C \supset D) \vee {\sim}E$ 1, Add.
    3. ${\sim}E \vee (C \supset D)$ 2, Com.
    4. $E \supset (C \supset D)$ 3, Impl.
    5. $(E \cdot C) \supset D$ 4, Exp.

18.

F	G	H	I	J	K	L
t	t	f	f	t	f	f

19. 2. ${\sim}M \vee N$ 1, Impl.
    3. $({\sim}M \vee N) \vee O$ 2, Add.
    4. ${\sim}M \vee (N \vee O)$ 3, Assoc.
    5. $M \supset (N \vee O)$ 4, Impl.
20. 3. ${\sim}Q \supset {\sim}P$ 1, Trans.
    4. ${\sim}Q \supset Q$ 3, 2, H.S.
    5. ${\sim}{\sim}Q \vee Q$ 4, Impl.
    6. $Q \vee Q$ 5, D.N.
    7. Q 6, Taut.
21. 5. ${\sim}({\sim}S \vee {\sim}V)$ 3, Impl.
    6. ${\sim}{\sim}(S \cdot V)$ 5, De M.
    7. $S \cdot V$ 6, D.N.
    8. ${\sim}({\sim}R \vee {\sim}T)$ 4, Impl.
    9. ${\sim}{\sim}(R \cdot T)$ 8, De M.

10.	$R \cdot T$	9, D.N.
11.	R	10, Simp.
12.	S	7, Simp.
13.	$R \cdot S$	11, 12, Conj.
14.	$T \supset U$	1, 13, M.P.
15.	$T \cdot R$	10, Com.
16.	T	15, Simp.
17.	U	14, 16, M.P.
18.	$V \cdot S$	7, Com.
19.	V	18, Simp.
20.	$\sim U$	2, 19, M.P.
21.	$U \vee \sim R$	17, Add.
22.	$\sim R$	21, 20, D.S.

Chapter 10 Quantification Theory

READ PAGES 340–343 OF THE TEXT

10.1 Singular Propositions

In the two preceding chapters of the text, techniques were developed for determining the validity or invalidity of arguments like the following:

$$\begin{array}{ll} 1.\ (A \cdot B) \supset {\sim}C & \\ 2.\ C \vee (D \cdot E) & \\ 3.\ A \equiv B & /\therefore A \supset D \end{array}$$

This argument is composed of simple statements and truth-functional compound statements, and its validity depends only on the way in which the simple statements are truth-functionally combined into compound statements. The validity of the argument does not depend on the inner logical structure of the constituent simple statements.

In the present chapter, on the other hand, we shall be dealing with arguments whose validity depends on the inner logical structure of noncompound statements. The following is a typical example of the type of argument which we shall be studying in this chapter:

All humans are mortal.
Socrates is human.
Therefore, Socrates is mortal.

You can see that each of the three statements in this argument is a simple statement (that is, not a truth-functional compound statement) and that the validity of the argument depends on the inner logical structure of the simple statements involved. The validity of this particular argument, as well as the validity of some of the other arguments with which we shall be dealing in this chapter, can be determined by applying the principles already developed in the chapters on categorical syllogisms, but in order to deal with *all* arguments of the general type whose validity depends on the inner logical structure of simple statements, some additional symbols and rules of inference are required.

The small letters *a* through *w* are to be used as **individual constants,** that is, as names of individual entities such as people, cities, material things, and so on. For example, *s* could be used to denote Socrates, *a* to denote Aristotle, *c* to denote Chicago, and so on. The small letters *x, y,* and *z* should not be used as individual constants.

Capital letters are used as **attribute constants,** that is, as names of attributes which may be predicated of individuals. For example, *H* could be used to symbolize the attribute of being human, *M* the attribute of being mortal, *L* the attribute of being large, and so on.

"Socrates is human" (called a **singular proposition** because it says something about a single individual entity) can be symbolized as *Hs.* Similarly, "Aristotle is human" can be symbolized as *Ha,* and "Chicago is large" can be symbolized as *Lc.* In general, to symbolize the statement that a certain individual has a certain attribute, write a capital letter standing for the attribute in question, followed by a small letter standing for the individual in question.

The small letter *x* is to be used as an **individual variable** to stand for any individual whatever, just as in algebra *x* is used to stand for any number whatever.

Where *H* symbolizes the attribute of being human, *Hx* is a **propositional function,** that is, a formula which contains an individual variable and which becomes a statement when an individual constant is substituted for the individual variable. *Hs, Ha, Hc,* and so on, are called **substitution instances** of the propositional function *Hx.* These substitution instances, being statements, are either true or false, but *Hx* is neither true nor false, for it is not itself a statement; it only represents a form which various statements can have.

READ PAGES 343–346 OF THE TEXT

10.2 Quantification

The statement "Everything is human" can be rephrased as "Given any x, x is human," which can be symbolized as $(x)\,Hx$, where the symbol "(x)," called the **universal quantifier,** is used to symbolize the phrase "given any x."

The statement "Something is human" can be rephrased as "There is at least one x such that x is human," which can be symbolized as $(\exists x)\,Hx$, where the symbol "$(\exists x)$," called the **existential quantifier,** is used to symbolize the phrase "there is at least one x such that."

Using symbols already introduced, each formula on the left below can be used to symbolize the statement on its right:

$\sim Hs$	Socrates is not human.
$(x)\ \sim Hx$	Nothing is human.
$(\exists x)\ \sim Hx$	Something is not human.
$\sim (x)\,Hx$	It is not the case that everything is human.
$\sim (\exists x)\,Hx$	It is not the case that something is human.

Be sure you understand that $(x) \sim Hx$ is not equivalent to $\sim (x)\ Hx$, for the first formula symbolizes the false statement that nothing is human, whereas the second formula symbolizes the true statement that it is not the case that everything is human. Similarly, $(\exists x) \sim Hx$ and $\sim (\exists x)\,Hx$ are not equivalent, for the first formula symbolizes the true statement that something is not human, whereas the second formula symbolizes the false statement that it is not the case that something is human.

There are, however, certain general relationships between universal and existential quantification, four of which are listed on page 346 of the text, where ϕ (the Greek letter *phi*) is used to stand for any attribute whatever. You should study these equivalences once again, making sure that you can express them easily in ordinary English. If you have trouble with any one of the four, you can check its translation as follows:

1. "Everything is ϕ" is equivalent to "It is not the case that something is not ϕ."
2. "Something is ϕ" is equivalent to "It is not the case that nothing is ϕ."

3. "Nothing is ϕ" is equivalent to "It is not the case that something is ϕ."
4. "Something is not ϕ" is equivalent to "It is not the case that everything is ϕ."

READ PAGES 346–352 OF THE TEXT

10.3 Traditional Subject–Predicate Propositions

The statement "All humans are mortal" (called a universal affirmative or ***A*** proposition in traditional logic) can be rephrased as "Given any *x*, if *x* is human then *x* is mortal," which can be symbolized as $(x)(Hx \supset Mx)$.

The statement "No humans are mortal" (called a universal negative or ***E*** proposition in traditional logic) can be rephrased as "Given any *x*, if *x* is human then *x* is not mortal," which can be symbolized as $(x)(Hx \supset \sim Mx)$.

The statement "Some humans are mortal" (called a particular affirmative or ***I*** proposition in traditional logic) can be rephrased as "There is at least one *x* such that *x* is human and *x* is mortal," which can be symbolized as $(\exists x)(Hx \cdot Mx)$.

The statement "Some humans are not mortal" (called a particular negative or ***O*** proposition in traditional logic) can be rephrased as "There is at least one *x* such that *x* is human and *x* is not mortal," which can be symbolized as $(\exists x)(Hx \cdot \sim Mx)$.

Not only can the four standard-form statements listed above be symbolized in the ways indicated, but any statement which has the same meaning as any one of the above statements can also be symbolized in the same way.

Where ϕ and ψ (the Greek letters *phi* and *psi*) are used to stand for any attributes whatever, the form of the four propositions illustrated above can be represented, as in the diagram on page 350 of the text, which you should now study again. As you can see, the ***A*** and ***O*** propositions are contradictories (one must be true and one false), because the ***A*** says that all *phi* are *psi* and the ***O*** says that some *phi* are not *psi*. Likewise, ***E*** and ***I*** are contradictory, because ***E*** says that no *phi* are *psi* whereas ***I*** says that some *phi* are *psi*.

In translating from ordinary English into logical symbolism, you must be careful to translate an ***I*** proposition such as "Some humans are mortal" as $(\exists x)(Hx \cdot Mx)$ rather than as $(\exists x)(Hx \supset Mx)$. "Some humans are mortal" implies the existence of some humans, as is reflected in the fact that $(\exists x)(Hx \cdot Mx)$ is false if Hx has no true substitution instance. On the other hand, $(\exists x)(Hx \supset Mx)$, which is equivalent to $(\exists x)(\sim Hx \vee Mx)$, is automatically true if Hx has no true substitution instance, and so $(\exists x)(Hx \supset Mx)$ cannot be a correct symbolization of "Some humans are mortal."

For similar reasons, you should be careful to translate an ***O*** proposition such as "Some humans are not mortal" as $(\exists x)(Hx \cdot \sim Mx)$ rather than as $(\exists x)(Hx \supset \sim Mx)$. And you should translate an ***E*** proposition such as "No humans are mortal" as $(x)(Hx \supset \sim Mx)$ rather than as $(x) \sim (Hx \supset Mx)$.

SOLUTIONS

to selected exercises on pages 352–353

Remember that there are a great many different ways in which ***A, E, I,*** and ***O*** propositions can be phrased in ordinary English. You should first be sure that you understand the intended meaning of a sentence before trying to express that meaning in symbols.

Page 352, I, #2: $(x)(Sx \supset \sim Mx)$

Page 352, I, #6: $(x)(Ax \supset Dx)$

Page 353, I, #11: $(\exists x)(Cx \cdot Px)$

Page 353, I, #16: $(x)(Ex \supset Ux)$

In part II of these exercises you are asked to find a normal-form formula logically equivalent to the given formula. A **normal-form formula** is a formula in which negation signs apply only to *simple* predicates. The kind of simplification required to arrive at a normal-form formula is explained on pages 351–352 of the text. This explanation should be read again now if you are uncertain how to proceed. Notice that the successive steps are all based either on the four logical equivalences listed on page 346 of the text or on the various logical equivalences accompanying the rule of replacement in the preceding chapter of the text on page 319.

Page 353, II, #2: $(\exists x)(Cx \cdot Dx)$

Page 353, II, #6: $(\exists x)(Kx \cdot Lx)$

READ PAGES 353–360 OF THE TEXT

10.4 Proving Validity

In order to construct formal proofs of validity for various arguments containing universally and existentially quantified propositions, the following four additional rules of inference are required:

UI (Universal Instantiation):

$(x)\ \phi x$
$\therefore \phi v$ (where v is any individual symbol)

ϕx can be any propositional function of x, and v can be either one of the individual *constants* a through w (which are used as names of particular individuals) or v can be the special individual symbol y (which represents any arbitrarily selected individual whatever).

An example of a use of **UI** in which v is an individual constant occurs in the following formal proof of validity for the argument "All Greeks are mortal. Aristotle is a Greek. Therefore, Aristotle is mortal."

1. $(x)(Gx \supset Mx)$
2. Ga $\quad /\therefore Ma$
3. $Ga \supset Ma$ $\quad$ 1, **UI**
4. Ma $\quad$ 3, 2, M.P.

Line 1 is true if and only if all substitution instances of the propositional function $Gx \supset Mx$ are true. But if all substitution instances of $Gx \supset Mx$ are true, then (by **UI**) it follows that $Ga \supset Ma$ (which is line 3) must be true also.

UI can also be used to justify an inference from $(x)\ \phi x$ to ϕv where v is the special individual symbol y, which represents any arbitrarily selected individual whatever. An example of this use of **UI** occurs in the following formal proof of validity for the argument "All Greeks are humans. All humans are mortal. Therefore, all Greeks are mortal."

1. $(x)(Gx \supset Hx)$
2. $(x)(Hx \supset Mx)$ $\quad /\therefore (x)(Gx \supset Mx)$
3. $Gy \supset Hy$ $\quad$ 1, **UI**
4. $Hy \supset My$ $\quad$ 2, **UI**
5. $Gy \supset My$ $\quad$ 3, 4, H.S.
6. $(x)(Gx \supset Mx)$ $\quad$ 5, **UG**

Line 1 is true if and only if all substitution instances of the propositional function $Gx \supset Hx$ are true. But if all substitution instances of $Gx \supset Hx$ are true, then (where y represents *any* arbitrarily selected individual) it follows (by **UI**) that $Gy \supset Hy$ (which is line 3) must be true also. Similarly, line 4 follows from line 2. And the deduction of line 5 by H.S. is obvious. Now if line 5, $Gy \supset My$, is true where y is *any* arbitrarily selected individual, then it follows that all substitution instances of the propositional function $Gx \supset Mx$

are true, which means that $(x)(Gx \supset Mx)$ is true. Here we have appealed to a principle of inference which may be stated as follows:

UG (Universal Generalization):
ϕy (where y denotes any arbitrarily selected individual)
$\therefore (x)\,\phi x$

Since y denotes *any* arbitrarily selected individual, what is true of y must be true of all individuals. The symbol y can be introduced into a proof only by using **UI**, and it is only the presence of y in a line which permits the use of **UG** in the next line.

The other two new rules involve existentially quantified propositions.

EI (Existential Instantiation):
$(\exists x)\,\phi x$
$\therefore \phi v$ (where v is any individual constant a through w having *no previous occurrence* in the proof)

An example of **EI** occurs in the following formal proof of validity for the argument "All Greeks are mortal. There are Greeks. Therefore, there are mortals."

1.	$(x)(Gx \supset Mx)$	
2.	$(\exists x)\,Gx$	$/\therefore (\exists x)\,Mx$
3.	Gd	2, **EI**
4.	$Gd \supset Md$	1, **UI**
5.	Md	4, 3, M.P.
6.	$(\exists x)\,Mx$	5, **EG**

Line 2 is true if and only if there is some individual who is Greek. Now we do not know the name of that individual, but we have at our disposal a number of names (the individual constants a through w) and we can choose one of these names and use it to denote the individual who is Greek, so long as the name we choose has not already been used in the proof to denote some other individual. In the proof above we chose the name d. We could have chosen any other name a through w, since none of these names had been previously used in the proof. Now since line 2 above says that there is a Greek, and since we have chosen d to denote that Greek, line 3 follows validly (by **EI**). The deduction of lines 4 and 5 is obvious. Now if line 5, Md, is true, then it follows that there is some individual who is mortal, which means that $(\exists x)\,Mx$ is true. Here we have appealed to a principle of inference which may be stated as follows:

EG (Existential Generalization)
ϕv (where v is any individual symbol)
$\therefore (\exists x)\, \phi x$

If some substitution instance of ϕx is true, then it follows that $(\exists x)\, \phi x$ must be true also.

Before going on to the exercises, you should read once again the restriction on the use of **EI**, and then turn to page 359 of the text where the misuse of **EI** is illustrated in line 4 of the "proof." The premisses of that argument merely say that there is some individual which is an alligator kept in captivity and that there is some individual which is a bird kept in captivity, but the premisses obviously do not say (or imply) that these two individuals are identical. Now in line 3 the name a is used to denote an alligator kept in captivity. Hence, in line 4 it would be wrong to use the name a again to denote a bird kept in captivity, since this would involve assuming that the bird and the alligator are identical, which is neither affirmed nor implied by the premisses. The restriction on the use of **EI** clearly serves to prevent all such mistakes.

The restriction on the use of **EI** may also be violated in another way, as in line 4:

1. $(x)\,(Gx \supset Mx)$	
2. $(\exists x)\, Gx$	$/\therefore (\exists x)\, Mx$
3. $Ga \supset Ma$	1, **UI**
4. Ga	2, **EI**
5. Ma	3, 4, M.P.
6. $(\exists x)\, Mx$	5, **EG**

Line 4 is wrong because it violates the restriction on the use of **EI** (since a has a previous occurrence in the proof). This mistake can be eliminated, however, by simply interchanging lines 3 and 4; and all similar mistakes can be avoided by using **EI** before **UI**.

SOLUTIONS
to selected exercises on pages 360–361

If the premisses and conclusion of an argument are all universally quantified propositions, use **UI** to introduce y at the beginning of the proof, and use **UG** at the end of the proof.

If one premiss of an argument is a universally quantified proposition.

the other premiss an existentially quantified proposition, and the conclusion an existentially quantified proposition, use **EI** and then **UI** at the beginning of the proof, and use **EG** at the end of the proof.

If one premiss of an argument is a universally quantified proposition, the other premiss a singular proposition, and the conclusion a singular proposition, **UI** is used at the beginning of the proof, and no quantification rule is needed at the end of the proof.

Page 360, I, #2:

1. $(x)\ (Dx \supset \sim Ex)$	
2. $(x)\ (Fx \supset Ex)$	$/\therefore (x)\ (Fx \supset \sim Dx)$
3. $Fy \supset Ey$	2, **UI**
4. $Dy \supset \sim Ey$	1, **UI**
5. $\sim \sim Ey \supset \sim Dy$	4, Trans.
6. $Ey \supset \sim Dy$	5, D.N.
7. $Fy \supset \sim Dy$	3, 6, H.S.
8. $(x)\ (Fx \supset \sim Dx)$	7, **UG**

Page 360, I, #6:

1. $(\exists x)\ (Px \cdot \sim Qx)$	
2. $(x)\ (Px \supset Rx)$	$/\therefore (\exists x)\ (Rx \cdot \sim Qx)$
3. $Pa \cdot \sim Qa$	1, **EI**
4. Pa	3, Simp.
5. $Pa \supset Ra$	2, **UI**
6. Ra	5, 4, M.P.
7. $\sim Qa \cdot Pa$	3, Com.
8. $\sim Qa$	7, Simp.
9. $Ra \cdot \sim Qa$	6, 8, Conj.
10. $(\exists x)\ (Rx \cdot \sim Qx)$	9, **EG**

Check your symbolization of each argument in part II against the symbolization given here before trying to construct a formal proof of validity. There may be more than one correct symbolization of an argument, just as there may be more than one correct proof, but in general two alternative symbolizations must be logically equivalent in order for both to be correct.

Page 360, II, #2:

1. $(x)\ (Dx \supset Ex)$	
2. $(\exists x)\ (Fx \cdot \sim Ex)$	$/\therefore (\exists x)\ (Fx \cdot \sim Dx)$
3. $Fa \cdot \sim Ea$	2, **EI**
4. $Da \supset Ea$	1, **UI**
5. $\sim Ea \cdot Fa$	3, Com.
6. $\sim Ea$	5, Simp.
7. $\sim Da$	4, 6, M.T.
8. Fa	3, Simp.

9. $Fa \cdot \sim Da$ — 8, 7, Conj.
10. $(\exists x)\ (Fx \cdot \sim Dx)$ — 9, **EG**

Notice in lines 3 and 4 that **EI** is used before **UI** in order to avoid violating the restriction on **EI.**

Page 361, II, #6:

1. $(x)\ (Qx \supset Px)$
2. $(\exists x)\ (Rx \cdot Qx)$ — $/\therefore (\exists x)\ (Px \cdot Rx)$
3. $Ra \cdot Qa$ — 2, **EI**
4. $Qa \supset Pa$ — 1, **UI**
5. $Qa \cdot Ra$ — 3, Com.
6. Qa — 5, Simp.
7. Pa — 4, 6, M.P.
8. Ra — 3, Simp.
9. $Pa \cdot Ra$ — 7, 8, Conj.
10. $(\exists x)\ (Px \cdot Rx)$ — 9, **EG**

Notice in lines 3 and 4 that **EI** is used before **UI** in order to avoid violating the restriction on **EI.** Notice also that the first premiss affirms *not* that all pacifists are Quakers but rather that all Quakers are pacifists.

READ PAGES 361–365 OF THE TEXT

10.5 Proving Invalidity

To prove the invalidity of an argument such as the following

1. $(x)\ (Ax \supset Bx)$
2. $(\exists x)\ (Bx \cdot Cx)$ — $/\therefore (\exists x)\ (Ax \cdot Cx)$

it suffices to prove that it is *logically* possible for the premisses to be true and the conclusion false. Now it is logically possible for the universe to contain only one individual, and if the universe did contain only one individual then (where *a* denoted that individual) the argument above would be logically equivalent to

1. $Aa \supset Ba$
2. $Ba \cdot Ca$ — $/\therefore Aa \cdot Ca$

which is proved invalid by showing that it is possible for the premisses to be true and the conclusion false, as in the following case:

Aa	Ba	Ca
f	t	t

Thus, we have proved the invalidity of the original argument by showing that it is logically possible for the statements made by its premisses to be true while the statement made by its conclusion is false. (We are assuming throughout this section that the arguments with which we are dealing satisfy the conditions stated in the footnote on page 363 of the text.)

In the above proof of invalidity we have appealed to the general principle that if the universe contained only one individual (denoted by a) then to affirm $(x)\,\phi x$ would be logically equivalent to affirming ϕa, and to affirm $(\exists x)\,\phi x$ would be logically equivalent to affirming ϕa.

Of course, if the universe contained two individuals (denoted by a and b) then to affirm $(x)\,\phi x$ would be logically equivalent to affirming $\phi a \cdot \phi b$, whereas to affirm $(\exists x)\,\phi x$ would be logically equivalent to affirming $\phi a \vee \phi b$.

The logical equivalences stated in the preceding paragraph are used in proving the invalidity of an argument such as the following:

$$\begin{array}{ll} 1. & (x)\,(Dx \supset Fx) \\ 2. & (\exists x)\,(Gx \cdot Dx) \quad /\therefore (x)\,(Gx \supset Fx) \end{array}$$

To prove the invalidity of the preceding argument it suffices to prove that it is *logically* possible for the premisses to be true and the conclusion false. This cannot be *proved* by considering a universe of only *one* individual, but we can reason as follows: It is logically possible for the universe to contain exactly *two* individuals, and if the universe did contain exactly two individuals then (where a and b denoted those two individuals) the preceding argument would be logically equivalent to

$$\begin{array}{ll} 1. & (Da \supset Fa) \cdot (Db \supset Fb) \\ 2. & (Ga \cdot Da) \vee (Gb \cdot Db) \quad /\therefore (Ga \supset Fa) \cdot (Gb \supset Fb) \end{array}$$

which is proved invalid by showing that it is possible for the premisses to be true and the conclusion false, as in either of the following two cases:

	Da	*Db*	*Fa*	*Fb*	*Ga*	*Gb*
	f	t	f	t	t	t
or	t	f	t	f	t	t

Thus, we have proved the invalidity of the original argument by showing that it is logically possible for the statements made by its premisses to be true while the statement made by its conclusion is false.

In using this general technique for proving invalidity, there is no easy way of determining immediately whether invalidity can be proved by considering a universe or model of one individual, or whether it is necessary to consider a model of two individuals. Usually when an argument has two existentially quantified premisses you will have to consider a model of two individuals, but there are exceptions even to this general rule. The best procedure is to try to prove invalidity by considering a model of one individual, and if that fails then try a model of two individuals. Some very complex arguments may require you to consider a model of three or more individuals.

Notice that in employing this technique for proving invalidity no use is made of the four quantification rules **UI**, **EI**, **UG**, and **EG**. Instead, we first decide to consider a possible universe or model containing a certain number of individuals, and then we translate the argument into a logically equivalent form, using whichever of the following logical equivalences are applicable.

For a model of *one* individual (denoted by *a*) :

$$(x)\ \phi x \equiv \phi a$$
$$(\exists\ x)\ \phi x \equiv \phi a$$

For a model of *two* individuals (denoted by *a* and *b*) :

$$(x)\ \phi x \equiv (\phi a \cdot \phi b)$$
$$(\exists\ x)\ \phi x \equiv (\phi a \vee \phi b)$$

For a model of *three* individuals (denoted by *a, b,* and *c*) :

$$(x)\ \phi x \equiv (\phi a \cdot \phi b \cdot \phi c)$$
$$(\exists\ x)\ \phi x \equiv (\phi a \vee \phi b \vee \phi c)$$

Notice the patterns in the preceding equivalences. Since $(x)\ \phi x$ says that everything has the property ϕ, the *dot* symbol occurs in the equivalences for $(x)\ \phi x$. Whereas, since $(\exists\ x)\ \phi x$ says that at least one individual has the property ϕ, the *wedge* symbol occurs in the equivalences for $(\exists\ x)\ \phi x$.

SOLUTIONS

to selected exercises on pages 365–366

Each proof of invalidity given here consists of (1) a statement of the possible universe or model that will be considered in order to prove that the premisses can be true while the conclusion is false, (2) a translation of the premisses and conclusion of the argument into logically equivalent truth-functional compound statements about the individuals in the possible universe or model being considered, and (3) a statement of the truth value assignments, any one of which proves that the premisses can be true while the conclusion is false.

Try conscientiously to work out solutions to these exercises *on your own.*

Page 365, I, #2:

$$\left.\begin{array}{l}(x)\ (Dx \supset {\sim}Ex)\\ (x)\ (Ex \supset Fx)\\ \therefore (x)\ (Fx \supset {\sim}Dx)\end{array}\right\}\ \begin{array}{l}\text{logically}\\ \text{equivalent}\\ \text{in } \boxed{a} \text{ to}\end{array}\ \left\{\begin{array}{l}Da \supset {\sim}Ea\\ Ea \supset Fa\\ \therefore Fa \supset {\sim}Da\end{array}\right.$$

proved invalid by

Da	Ea	Fa
t	f	t

Page 365, I, #6:

$$\left.\begin{array}{l}(x)\ (Px \supset {\sim}Qx)\\ (x)\ (Px \supset {\sim}Rx)\\ \therefore (x)\ (Rx \supset {\sim}Qx)\end{array}\right\}\ \begin{array}{l}\text{logically}\\ \text{equivalent}\\ \text{in } \boxed{a} \text{ to}\end{array}\ \left\{\begin{array}{l}Pa \supset {\sim}Qa\\ Pa \supset {\sim}Ra\\ \therefore Ra \supset {\sim}Qa\end{array}\right.$$

proved invalid by

Pa	Qa	Ra
f	t	t

Page 365, II, #2:

$$\left.\begin{array}{l}(x)\ (Dx \supset {\sim}Ex)\\ (\exists x)\ (Fx \cdot Ex)\\ \therefore (\exists x)\ (Dx \cdot {\sim}Fx)\end{array}\right\}\ \begin{array}{l}\text{logically}\\ \text{equivalent}\\ \text{in } \boxed{a} \text{ to}\end{array}\ \left\{\begin{array}{l}Da \supset {\sim}Ea\\ Fa \cdot Ea\\ \therefore Da \cdot {\sim}Fa\end{array}\right.$$

proved invalid by

Da	Ea	Fa
f	t	t

Page 365, II, #6:

$$\left.\begin{array}{l}(\exists x)\ (Px \cdot Qx)\\ (\exists x)\ (Qx \cdot {\sim}Rx)\\ \therefore (\exists x)\ (Px \cdot {\sim}Rx)\end{array}\right\}\ \begin{array}{l}\text{logically}\\ \text{equivalent}\\ \text{in } \boxed{a,b} \text{ to}\end{array}\ \left\{\begin{array}{l}(Pa \cdot Qa) \vee (Pb \cdot Qb)\\ (Qa \cdot {\sim}Ra) \vee (Qb \cdot {\sim}Rb)\\ \therefore (Pa \cdot {\sim}Ra) \vee (Pb \cdot {\sim}Rb)\end{array}\right.$$

proved invalid by

	Pa	Pb	Qa	Qb	Ra	Rb
	t	f	t	t	t	f
or	f	t	t	t	f	t

READ PAGES 366–369 OF THE TEXT

10.6 Asyllogistic Inference

The techniques for proving validity and invalidity that were developed in previous sections of this chapter can be applied both to arguments which contain more than two quantified propositions as premisses and to arguments in which the propositional functions that are quantified are more complicated than those previously encountered.

Notice the way in which the following three statements are symbolized:

All motives are either altruistic or selfish. $(x)\,[Mx \supset (Ax \vee Sx)]$

Beer and caviar are nutritious. $(x)\,[(Bx \vee Cx) \supset Nx]$ (Notice that the wedge is used to convey the intended meaning, even though the word "and" occurs in the original statement.)

All except diamonds are rejected. All but diamonds are rejected. Diamonds alone are not rejected. (These are traditionally called exceptive propositions and may be translated as $(x)\,(Dx \supset \sim Rx) \cdot (x)\,(\sim Dx \supset Rx)$. They may also be translated as $(x)\,(Rx \equiv \sim Dx)$, which can be read as, "Anything is rejected if and only if it is not a diamond.")

SOLUTIONS
to selected exercises on pages 369–370

Page 369, I, #2: $(\exists x)\,[Fx \cdot (Ex \supset Cx)]$

Notice that "edible only if cooked" has the same meaning as "if edible then cooked."

Page 369, I, #6: $(x)\,\{[Bx \cdot (Wx \equiv Lx)] \supset \sim Sx\}$

Notice that "a *P* who is *Q* is *R*" is symbolized as $(x)\,[(Px \cdot Qx) \supset Rx]$. The word "who" indicates that an additional attribute is to be *conjoined* to the subject term.

SOLUTIONS
to selected exercises on pages 370–373

The more familiar you become with the nineteen rules of inference and the four quantification rules, the easier it will be for you to determine whether an argument is valid or invalid by simply studying its symbolization.

Page 370, II, #2:

$$(\exists x)\,\{(Ex \cdot Fx) \cdot [(Ex \vee Fx) \supset (Gx \cdot Hx)]\}$$
$$\therefore (x)\,(Ex \supset Hx)$$

logically equivalent in $\boxed{a,b}$ to

$$\{(Ea \cdot Fa) \cdot [(Ea \vee Fa) \supset (Ga \cdot Ha)]\} \vee \{(Eb \cdot Fb) \cdot [(Eb \vee Fb) \supset (Gb \cdot Hb)]\}$$
$$\therefore (Ea \supset Ha) \cdot (Eb \supset Hb)$$

proved invalid by

Ea	Eb	Fa	Fb	Ga	Gb	Ha	Hb
t	t	t	t	t	t	t	f
t	t	t	t	t	f	t	f
t	t	t	f	t	t	t	f
t	t	t	f	t	f	t	f
t	t	t	t	t	t	f	t
t	t	t	t	f	t	f	t
t	t	f	t	t	t	f	t
t	t	f	t	f	t	f	t

Page 370, II, #6:

1.	$(x)\ [Wx \supset (Xx \supset Yx)]$	
2.	$(\exists x)\ [Xx \cdot (Zx \cdot \sim Ax)]$	
3.	$(x)\ [(Wx \supset Yx) \supset (Bx \supset Ax)]$	$/\therefore (\exists x)\ (Zx \cdot \sim Bx)$
4.	$Xa \cdot (Za \cdot \sim Aa)$	2, **EI**
5.	Xa	4, Simp.
6.	$Wa \supset (Xa \supset Ya)$	1, **UI**
7.	$(Wa \cdot Xa) \supset Ya$	6, Exp.
8.	$(Xa \cdot Wa) \supset Ya$	7, Com.
9.	$Xa \supset (Wa \supset Ya)$	8, Exp.
10.	$Wa \supset Ya$	9, 5, M.P.
11.	$(Wa \supset Ya) \supset (Ba \supset Aa)$	3, **UI**
12.	$Ba \supset Aa$	11, 10, M.P.
13.	$(Za \cdot \sim Aa) \cdot Xa$	4, Com.
14.	$Za \cdot \sim Aa$	13, Simp.
15.	$\sim Aa \cdot Za$	14, Com.
16.	$\sim Aa$	15, Simp.
17.	$\sim Ba$	12, 16, M.T.
18.	Za	14, Simp.
19.	$Za \cdot \sim Ba$	18, 17, Conj.
20.	$(\exists x)\ (Zx \cdot \sim Bx)$	19, **EG**

Page 371, III, #2:

1.	$(x)\ [Tx \supset (Ex \vee Ux)]$	
2.	$(\exists x)\ (Tx \cdot \sim Ux)$	$/\therefore (\exists x)\ (Ex \cdot Tx)$
3.	$Ta \cdot \sim Ua$	2, **EI**
4.	$Ta \supset (Ea \vee Ua)$	1, **UI**
5.	Ta	3, Simp.
6.	$Ea \vee Ua$	4, 5, M.P.
7.	$\sim Ua \cdot Ta$	3, Com.
8.	$\sim Ua$	7, Simp.
9.	$Ua \vee Ea$	6, Com.
10.	Ea	9, 8, D.S.

11.	$Ea \cdot Ta$	10, 5, Conj.
12.	$(\exists x)\ (Ex \cdot Tx)$	11, **EG**

Page 371, III, #6:

1.	$(x)\ (Gx \supset Ex)$	
2.	$(x)\ (Wx \supset \sim Sx)$	
3.	$(\exists x)\ (Wx \cdot \sim Ex)$	$/\therefore (\exists x)\ \sim (Gx \vee Sx)$
4.	$Wa \cdot \sim Ea$	3, **EI**
5.	$Wa \supset \sim Sa$	2, **UI**
6.	Wa	4, Simp.
7.	$\sim Sa$	5, 6, M.P.
8.	$\sim Ea \cdot Wa$	4, Com.
9.	$\sim Ea$	8, Simp.
10.	$Ga \supset Ea$	1, **UI**
11.	$\sim Ga$	10, 9, M.T.
12.	$\sim Ga \cdot \sim Sa$	11, 7, Conj.
13.	$\sim (Ga \vee Sa)$	12, De M.
14.	$(\exists x)\ \sim (Gx \vee Sx)$	13, **EG**

Page 372, IV, #2:

1.	$(x)\ [(Dx \vee Lx) \supset Px]$	
2.	$(x)\ [(Px \vee Ex) \supset Rx]$	$/\therefore (x)\ (Dx \supset Rx)$
3.	$(Dy \vee Ly) \supset Py$	1, **UI**
4.	$\sim (Dy \vee Ly) \vee Py$	3, Impl.
5.	$(\sim Dy \cdot \sim Ly) \vee Py$	4, De M.
6.	$Py \vee (\sim Dy \cdot \sim Ly)$	5, Com.
7.	$(Py \vee \sim Dy) \cdot (Py \vee \sim Ly)$	6, Dist.
8.	$Py \vee \sim Dy$	7, Simp.
9.	$\sim Dy \vee Py$	8, Com.
10.	$(\sim Dy \vee Py) \vee Ey$	9, Add.
11.	$\sim Dy \vee (Py \vee Ey)$	10, Assoc.
12.	$Dy \supset (Py \vee Ey)$	11, Impl.
13.	$(Py \vee Ey) \supset Ry$	2, **UI**
14.	$Dy \supset Ry$	12, 13, H.S.
15.	$(x)\ (Dx \supset Rx)$	14, **UG**

Page 372, IV, #6:

1.	$(x)\ \{[Cx \cdot (Lx \vee Ox)] \supset \sim Fx\}$	
2.	$(x)\ (\sim Fx \supset \sim Ex)$	$/\therefore (x)\ [(Cx \cdot Lx) \supset \sim Ex]$
3.	$[Cy \cdot (Ly \vee Oy)] \supset \sim Fy$	1, **UI**
4.	$\sim Fy \supset \sim Ey$	2, **UI**
5.	$[Cy \cdot (Ly \vee Oy)] \supset \sim Ey$	3, 4, H.S.
6.	$[(Cy \cdot Ly) \vee (Cy \cdot Oy)] \supset \sim Ey$	5, Dist.
7.	$\sim [(Cy \cdot Ly) \vee (Cy \cdot Oy)] \vee \sim Ey$	6, Impl.
8.	$[\sim (Cy \cdot Ly) \cdot \sim (Cy \cdot Oy)] \vee \sim Ey$	7, De M.

9.	$\sim Ey \vee [\sim (Cy \cdot Ly) \cdot \sim (Cy \cdot Oy)]$	8, Com.
10.	$[\sim Ey \vee \sim (Cy \cdot Ly)] \cdot [\sim Ey \vee \sim (Cy \cdot Oy)]$	9, Dist.
11.	$\sim Ey \vee \sim (Cy \cdot Ly)$	10, Simp.
12.	$\sim (Cy \cdot Ly) \vee \sim Ey$	11, Com.
13.	$(Cy \cdot Ly) \supset \sim Ey$	12, Impl.
14.	$(x)\ [(Cx \cdot Lx) \supset \sim Ex]$	13, UG

EXAMINATION
on Chapter 10

Write your answers on a separate sheet of paper, then check them against the answers given at the end of the examination. If you miss a question, restudy the appropriate part of the text.

Part I.

1. Are the two following formulas contradictory?

$$(x)\ (Fx \supset Gx)$$
$$(x) \sim (Fx \supset Gx)$$

2. Are the two following formulas logically equivalent?

$$\sim (x) \sim (Fx \cdot \sim Gx)$$
$$(\exists x) \sim (Fx \supset Gx)$$

3. Is it true that an argument must be valid if it is impossible to prove its invalidity in a universe or model of one individual?
4. Symbolize the following statements by using propositional functions and quantifiers:

   (a) No non-*S* are non-*P*.
   (b) Some *S* are not non-*P*.

5. Use the technique for proving invalidity introduced in this chapter to prove the invalidity of the relationship of subalternation between ***E*** and ***O*** propositions. [If you have not studied Chapter 5, omit this question.]
6. Is it true that, if we assume that there is at least one individual in the universe, then if the universal quantification of a propositional function is true, then its existential quantification must be true also?

Part II. Translate each of the following statements into the logical notation of propositional functions and quantifiers, in each case using the abbreviations suggested:

7. All students except freshmen are eligible. (*Sx*—*x* is a student. *Fx*—*x* is a freshman. *Ex*—*x* is eligible.)

8. Only company-employees are not eligible. (*Cx*—*x* is a company-employee. *Ex*—*x* is eligible.)
9. If something is a whale, then it is a mammal. (*Wx*—*x* is a whale. *Mx*—*x* is a mammal.)
10. Nothing is both a whale and a fish. (*Wx*—*x* is a whale. *Fx*—*x* is a fish.)
11. Nothing can be a whale without being a mammal. (*Wx*—*x* is a whale. *Mx*—*x* is a mammal.)
12. No one who is not registered may take a course. (*Tx*—*x* may take a course. *Rx*—*x* is registered.)
13. There are no books on the desk. (*Bx*—*x* is a book. *Dx*—*x* is on the desk.)
14. There are no students who are both lazy and deserving. (*Sx*—*x* is a student. *Lx*—*x* is lazy. *Dx*—*x* is deserving.)
15. Everything enjoyable is either immoral, illegal, or fattening. (*Ex*—*x* is enjoyable. *Mx*—*x* is moral. *Lx*—*x* is legal. *Fx*—*x* is fattening.)
16. A professor is a good lecturer if and only if both well informed and entertaining. (*Px*—*x* is a professor. *Gx*—*x* is a good lecturer. *Wx*—*x* is well informed. *Ex*—*x* is entertaining.)
17. Only citizens can vote. (*Cx*—*x* is a citizen. *Vx*—*x* can vote.)
18. Some students work hard only if they are behind. (*Sx*—*x* is a student. *Wx*—*x* works hard. *Bx*—*x* is behind.)
19. No student is deserving unless he works hard. (*Sx*—*x* is a student. *Dx*—*x* is deserving. *Wx*—*x* works hard.)
20. Not all students who are deserving are both intelligent and hard-working. (*Sx*—*x* is a student. *Dx*—*x* is deserving. *Ix*—*x* is intelligent. *Hx*—*x* is hard-working.)
21. Any student is deserving if intelligent and hard-working. (*Sx*—*x* is a student. *Dx*—*x* is deserving. *Ix*—*x* is intelligent. *Hx*—*x* is hard-working.)
22. No man who is a pacifist will be drafted if he believes in God. (*Mx*—*x* is a man. *Px*—*x* is a pacifist. *Dx*—*x* is drafted. *Gx*—*x* believes in God.)
23. None but the insecure are aggressive. (*Ix*—*x* is insecure. *Ax*—*x* is aggressive.)
24. A man who is happy if and only if he is wealthy is actually spiritually impoverished. (*Mx*—*x* is a man. *Hx*—*x* is happy. *Wx*—*x* is wealthy. *Sx*—*x* is spiritually impoverished.)
25. Both supporters and critics of the administration are free to express their opinions. (*Sx*—*x* is a supporter of the administration. *Cx*—*x* is a critic of the administration. *Fx*—*x* is free to express his opinion.)
26. All members and only members are eligible. (*Mx*—*x* is a member. *Ex*—*x* is eligible.)

Part III. For each of the following arguments, either construct a formal proof of validity or prove invalidity by the method developed in this chapter.

27. 1. $(x)[(Ax \vee Bx) \supset Cx]$
    2. $(\exists x)(Ax \cdot Dx)$
    3. $(\exists x)(Ax \cdot Ex)$
    4. $(\exists x)(Bx \cdot \sim Cx)$ $\quad /\therefore (\exists x)(Dx \cdot Ex)$
28. 1. $(x)(Fx \supset Gx)$
    2. $(\exists x)(Hx \cdot Gx)$
    3. $(\exists x)(Hx \cdot \sim Gx)$ $\quad /\therefore (x)(Fx \supset \sim Hx)$
29. 1. $(x)[(Ix \vee Jx) \supset (Kx \cdot Lx)]$ $\quad /\therefore (x)(Ix \supset Lx)$
30. 1. $(x)[Mx \supset (Nx \equiv Ox)]$
    2. $(x)(Mx \supset Px)$
    3. $(\exists x)[Mx \cdot (Nx \cdot \sim Ox)]$ $\quad /\therefore (x)(Px \supset Mx)$
31. 1. $(x)(Qx \supset Rx)$
    2. $(\exists x)(Qx \cdot Sx)$
    3. $(\exists x)(Rx \cdot \sim Qx)$ $\quad /\therefore (\exists x)(Rx \cdot \sim Sx)$
32. 1. $(x)(Tx \supset Ux)$
    2. $(x)[(Ux \cdot Tx) \supset Vx]$ $\quad /\therefore (x)[Tx \supset (Ux \cdot Vx)]$

ANSWERS

1. No. [The formulas could both be false, and therefore they are not contradictory.]
2. Yes.
3. No.
4. a. $(x)(\sim Sx \supset Px)$
   b. $(\exists x)(Sx \cdot Px)$
5. $(x)(Sx \supset \sim Px)$, $\therefore (\exists x)(Sx \cdot \sim Px)$ } logically equivalent in $\boxed{a}$ to { $Sa \supset \sim Pa$, $\therefore Sa \cdot \sim Pa$

   proved invalid by

Sa	Pa
f	t
or f	f

6. Yes.
7. $(x)[Sx \supset (Ex \equiv \sim Fx)]$
8. $(x)(\sim Ex \supset Cx)$
9. $(x)(Wx \supset Mx)$
10. $(x)(Wx \supset \sim Fx)$
11. $(x)(Wx \supset Mx)$
12. $(x)(Tx \supset Rx)$
13. $(x)(Bx \supset \sim Dx)$
14. $(x)[Sx \supset \sim(Lx \cdot Dx)]$
15. $(x)\{Ex \supset [(\sim Mx \vee \sim Lx) \vee Fx]\}$

16. $(x)\{Px \supset [Gx \equiv (Wx \cdot Ex)]\}$
17. $(x)(Vx \supset Cx)$
18. $(\exists x)[Sx \cdot (Wx \supset Bx)]$
19. $(x)[Sx \supset (Dx \supset Wx)]$
20. $(\exists x)[(Sx \cdot Dx) \cdot \sim(Ix \cdot Hx)]$
21. $(x)\{Sx \supset [(Ix \cdot Hx) \supset Dx]\}$
22. $(x)[(Mx \cdot Px) \supset (Gx \supset \sim Dx)]$
23. $(x)(Ax \supset Ix)$
24. $(x)\{[Mx \cdot (Hx \equiv Wx)] \supset Sx\}$
25. $(x)[(Sx \vee Cx) \supset Fx]$
26. $(x)(Ex \equiv Mx)$
27.

5.	$Ba \cdot \sim Ca$	4, **EI**
6.	Ba	5, Simp.
7.	$Ba \vee Aa$	6, Add.
8.	$Aa \vee Ba$	7, Com.
9.	$(Aa \vee Ba) \supset Ca$	1, **UI**
10.	Ca	9, 8, M.P.
11.	$\sim Ca \cdot Ba$	5, Com.
12.	$\sim Ca$	11, Simp.
13.	$Ca \vee (\exists x)(Dx \cdot Ex)$	10, Add.
14.	$(\exists x)(Dx \cdot Ex)$	13, 12, D.S.

28. This argument is logically equivalent in $\boxed{a,b}$ to

1. $(Fa \supset Ga) \cdot (Fb \supset Gb)$
2. $(Ha \cdot Ga) \vee (Hb \cdot Gb)$
3. $(Ha \cdot \sim Ga) \vee (Hb \cdot \sim Gb)$ $\quad /\therefore (Fa \supset \sim Ha) \cdot (Fb \supset \sim Hb)$

which is proved invalid by

	Fa	*Fb*	*Ga*	*Gb*	*Ha*	*Hb*
	t	f	t	f	t	t
or	f	t	f	t	t	t

29.

2.	$(Iy \vee Jy) \supset (Ky \cdot Ly)$	1, **UI**
3.	$\sim(Iy \vee Jy) \vee (Ky \cdot Ly)$	2, Impl.
4.	$\sim(Iy \vee Jy) \vee (Ly \cdot Ky)$	3, Com.
5.	$[\sim(Iy \vee Jy) \vee Ly] \cdot [\sim(Iy \vee Jy) \vee Ky]$	4, Dist.
6.	$\sim(Iy \vee Jy) \vee Ly$	5, Simp.
7.	$Ly \vee \sim(Iy \vee Jy)$	6, Com.
8.	$Ly \vee (\sim Iy \cdot \sim Jy)$	7, De M.
9.	$(Ly \vee \sim Iy) \cdot (Ly \vee \sim Jy)$	8, Dist.
10.	$Ly \vee \sim Iy$	9, Simp.
11.	$\sim Iy \vee Ly$	10, Com.
12.	$Iy \supset Ly$	11, Impl.
13.	$(x)(Ix \supset Lx)$	12, **UG**

30.

4.	$Ma \cdot (Na \cdot \sim Oa)$	3, **EI**
5.	Ma	4, Simp.

6.	$Ma \supset (Na \equiv Oa)$	1, **UI**
7.	$Na \equiv Oa$	6, 5, M.P.
8.	$(Na \supset Oa) \cdot (Oa \supset Na)$	7, Equiv.
9.	$Na \supset Oa$	8, Simp.
10.	$\sim Na \vee Oa$	9, Impl.
11.	$\sim Na \vee \sim \sim Oa$	10, D.N.
12.	$\sim (Na \cdot \sim Oa)$	11, De M.
13.	$(Na \cdot \sim Oa) \cdot Ma$	4, Com.
14.	$Na \cdot \sim Oa$	13, Simp.
15.	$(Na \cdot \sim Oa) \vee (x)\ (Px \supset Mx)$	14, Add.
16.	$(x)\ (Px \supset Mx)$	15, 12, D.S.

31. This argument is logically equivalent in $\boxed{a,b}$ to

1. $(Qa \supset Ra) \cdot (Qb \supset Rb)$
2. $(Qa \cdot Sa) \vee (Qb \cdot Sb)$
3. $(Ra \cdot \sim Qa) \vee (Rb \cdot \sim Qb)$ $\quad /\therefore (Ra \cdot \sim Sa) \vee (Rb \cdot \sim Sb)$

which is proved invalid by

	Qa	Qb	Ra	Rb	Sa	Sb
	t	f	t	t	t	t
or	f	t	t	t	t	t

32.

3.	$Ty \supset Uy$	1, **UI**
4.	$Ty \supset (Ty \cdot Uy)$	3, Abs.
5.	$Ty \supset (Uy \cdot Ty)$	4, Com.
6.	$(Uy \cdot Ty) \supset Vy$	2, **UI**
7.	$Ty \supset Vy$	5, 6, H.S.
8.	$\sim Ty \vee Uy$	3, Impl.
9.	$\sim Ty \vee Vy$	7, Impl.
10.	$(\sim Ty \vee Uy) \cdot (\sim Ty \vee Vy)$	8, 9, Conj.
11.	$\sim Ty \vee (Uy \cdot Vy)$	10, Dist.
12.	$Ty \supset (Uy \cdot Vy)$	11, Impl.
13.	$(x)\ [Tx \supset (Ux \cdot Vx)]$	12, **UG**

Part Three *Induction*

Chapter 11
Analogy and Probable Inference

READ PAGES 377–380 OF THE TEXT

11.1 Argument by Analogy

In the preceding six chapters of the text you studied deductive arguments; in these next four chapters you will be studying inductive arguments. An argument is deductive if it is claimed that if the premisses are true then the conclusion *must* be true also. If this claim is correct then the deductive argument is said to be valid; and if the claim is incorrect then the deductive argument is said to be invalid.

An argument is **inductive** if it is claimed that if the premisses are true then the conclusion is *probably* true. Inductive arguments are not characterized as valid or invalid, but they may be characterized as being relatively strong or weak, depending upon how probable it is that the conclusion would be true if the premisses were true.

One common type of inductive argument is the **argument by analogy,** in which it is inferred that a certain entity has a certain attribute on the grounds that the entity is analogous to other entities which have that attribute. The form of a typical analogical argument is schematically represented on page 380 of the text, where if d is analogous to (similar to) a, b, and c in respects P and Q, and if a, b, and c all have the additional attribute R, then it can be inferred inductively (that is, with probability) that d also has the attribute R. Arguments by analogy may differ from this form in the number of entities involved and in the number of attributes or respects in which the entities are analogous, but no matter how strong the evidence presented in the premisses, all arguments by analogy are inductive, because the only claim that can be made legitimately is that if the premisses are true then the conclusion is *probably* true also.

Analogies can also be used for purposes other than constructing analogical arguments. Two of these nonargumentative uses of analogy are (1) to make description more vivid through the use of analogies in metaphors and similes, and (2) to facilitate explanation by making the unfamiliar more intelligible through analogy with the familiar.

SOLUTIONS
to selected exercises on pages 380–385

It is very important in these last four chapters of the text, as it has been in the earlier chapters, that you work conscientiously on each set of exercises *on your own*. You should find the passages quoted in the exercises to be informative and interesting in their own right, as well as being helpful illustrations of the principles developed in the text.

Page 380, #2: Nonargumentative use of analogy.

Page 381, #6: Analogical argument.

Page 382, #11: Nonargumentative use of analogy.

Page 383, #16: Nonargumentative use of analogy.

Page 384, #21: Analogical argument.

READ PAGES 386–389 OF THE TEXT

11.2 Appraising Analogical Arguments

Because analogical arguments are inductive rather than deductive, it would not be proper to appraise them as being either valid or invalid, for it is not being claimed that if the premisses are true then the conclusion *must* be true also. In an analogical argument it is being claimed that if the premisses are true then the conclusion is *probably* true, and analogical arguments can be appraised as being relatively strong or weak, depending upon how probable it is that the conclusion would be true if the premisses were true. In other words, one analogical argument is said to be stronger than a second analogical argument if the premisses of the first argument support its conclusion with a degree of probability which is greater than the degree of probability with which the premisses of the second argument support its conclusion. The text presents six criteria for appraising the relative strength of analogical arguments. In restating these criteria below, we shall refer to the symbols in the following typical analogical argument:

> *a, b, c,* and *d* all have the attributes *P* and *Q*.
> *a, b,* and *c* all have the attribute *R*.
> Therefore, *d* probably has the attribute *R*.

The relative strength of analogical arguments can be compared by appealing to any of the following six criteria:

1. The greater the number of entities between which the analogies are said to hold, the stronger the argument. The entities referred to are the *a, b, c,* and so on, of the preceding schematic argument.
2. The greater the number of respects in which the entities are said to be analogous, the stronger the argument. The respects referred to are the *P, Q,* and so on, of the preceding schematic argument.
3. The "weaker" the conclusion relative to the premisses, the stronger the argument. For example, if Smith's new watch varies from the correct time by no more than five seconds per week, and if Jones buys a new watch of the same make and model, then if Jones draws the relatively "strong" conclusion that his new watch will also vary from the correct time by no more than five seconds per week, his argument is not as strong as it would be if he had drawn the relatively "weaker" conclusion that his new watch will vary from the correct time by no more than thirty seconds per week.
4. The greater the number of disanalogies (dissimilarities, points of difference) between the entity referred to in the conclusion and the other entities in the premisses, the weaker the argument. Using the symbols in the preceding schematic argument, the greater the number of disanalogies between *d* and the other entities *a, b,* and *c,* the weaker the argument. In other words, the greater the number of respects in which *d* differs from *a, b,* and *c,* the more probable it is that *d* will also differ from *a, b,* and *c* in not having the attribute *R*.
5. Using once again the symbols in the preceding schematic argument, the greater the number of dissimilarities among the entities *a, b,* and *c,* the stronger the argument. In other words, assuming that *a, b, c,* and *d* all have the attributes *P* and *Q*, and that *a, b,* and *c* have the attribute *R*, then the probability of *d* also having *R* is increased if it can be shown that *a, b,* and *c* are similar *only* in respects *P, Q,* and *R* and that in other respects they are dissimilar.

The reason for this is that if *a, b,* and *c* are similar only in respects *P, Q,* and *R* but dissimilar in other respects, then there is a greater probability that having attributes *P* and *Q* is causally related to having *R,* and that therefore if *d* has *P* and *Q,* then it is very probable that *d* also has *R.*

For example, let *a, b, c,* and *d* be automobiles, let *P* be the attribute of being serviced at Joe's Garage, let *Q* be the attribute of being serviced at the mileages recommended by the manufacturer, and let *R* be the attribute of running perfectly after 100,000 miles. Then the more dissimilarities that can be pointed out among *a, b,* and *c* (for example, that they are different makes and models, driven by different people in different ways), the more probable it is that running perfectly after 100,000 miles is caused by being serviced on schedule at Joe's Garage rather than being caused by some other factors, and therefore the more probable it is that if *d* is serviced on schedule at Joe's Garage then *d* will run perfectly after 100,000 miles.

6. Using once again the symbols in the preceding schematic argument, in order for an analogical argument to be strong, the attributes *P, Q,* etc., must be *relevant* to the attribute *R.* In general, one attribute is relevant to another attribute if the two attributes are causally related in some way.

SOLUTIONS

to selected exercises on pages 390–398

In the first set of exercises, the addition of a premiss can make the resulting argument either more probable or less probable or neither more nor less probable. The last alternative is the correct answer where the additional premiss is irrelevant to the conclusion of the argument.

Page 390, I, #2:

a. less, b. more, c. neither, d. more, e. more, f. more.

Page 392, II, #2: Structure of the analogical argument:

Dr. Haldane's clock, *Hamlet,* and living organisms all have the attributes of being produced by a process involving careful selection, and of being alterable in a random way (by shooting a bullet through the clock, by introducing a typographical error into *Hamlet,* and by radiation from a bomb causing a mutation in an organism).

Dr. Haldane's clock and *Hamlet* both have the attribute that random alterations would almost invariably be detrimental.

Therefore, living organisms have the attribute that random alterations (mutations) would almost invariably be detrimental.

Evaluation of the argument in terms of the six criteria:

1. Living organisms are held to be analogous to only *two* entities, which is not enough to make the argument very strong, according to the first criterion. On the other hand, if Dr. Haldane's clock is regarded as implicitly representing all carefully constructed mechanisms, and if *Hamlet* is regarded as implicitly representing all carefully constructed works of art, then living organisms are actually held to be analogous to a great many entities, and thus by the first criterion the argument is fairly strong, or cogent.
2. There are only two respects in which, according to the explicitly stated premisses, the entities are said to be analogous. This is not very many, and thus by the second criterion the argument is rather weak. On the other hand, the author may be assuming that there are other respects (in which the entities are analogous) which are so obvious that the reader can be expected to supply them for himself (for example, all the entities consist of interdependent parts, so that if one part is altered the structure and value of the whole is altered). If the argument is thus understood as an enthymeme, it becomes correspondingly stronger.
3. If we assume that the premisses implicitly affirm that the effect of shooting a bullet through a clock and the effect of introducing a random typographical error into *Hamlet* would almost invariably be detrimental, then the conclusion is just as strong as the premisses, and so by the third criterion the argument is relatively weak.
4. There are a great many disanalogies between living organisms on the one hand and mechanisms and works of art on the other hand, but there is one particular disanalogy which is so basic that it actually destroys whatever strength the argument might otherwise have. With respect to mechanisms and works of art it is generally true to say that the probability of a great many random alterations being detrimental is greater than the probability of any one alteration being detrimental; whereas with respect to living organisms it is by no means true that the probability of the long-range effect of a great many different mutations in a great many different organisms being detrimental is greater than the probability of the effect of a single mutation in a single organism being detrimental. After all, the species have evolved into their present state of adaptation to the environment through a process of mutation and *natural selection*. Therefore, there would seem to be a high probability that further mutations will result (through natural selection) in even better adaptation in the long run. So although any given mutation is almost invariably detrimental, the long-range effect of many mutations is more likely to be beneficial than detrimental, and in this very important respect living organisms are

disanalogous to mechanisms and works of art. Using the distinction (introduced in Chapter 3 of the text) between the distributive and the collective sense of a class term, we can say that mutations (taken distributively) are almost invariably detrimental, even though mutations (taken collectively) are not detrimental in the long run. This is similar to the example that improbable events (taken distributively) almost never occur, even though improbable events (taken collectively) occur every day.

5. There are only two kinds of entities (mechanisms and works of art) to which living organisms are said to be analogous. But mechanisms and works of art are quite dissimilar to each other, and so by the fifth criterion the argument is moderately strong.
6. Producing a random alteration in an entity whose parts have been carefully selected (and are assumed to be interdependent) is certainly causally relevant to the structure and value of that entity, and so by the sixth criterion the argument is quite strong.

Page 393, II, #6: Structure of the analogical argument:

Measurements of space and measurements of time both have the following two attributes:

1. We can never measure again the *same* interval, for "we can never find again an interval of time that has passed," and "we never find again the *same* length, which has been displaced by the motion of the stars and put out of shape by the molecular motion which never ceases."
2. We can measure again approximately equal intervals, for in the case of space "we find that the dimensions of a solid body are the same today as they were yesterday," and "in an analogous manner we may say that *approximately* we find again the same interval of time. This is what happens when in the course of several succeeding nights an astronomer measures the time separating the passage of the meridian by two fixed stars. He finds that this interval of time is the same. We know very well that the identity cannot be absolute, but the equality is very near."

Our measurements of space are sufficient for the requirements of our science.

Therefore, our measurements of time are sufficient for the requirements of our science.

Evaluation of the argument in terms of the six criteria:

1. There is only one *kind* of entity (measurements of space) to which measurements of time are said to be analogous, which is not very many. On the other hand, there are many instances of this kind, and so by the first criterion the argument is fairly strong.

2. There are only two respects in which the entities are said to be analogous, according to the stated premisses. In terms of their sheer number, that is not enough to make the argument very strong, according to the second criterion.
3. The conclusion is just as strong as the premisses, and so by the third criterion the argument is relatively weak.
4. There may be some minor disanalogies between measurements of space and measurements of time, but the major disanalogy which was traditionally thought to exist is only apparent, for, as Borel points out, it is no more possible to measure again exactly the *same* interval of space as it is to measure again the same interval of time. Therefore, by the fourth criterion the argument is quite strong.
5. There is only one kind of entity (measurements of space) to which measurements of time are said to be analogous, and measurements of space are presumably not very dissimilar to one another, so by the fifth criterion the argument is rather weak.
6. The second attribute which the premisses affirm to hold of measurements of time is relevant to the attribute which the conclusion affirms to hold of measurements of time, and so by the sixth criterion the argument is quite strong.

EXAMINATION
on Chapter 11

Examination questions on Chapter 11 will be included in the examination at the end of Chapter 12.

Chapter 12
Causal Connections: Mill's Methods of Experimental Inquiry

READ PAGES 399–405 OF THE TEXT

12.1 The Meaning of "Cause"

The word "cause" may have different meanings in different contexts. "*A* causes *B*" may mean that *A* is a **necessary condition** of *B*, which means that *B* cannot occur in the absence of *A*. For example, a certain germ may be said to cause a particular illness in the sense that the presence of the germ is a necessary condition for the occurrence of the illness.

Or, "*A* causes *B*" may mean that *A* is a **sufficient condition** of *B*, which means that if *A* occurs then *B* must occur also. For example, being at the center of an atomic bomb explosion is a sufficient condition for death.

There may be several necessary conditions for the occurrence of a particular event, and all those necessary conditions must obviously be included in any sufficient condition.

When we are interested in *preventing* a certain event, we try to discover the *necessary* conditions for that event, since the event can be prevented if any of its necessary conditions can be prevented. On the other hand, when we are interested in *producing* a certain event, we try to discover the *sufficient* conditions for that event, since the event can be produced only if we can produce its sufficient conditions.

The word "cause" may have still a different meaning in a situation in which there are certain constant conditions that are ordinarily present, so that when it is said that *A* causes *B* what is meant is that it is *A* which makes the difference between the occurrence and nonoccurrence of *B* in that situation. In the example used in the text, the policyholder was the cause of the fire in the sense that, in the situation in which all the other conditions were constant, it was the policyholder's action which made the difference between the occurrence and nonoccurrence of the fire.

A distinction can also be made between **remote** and **proximate** causes. If *A* causes *B*, and *B* causes *C*, and *C* causes *D*, then *A*, *B*, and *C* are each causes of *D*, but *C* is said to be the proximate cause of *D*, whereas *B* is a remote cause and *A* is an even more remote cause.

If *A* is the cause of *B* in the sense of necessary condition then *A* can be inferred from *B*, and if *A* is the cause of *B* in the sense of sufficient condition then *B* can be inferred from *A*.

"*A* causes *B*" is sometimes intended to mean that *A* is a necessary and sufficient condition of *B*, which means that *B* occurs if and only if *A* occurs. It is this conception of cause as necessary and sufficient condition which is being used by those who hold that there is a unique cause for any effect. On the other hand, there are those who hold that there can be a plurality of causes, that is, that the same effect can be caused in a number of different ways; for example, death can be caused either by a bullet, or by a heart attack, or by an automobile accident, and so on. Those who believe that there is a unique cause for any effect respond that if the effect (death) is specified with sufficient precision, that is, if we talk not about death in general but about a *specific* kind of death, then the apparent plurality of causes will disappear, for it will be found that each specific kind of death has a specific (unique) kind of cause which is the necessary and sufficient condition for that kind of death. The view that there is a unique cause for any effect is thus supported by arguing that whenever scientists have analyzed a specific kind of event in sufficient detail they have been able to discover a single or unique cause for it.

Although the word "cause" may have any of the different meanings just discussed, to say that *A* causes *B* is always to imply that any other event like *A* would (in a similar situation) cause another event like *B*. Cause and effect are uniformly connected in the sense that similar causes produce similar effects. Thus, to say that circumstance *C* is causally connected to phenomenon *E* is to imply that they constitute an instance or example of a general causal law to the effect that events like *C* are causally connected to events like *E*. A causal law, then, is a statement that such and such a circumstance is always accompanied by such and such a phenomenon, regardless of when or where it occurs.

Causal laws may be based on inductive generalization from past experience. The most elementary type of induction is by **simple enumeration,** the schematic form of which is given in the middle of page 404 of the text. This argument form should now be read again. On the basis of three instances of *E* being accompanied by *C,* the inductive generalization is drawn that *every* instance of *E* is accompanied by *C*. Each premiss in this argument is said to be a **confirming instance** of the generalization in the conclusion. But such an induction by simple enumeration is not a very trustworthy argument, for *by definition* the premisses contain only *confirming* instances of the generalization and all possible negative or disconfirming instances are necessarily excluded from the premisses. Thus, there is no reason to believe that the instances reported by the premisses are anything more than mere coincidences.

In order to test causal laws more reliably, it is necessary to employ the methods of induction discussed in the next section of the text.

READ PAGES 406–408 OF THE TEXT

12.2 Mill's Methods

Mill's methods of inductive inference are more reliable than induction by simple enumeration, but even with Mill's methods we can never attain certainty through induction.

The first of the five methods of inductive inference analyzed by Mill is the **Method of Agreement,** which is stated on page 407 of the text. Read this statement again, then look at the example of the application of the Method of Agreement at the bottom of page 406 of the text. You will notice in the example that all instances of *s* which were examined *agree* in being accompanied by *F,* and *F* was the *only* antecedent circumstance (among those investigated) which accompanied every instance of *s*. From this data the conclusion can then be drawn that *F* is probably the cause of *s*.

We cannot, of course, be certain that *F* caused *s,* since perhaps there was some other antecedent circumstance, say *G* (exposure to a certain kind of flu), which was not investigated but which in fact accompanied every instance of *s*. Or perhaps if we investigated more instances of *s* we would find that some of them were not accompanied by *F,* and then we would have to look for some other antecedent circumstance that accompanied every instance of *s*. Or, since each student ate either *A* or *B,* perhaps *A* and *B* were each a cause of *s* (in the sense of sufficient condition).

The point is that, like all patterns of inductive inference, the

Method of Agreement does not establish a causal connection with *certainty* but only with *probability*. All we can say is that, given the data contained in the table on page 406 of the text, it is more probable that *F* caused *s* than that some other circumstance caused *s*.

SOLUTIONS
to selected exercises on pages 408–410

Page 408, #2:

A B C occur together with *a b c*.
A D E occur together with *a d e*.
A F G occur together with *a f g*.
Therefore, *A* is the cause of *a*.

Where *A* is the drive of fear; *a* is the stopping of vocal behavior; *B C* and *D E* and *F G* are other circumstances which are present, respectively, in cases of extreme combat anxiety, acute stage fright, and frightened animals, and in which those cases presumably differ from one another; *b c* and *d e* and *f g* are other phenomena attending, respectively, cases of extreme combat anxiety, acute stage fright, and frightened animals. Actually, there should be as many premisses in the above argument as there are *individual instances* in which there is a stopping of vocal behavior and in which the drive of fear is the only antecedent circumstance present in all instances.

READ PAGES 410–413 OF THE TEXT

The **Method of Difference** is the second of Mill's methods of inductive inference. Read again the statement of this method on pages 410–411 of the text, then look at the example of the application of the Method of Difference on page 410 of the text. You will notice in the example that *s* occurs in instance 1 but not in instance *n*, and that the antecedent circumstances of these two instances are identical except that *F* occurs in instance 1 but not in instance *n*. From these data it can be inferred that *F* is probably the cause of *s* (at least in the sense of a necessary condition). The conclusion that *F* caused *s* is, of course, not certain but only probable. It is always possible that some other antecedent circumstance which was not investigated, say *G*, might have caused *s*. But relative to the evidence presented in the premisses, it is more probable that *F* caused *s* than that some other circumstance caused *s*.

SOLUTIONS
to selected exercises on pages 413–415

Page 413, #2:

A B C occur together with *a b c*.
B C occur together with *b c*.
Therefore, *A* is the cause of *a*.

Where *A* is the brain of a nereis; *a* is the inhibition of movement in response to certain stimuli; *B* and *C* are the other (usual) circumstances present in nereides (plural of "nereis"); *b* and *c* are the other (usual) phenomena attending the movement of nereides. Actually, there are as many arguments of the above form as there are cases in which the movements of a nereis are observed before and after the removal of its brain.

READ PAGES 415–416 OF THE TEXT

The **Joint Method of Agreement and Difference** is simply the use of both the Method of Agreement and the Method of Difference to reach the same conclusion. Look at the form of this method as schematized on page 415 of the text. In the Method of Agreement on the left, *A* is the only antecedent circumstance which accompanies both instances of *a*. The other antecedent circumstances accompany one or the other of the instances of *a* but not both. In the Method of Difference on the right, phenomenon *a* occurs when *A* occurs, but *a* does not occur without *A*, where all the other antecedent circumstances are present in both instances. The use of both methods jointly makes the conclusion more probable than it would be if only one method were used.

SOLUTIONS
to selected exercises on pages 416–420

Page 416, #2:

(1) *A B C* occur together with *a b c*.
A D E occur together with *a d e*.
A F G occur together with *a f g*.
. . . .
. . . .
. . . .
Therefore, *A* is the cause of *a*.

Where the instances are the members of the experimental group (to whom the experimenter said "Mmm-hmm" after each plural noun);

A is the circumstance of the experimenter saying "Mmm-hmm" after each plural noun; *B, C, D, E, F, G,* . . . are other circumstances in which the members of the experimental group presumably differed among themselves; *a* is the phenomenon of a great increase in the percentage of plural nouns spoken; and *b, c, d, e, f, g,* . . . are other phenomena attending the various members of the experimental group. This is of course the Method of Agreement.

(2) *A B C* occur together with *a b c*.
B C occur together with *b c*.
Therefore, *A* is the cause of *a*.

Where the instances are the first member of the experimental group and the first member of the control group; *A* is the circumstance of the experimenter saying "Mmm-hmm" after each plural noun; *B* and *C* are the other circumstances present in both instances; *a* is the phenomenon of a great increase in the percentage of plural nouns spoken; *b* and *c* are the other phenomena attending both instances. This is the Method of Difference, and there are as many uses of the form of argument above as there are "matching" pairs of members in the two groups.

READ PAGES 420–421 OF THE TEXT

According to the **Method of Residues**, if part of a phenomenon is already known to be the effect of certain antecedents, then the conclusion can be drawn that the residue of the phenomenon is the effect of the remaining antecedents. Study again the statement of the Method of Residues on page 420 of the text and the schematic form of the inference on the following page.

SOLUTIONS
to selected exercises on pages 422–424

Page 422, #2:

A B occur together with *a b*.
B is known to be the cause of *b*.
Therefore, *A* is the cause of *a*.

Where *A* is radium; *B* is uranium; *b* is the radioactivity known to be the effect of the uranium; and *a* is the residue of the radioactivity.

READ PAGES 424–427 OF THE TEXT

The **Method of Concomitant Variation** is the fifth and last of Mill's methods of experimental inquiry or inductive inference.

Study again the statement of this method on page 425 of the text and the two following schematic forms of the inference. In the schematic form of inference near the top of page 426 of the text, a is said to *vary directly* with A because a increases when A increases, and a decreases when A decreases. In the schematic form of inference near the middle of page 426 of the text, a is said to *vary inversely* with A because a decreases when A increases, and a increases when A decreases. In either case, a causal connection between A and a can be inferred with probability by the Method of Concomitant Variation.

SOLUTIONS
to selected exercises on pages 427–431

Page 427, #2:

$$A\ B\ C \quad \text{———} \quad a\ b\ c$$
$$A{+}B\ C \quad \text{———} \quad a{+}b\ c$$
$$A{+}{+}B\ C \quad \text{———} \quad a{+}{+}b\ c$$
$$A{+}{+}{+}B\ C \quad \text{———} \quad a{+}{+}{+}b\ c$$

Therefore, A is causally connected with a.

Where A is exposure to radiation; B and C are other circumstances roughly constant over the years; a is the incidence of leukemia; b and c are other phenomena roughly constant over the years; $A+$, $A{+}{+}$, and $A{+}{+}{+}$ are, respectively, exposure to an estimated average dose of 25, 250, and 650 roentgens; $a+$, $a{+}{+}$, and $a{+}{+}{+}$ are, respectively, incidences of leukemia which are proportional ("within the reliability of the numbers") to the estimated doses of radiation listed above.

READ PAGES 431–442 OF THE TEXT

12.3 Criticisms of Mill's Methods

12.4 Vindication of Mill's Methods

Mill's five Methods of inductive inference are subject to the following limitations:

1. Mill's Methods do not tell us how to determine whether the antecedent circumstances have been properly analyzed. For example, the "scientific drinker," who drank scotch and soda one night, bourbon and soda the next night, etc., concluded on the basis of the Method of Agreement that it was the soda which was making him drunk. But he made an improper analysis of the antecedent

circumstances, for he failed to recognize that the alcoholic content of his drinks was also an antecedent circumstance which accompanied all instances of the phenomenon of getting drunk. The point is that Mill's Methods by themselves provide no criteria for determining whether an analysis of the antecedent circumstances is proper or improper, and without a proper analysis Mill's Methods may lead us to the wrong conclusion. Therefore, Mill's Methods by themselves are *not sufficient* for discovering causal connections, and it would be extravagant to claim that they are sufficient.

2. Mill's Methods are also subject to the limitation that they do not tell us which antecedent circumstances to investigate. We obviously cannot investigate all of the infinite number of antecedent circumstances, so we must content ourselves with trying to investigate all those antecedent circumstances which are causally relevant to the phenomenon in question. But Mill's Methods do not tell us which antecedent circumstances are causally relevant, and if we ignore a relevant circumstance (as in the example of the frustration–aggression experiment discussed on page 433ff of the text), Mill's Methods may lead us to the wrong conclusion. Thus, once again we can see that Mill's Methods by themselves are *not sufficient* for discovering causal connections, for they provide no criteria for determining which antecedent circumstances are causally relevant.

3. Mill's Methods are also subject to the obvious limitation that the inference made is only probable and never certain, demonstrative, or conclusive, in the sense of being a deductively valid proof. There are at least three reasons why Mill's Methods lead to conclusions which are only probable but not certain: (a) we can never investigate all antecedent circumstances, and we can never be certain that we have investigated all *relevant* antecedent circumstances, so that we may not have investigated that particular antecedent circumstance which is in fact the cause of the phenomenon in question; (b) we can never be certain that the antecedent circumstances which were investigated were properly analyzed; and (c) no matter how many instances are appealed to as evidence for a generalization which states a uniform causal connection, the generalization by its very nature covers instances which are as yet unobserved, and one of these instances may disprove the generalization. For these three reasons it would be wrong to claim that Mill's Methods can establish a causal connection with *certainty*.

4. Mill's Methods are also subject to the limitation that a person of average intelligence cannot simply use them in a *mechanical* or *automatic* way to discover new causal connections. First of all, it takes more than average intelligence to understand what science has already discovered and thus to reach the frontiers of science where

new discoveries are to be made. And, second, it takes more than average intelligence to be able to select and analyze properly those antecedent circumstances which are in fact causally relevant to the phenomenon in question. For these reasons it would be somewhat extravagant to apply to Mill's Methods Bacon's remark that "our method of discovering the sciences is such as to leave little to the acuteness and strength of wit."

Subject to the limitations listed above, Mill's Methods represent perfectly acceptable patterns of inductive inference, and their role can perhaps be most accurately described in the following way: In trying to discover the cause of a given phenomenon *a*, one first selects those antecedent circumstances (for example, *A*, *B*, *C*) which one believes to be causally related to *a*, and then one formulates a series of alternative hypotheses, for example, that *A* causes *a*, that *B* causes *a*, that *C* causes *a*. Then one performs controlled experiments, the results of which can be structured to fit one or more of Mill's Methods in such a way that all but one of the hypotheses can be eliminated. Mill's Methods can thus be seen as basic patterns of inductive inference which can be used to show how certain experimental data confirm or disconfirm various hypotheses about causal connections.

SOLUTIONS
to selected exercises on pages 442–457

Page 443, #2:

(1) *A B* occur together with *a b*.
A C occur together with *a c*.
A D occur together with *a d*.
A E occur together with *a e*.
Therefore, *A* is the cause of *a*.

Where the instances are the individual test plats, *A* is the circumstance of fertilizing with potash; *B*, *C*, *D*, *E* are, respectively, the application of zero, two, four, and six tons of limestone per acre; *a* is the phenomenon of an increased yield; *b*, *c*, *d*, *e* are other phenomena which occurred in the test plats. This is, of course, the Method of Agreement.

(2) *A B C D* occur together with *a b c d*.
B C D occur together with *b c d*.
Therefore, *A* is the cause of *a*.

Where the instances are the individual test plats, *A* is the circumstance of fertilizing with potash; *B* is the circumstance of applying six tons of limestone per acre; *C* and *D* are other circumstances present in both instances; a is the phenomenon of an increased yield; b, c, and d are other phenomena attending both instances. This is the Method of Difference, and there are three other uses of this method, where B is, respectively, four, two, and zero tons of limestone per acre.

Page 446, #6:

$$A\ B\ C \quad \underline{\qquad\qquad} \quad a\ b\ c$$
$$A{-}\ B\ C \quad \underline{\qquad\qquad} \quad a{-}\ b\ c$$

Therefore, A is causally connected with a.

Where A is a normal diet high in saturated fats; B and C are other circumstances roughly constant over the years; a is a "normal" rate of cardiovascular disease of 47.7 per cent over eight years; b and c are other phenomena roughly constant over the years. $A-$ is a diet high in unsaturated fats (and therefore presumably low in saturated fats); $a-$ is a rate of cardiovascular disease of 31.3 per cent over eight years. This is the Method of Concomitant Variation.

Page 449, #11:

$$A\ B\ C \quad \underline{\qquad\qquad} \quad a\ b\ c$$
$$A{-}\ B\ C \quad \underline{\qquad\qquad} \quad a{-}\ b\ c$$

Therefore, A is causally connected with a.

Where A is the normal procedure of imprisonment upon conviction; B and C are other circumstances roughly constant over the years; a is the "normal" rate of parole revocation of 52 per cent over five years; b and c are other phenomena roughly constant over the years. $A-$ is no imprisonment upon conviction (but rather immediate parole and intensive care); $a-$ is a rate of parole revocation of 28 per cent over five years. This is the Method of Concomitant Variation.

EXAMINATION on Chapter 12

Write your answers on a separate sheet of paper, then check them against the answers given at the end of the examination. If you miss a question, restudy the appropriate part of the text. Several of the questions below are on Chapter 11, the rest on Chapter 12.

1. What is wrong with the following formulation of Mill's Method of Agreement?

   If two or more instances of the phenomenon under investigation have some circumstance in common, that circumstance is the cause (or effect) of the given phenomenon.
2. One can legitimately infer cause from effect only if the word "cause" is used in the sense of

a. necessary condition.
b. sufficient condition.
c. proximate cause.
d. none of the above.

3. Is it true that *all* the necessary conditions for an event must be included in *any* sufficient condition?
4. If the person who used Mill's Method of Agreement to determine that the cause of six cases of indigestion was probably the eating of canned pears then wished to check his conclusion by using Mill's Method of Difference, what additional evidence would he have to examine?
5. If one were interested in eliminating some undesirable phenomenon, would one be primarily interested in discovering the cause of that phenomenon in the sense of a necessary condition or in the sense of a sufficient condition?
6. What is the unique weakness of "induction by simple enumeration"?
7. If C is a necessary condition for the occurrence of E, is it necessarily true that C causally implies E?
8. Why is the following not a correct application of Mill's Method of Difference?

instance	*antecedent circumstances*	*phenomenon*
1	$A\ B\ C\ D\ E$	s
n	$-\ B\ C\ D\ -$	—

Therefore, A is the cause, or the effect, or an indispensable part of the cause, of s.

9. Which of the following (possibly more than one) are among the too extravagant claims sometimes made for Mill's Methods?
   a. The Methods are useful for showing how causal laws can be inferred with probability from certain data.
   b. The Methods constitute a simple, mechanical device which permits anyone to discover causal connections.
   c. The Methods can be used to demonstrate conclusively the existence of particular causal connections.
   d. The Methods constitute a complete account of scientific method.
   e. The Methods are sufficient instruments for the discovery of scientific laws.
10. The following argument by analogy has eight additional premisses suggested for it. For each of these alternative premisses, state whether its addition would make the resulting argument more probable, less probable, or neither more nor less probable. Base your answers on the criteria for appraising analogical arguments, *not* on additional facts not stated in the argument.

Joe College has received grades between 85 and 95 on every homework, quiz, and hour exam in logic during the semester. His average going into the final exam is 90. Therefore, he can expect, with some degree of probability, to get at least a 90 on the final exam.

a. Suppose that Joe was in a section which had ten one-hour exams during the semester instead of the usual three.
b. Suppose that his homework grades were consistently better than his quiz and hour exam grades.
c. Suppose that he studied only moderately hard during the semester but studied very hard for the final exam.
d. Suppose that his grades during the semester were all either 85 or 95, rather than being randomly distributed between 85 and 95 (assuming that his average in both cases was the same).
e. Suppose that all the one-hour exams were made up by his instructor, whereas only one fifth of the final exam was made up by his instructor.
f. Suppose that each of the hour exams had been made up by a different instructor.
g. Suppose that Joe expects to get at least a 92 on the final exam.
h. Suppose that Joe expects to get at least an 88 on the final exam.

ANSWERS

1. The instances of the phenomenon under investigation must have *only one* circumstance in common.
2. (a) Necessary condition.
3. Yes.
4. He would have to find out whether or not indigestion occurred in those people who ate exactly the same foods (except for the canned pears) as one of the six people who were found to have indigestion.
5. Necessary condition.
6. By definition the premisses of an induction by simple enumeration contain only confirming instances of the generalization in the conclusion and all possible negative or disconfirming instances are necessarily excluded from the premisses, so that there is no reason to believe that the instances reported by the premisses are anything more than mere coincidence.
7. No.
8. It would be correct only if the antecedent circumstance *E* were also present in instance *n*.
9. b, c, d, e.
10. a. More.
    b. Less.
    c. Less [see criterion #4].
    d. Neither.
    e. Less.
    f. More.
    g. Less.
    h. More.

Chapter 13
Science and Hypothesis

READ PAGES 458–461 OF THE TEXT

13.1 The Values of Science

Scientific knowledge has practical value insofar as its technological applications benefit humanity, and scientific knowledge has intrinsic value insofar as it satisfies our desire to understand the universe. To understand is not simply to observe and record phenomena but to explain them, that is, to unify the various phenomena in each particular field of investigation by formulating causal laws stating the interrelations between the phenomena. These separate laws can in turn be unified by comprehensive theories which explain individual laws as special cases of more general and fundamental principles.

READ PAGES 461–467 OF THE TEXT

13.2 Explanations: Scientific and Unscientific

An explanation of a certain fact consists of a set of statements from which the fact can be inferred. A scientific explanation usually consists of two kinds of statements: (1) statements of the antecedent circumstances (or "initial conditions") which precede the fact to be explained; and (2) statements of the relevant causal laws which indicate the causal connection between the antecedent circumstances and the fact to be explained.

There are a number of criteria which an explanation must satisfy in order to be acceptable. The two most obvious criteria are (1) the statements constituting the explanation must be *relevant* to the fact to be explained in the sense that the fact can be inferred from the statements, and (2) the statements constituting the explanation must be known to be true (or at least well confirmed).

One difference between scientific and unscientific explanations is that unscientific explanations are affirmed and believed *dogmatically*, whereas scientific explanations are proposed and accepted tentatively and provisionally, with an open-minded awareness that new evidence may require their revision or replacement. A scientific explanation is to be regarded as a hypothesis which is probable to the extent that it is confirmed by the evidence, whereas an unscientific explanation is put forward and accepted without regard to the evidence. Scientific explanations are testable, either directly through sense experience or at least indirectly.

Indirect testing of a hypothesis involves deducing from the hypothesis statements which are themselves directly testable. If any of these latter statements are found to be false, then one can infer (by *modus tollens*) that the hypothesis is false also. Of course it may not be possible to deduce any directly testable statements from the hypothesis alone, especially if the hypothesis is of a fairly high level of abstractness or generality. Additional premisses may be required, in which case if one of the directly testable statements which is deduced is found to be false, one can infer only that *either* the hypothesis is false *or* one of the additional premisses is false.

If the directly testable statements deduced from a hypothesis are found to be true, then they are said to constitute *confirming evidence* for the truth of the hypothesis, but they do not *conclusively* prove the truth of the hypothesis. The hypothesis could be false even though the statements deduced from it were true, because (as you will recall from Chapter 1) a valid argument can have false premisses and a true conclusion. To conclude that a hypothesis must be true because it implies certain true statements is to commit the Fallacy of Affirming the Consequent.

The notion of indirect testing can be used to describe the most fundamental difference between scientific and unscientific explanations. A scientific explanation of a certain fact can be indirectly tested by other facts, whereas an unscientific explanation cannot be indirectly tested by other facts. Thus, the office boy's explanation of his lateness is scientific because his claim that his bus was involved in an accident is indirectly testable by a number of other facts, whereas if someone said that the office boy was late because God willed him to be late that morning and God is omnipotent, this explanation would be unscientific because it is not indirectly testable by any other fact.

READ PAGES 467–472 OF THE TEXT

13.3 Evaluating Scientific Explanations

There are (at least) five conditions that a good scientific explanation or hypothesis should fulfill:

1. A good hypothesis should be *relevant* to the fact to be explained; that is, the fact should be deducible from the hypothesis. Of course, it is generally the case that the fact is not deducible from the hypothesis alone but only from the hypothesis in conjunction with additional statements of causal laws and antecedent circumstances (initial conditions).
2. A good hypothesis should be *testable,* either directly through sense experience or at least indirectly. An hypothesis is indirectly testable if directly testable statements are deducible from it.
3. Normally a new hypothesis is acceptable only if it is consistent or *compatible with previously well-established hypotheses.* The only exception to this condition occurs when the new hypothesis is better than the old hypothesis, either because it explains a wider range of facts or because it explains the same facts in a simpler way. In any case, the total set of hypotheses accepted at any one time should be self-consistent.
4. Of two or more alternative hypotheses, the one which has the greatest *predictive or explanatory power* is to be preferred, that is, the one which predicts or explains the widest range of observable facts.
5. Of two or more alternative hypotheses, the one which is the *simplest* is to be preferred.

READ PAGES 472–481 OF THE TEXT

13.4 The Detective as Scientist

The detective illustrates the method of the scientist when he first recognizes a problem (a fact in need of explanation), then formulates various preliminary hypotheses, then collects additional facts, then formulates a hypothesis which accounts for all the known facts, then deduces further conclusions from this hypothesis, and finally tests these conclusions to see whether the hypothesis is confirmed or disconfirmed.

READ PAGES 481–486 OF THE TEXT

13.5 Scientists in Action: The Pattern of Scientific Investigation

The goal of science is to formulate testable explanations or hypotheses to account for the observable facts of experience. The pattern of scientific investigation is exemplified in the procedures of scientists in action.

For example, Count Rumford recognized that the caloric theory of heat, which was generally accepted in his day, could not explain the amount of heat generated in the boring of cannon. After considerable experimentation and reflection he postulated the mechanical or kinetic theory of heat, which accounted more satisfactorily for the phenomena under investigation. This new theory or hypothesis was then submitted to further testing by Sir Humphrey Davy in a crucial experiment which confirmed the new kinetic theory and disconfirmed the old caloric theory.

The data of science should be objective in the sense of being public and repeatable, that is, open to investigation by any qualified observer.

READ PAGES 486–492 OF THE TEXT

13.6 Crucial Experiments and Ad Hoc Hypotheses

The basic structure of a **crucial experiment** is exemplified in the following *idealized* situation. H_1 and H_2 are rival hypotheses. H_1 entails that if circumstance C occurs then phenomenon P will occur; whereas H_2 entails that if circumstance C occurs then phenomenon P will not occur. To decide between H_1 and H_2 it is sufficient to produce circumstance C and then observe whether or not phenomenon P occurs. The occurrence of P would confirm H_1 and disconfirm H_2, whereas the nonoccurrence of P would disconfirm H_1 and confirm H_2.

This description of a crucial experiment is necessarily idealized because in practice no hypothesis of a fairly high level of abstractness or generality can actually be subjected to a decisively crucial experiment, since no such hypothesis *by itself* entails any directly testable conclusions. For example, the hypothesis that the earth is spherical does not *by itself* entail that the decks of a receding ship will disappear from view before the masthead. And the hypothesis that the earth is flat does not *by itself* entail that the decks of a receding ship will not disappear from view before the masthead. In both cases the deduction of testable conclusions can be made only if one assumes the additional hypothesis that light travels in straight lines. Thus, in general, no *individual* hypothesis can be subjected to a genuinely crucial experiment, although if one agrees to assume accepted scientific laws as additional premisses, then a hypothesis may be subjected to a hypothetically crucial experiment, since if the additional premisses are assumed to be true, then if the directly testable statement which is deduced from the hypothesis in conjunction with the additional premisses is found to be false, it follows that the hypothesis is false also.

READ PAGES 492–497 OF THE TEXT

13.7 Classification as Hypothesis

Hypotheses play an essential role not only in the more abstract and theoretical sciences such as physics and chemistry, but also in sciences which consist largely of description or classification, such as history and traditional biology.

If history is regarded as an attempt to discover a cosmic pattern or purpose which explains and accounts for the events of history, then this cosmic purpose functions as an explanatory hypothesis. If, on the other hand, history is regarded as an attempt to discover historical laws which explain past events and enable one to predict future events, then such laws function as explanatory hypotheses. And even if history is regarded simply as a description of past events, these past events are not now open to direct observation, so that any description of them is itself an hypothesis put forward to explain and account for the extant historical records and other data presently available to the historian. So it is clear that hypotheses are essential in all three of these interpretations of history.

Hypotheses also play an essential role in biology. Biological laws, like other scientific laws, are, of course, hypotheses. But even when biology is concerned only with description and classification, hypotheses are still essential, since to adopt one particular classification scheme from among many alternative schemes is, in effect, to adopt the hypothesis that that particular classification scheme will help more than any other in the discovery of additional characteristics of the entities being classified and in the discovery of the causal laws which explain the facts about those entities.

Given any collection of entities, there are many different possible schemes for classifying them. The choice among these schemes is to be made on the basis of one's purpose in classifying. The purpose of biology is to gain knowledge of the characteristics of living things and of the causal laws which explain the facts about living things. Hence, one should prefer that classification scheme which best serves these purposes. In other words, the choice of a particular classification scheme is an hypothesis to the effect that that particular scheme will be more fruitful than any other in suggesting causal laws and general explanatory hypotheses and in predicting additional characteristics of the entities being classified. If this hypothesis is not confirmed by future experience, then a new classification scheme should be adopted, as has occurred in the history of biology.

This does not imply that only one particular classification scheme is true. Any collection of entities can be classified accurately in different ways, and in this sense all accurate classifications are true. But some classifications are scientifically more useful than others. For example, it is more useful to classify a whale as a mammal than as something that lives in the water, because the former classification enables one to predict a greater range of additional characteristics of the whale and to discover a greater range of causal laws.

Classifications should be in terms of characteristics that are important, and a characteristic is important to the extent that the characteristic is causally related to many other characteristics, and hence involved in many causal laws. Thus, that classification scheme is best which is based on characteristics that are causally connected with the greatest number of other characteristics and thus involved in the greatest number of causal laws. But we cannot know in advance which characteristics these are, and thus the choice of a classification scheme at any time is no more than a hypothesis whose fruitfulness is constantly subject to the test of future experience. Subsequent investigations may indicate that some other classification scheme is preferable because other characteristics are more important. In such a case, the hypothesis that the original classification scheme was maximally fruitful would be rejected and replaced by a better hypothesis.

This view of classification schemes as hypotheses has a parallel in history, where the historian, in describing the past, must decide which facts to include in his description and which to omit. The historian, in general, bases his decision on his judgment as to which facts are most important, and thus his choice of events is, in effect, an hypothesis concerning which events are causally connected with a great number of other events and thus involved in a great number of causal laws, just as the biologist's choice of a classification scheme is, in effect, an hypothesis concerning which characteristics of living things are involved in the greatest number of causal laws.

SOLUTIONS
to selected exercises on pages 497–509

Page 497, #2: The datum to be explained is the fact that an antitoxin renders a toxin innocuous. The hypotheses proposed are that (1) the antitoxin destroys the toxin; (2) "the antitoxins did not act directly upon toxin, but affected it indirectly through the mediation of tissue cells"; and (3) there was a "reaction of toxin and antitoxin as a direct union, analogous to the chemical neutralization of an acid by a base." Although all three of these hypotheses presumably satisfy the criteria presented in Section 13.3, hypothesis (1) is said to be the *simplest*. But hypothesis (1) is disconfirmed by the evidence reported in the second paragraph of the passage, or at least hypothesis (1) is held to be incompatible with the presumably well-established hypothesis that something that is really *destroyed* cannot be re-created again simply by means of a temperature change from 70° C. to 100° C. Hypotheses (2) and (3) remain to be tested.

Page 499, #6: The data to be explained are Galileo's telescopic observations of the celestial bodies in the vicinity of Jupiter. The first datum is the observation on January 7, 1610 of "three stars near the body of the planet, two being to the east and one to the west of him [Jupiter]. They were all in a straight line, and parallel to the ecliptic, and they appeared brighter than other stars of the same magnitude." The first hypothesis considered by Galileo to explain and account for these observations was that these three celestial bodies were fixed stars. Given only the datum of January 7th, this first hypothesis satisfies all five of the criteria presented in Section 13.3, with the possible exception that the fact that the stars appeared brighter than other stars of the same magnitude might be held to be incompatible with previously well-established hypotheses concerning the relation of the brightness to the magnitude of fixed stars.

On January 8th, however, Galileo observed a very different arrangement of the stars: "all the three were on the west side of Jupiter, *nearer one another than before,* and almost at equal distances." Although Galileo "had not turned his attention to the extraordinary fact of the mutual approach of the stars" and thus continued to hold to his first hypothesis that they were fixed stars, he did formulate a second hypothesis to explain "how Jupiter could be found to the east of the three stars, when but the day before he had been to the west of two of them."

This second hypothesis was "that the motion of Jupiter was *direct*, . . . and that he had got before these two stars by his own motion." But Galileo recognized that this second hypothesis was "contrary to astronomical calculations," that is, contrary to previously well-established hypotheses concerning the motion of Jupiter (criterion #3), and so Galileo awaited further data to resolve this incompatibility between observation and generally accepted theory.

On January 10th Galileo observed that "two only of the stars appeared, and both on the east of the planet." This datum led Galileo to reject the second hypothesis [that the observations could be accounted for by Jupiter's motion] on the grounds that "it was obviously impossible that Jupiter could have advanced from west to east on the 8th of January, and from east to west on the 10th." In effect, Galileo was rejecting the second hypothesis on the grounds that it was incompatible with previously well-established hypotheses concerning the motion of Jupiter. Having thus rejected the second hypothesis, Galileo formulated a third hypothesis to explain and account for his observations. This third hypothesis was that "that phenomenon which he had observed arose from the motion of the stars." This third hypothesis presumably entails rejection of the first hypothesis that the celestial bodies which he observed were *fixed* stars.

On January 11th Galileo observed that "there were still only two stars, and both to the east of Jupiter; but the more eastern star was now *twice as large as the other one,* though on the preceding night they had been perfectly equal." Galileo considered this datum as further evidence against the first hypothesis [that the celestial bodies that he was observing were fixed stars], presumably reasoning that the first hypothesis was incompatible with the previously well-established hypothesis that fixed stars do not undergo such changes in magnitude.

Thus, Galileo was left with his third hypothesis [that the phenomenon which he had observed arose from the motion of the stars], which he then developed into a more specific fourth hypothesis: "that there were in the heaven three stars which revolved round Jupiter, in the same manner as Venus and Mercury revolved round the sun." Galileo's observations on January 12th confirmed this fourth hypothesis and again disconfirmed the first hypothesis. On January 13th Galileo observed a fourth star, which presumably led him to formulate a fifth hypothesis to the effect that Jupiter had four moons (instead of three).

Page 502, #11: The datum to be explained is the depopulation of the Indians as evidenced by the skulls, limbs, ribs, backbones, and some other vestiges of the human body, scattered promiscuously in great numbers. The hypotheses considered are (1) that there was a war or other violence which would have left warlike scars or signs of fear and suspicion, and (2) that there was a pestilential disease. Both of these hypotheses presumably satisfy the criteria presented in Section 13.3. But hypothesis (1) is disconfirmed by the evidence that no warlike scars were observed on the bodies of the remaining Indians and that no particular signs of fear and suspicion were noticed. Hypothesis (2) remains to be tested.

EXAMINATION
on Chapter 13

Write your answers on a separate sheet of paper, then check them against the answers given at the end of the examination. If you miss a question, restudy the appropriate part of the text.

1. What is the single most fundamental difference between a scientific and an unscientific explanation?
2. What is the logical (deductive) relationship between a fact to be explained and an explanation of that fact?
3. State the difference between indirect verification and direct verification.
4. What is the connection between the Fallacy of Affirming the Consequent and the fact that indirect verification of an hypothesis is never conclusive or certain?
5. What exactly is meant by the "predictive or explanatory power of an hypothesis"?
6. Distinguish three possible meanings of the phrase "*ad hoc* hypothesis."
7. Explain why a classification scheme is a kind of hypothesis.

ANSWERS

1. A scientific explanation of a certain fact can be indirectly tested by other facts, whereas an unscientific explanation cannot be indirectly tested by other facts.
2. The fact can be validly deduced from the explanation.
3. In the direct verification of a proposition, the truth or falsity of the proposition is determined immediately through sense experience; whereas in the indirect verification of a proposition, one first deduces from the proposition to be verified one or more other propositions which are capable of being tested directly, and then these other propositions are tested and found to be either true or false.
4. To hold that indirect verification is conclusive or certain is to commit the Fallacy of Affirming the Consequent.
5. The number or range of testable conclusions deducible from the hypothesis.
6. "*Ad hoc* hypothesis" can be defined in the following three ways:

a. An hypothesis that is specially formulated to account for some fact *after* that fact has been observed.
b. An hypothesis that accounts *only* for the particular fact or facts it was intended to explain and which has no other explanatory power, that is, which entails no other testable conclusions.
c. An hypothesis that is a mere descriptive generalization, without any explanatory power or theoretical scope.

7. To adopt a particular classification scheme is, in effect, to adopt the hypothesis that the classifying characteristics of that scheme are the most important, in the sense that they are involved in a greater number of causal laws and explanatory hypotheses than the classifying characteristics of any alternative classification scheme.

Chapter 14
Probability

READ PAGES 510–514 OF THE TEXT

14.1 Alternative Conceptions of Probability

The two alternative conceptions of probability explained in the text are the *a priori* (or "classical") theory and the relative-frequency theory.

According to the ***a priori* theory,** the probability that we assign to the occurrence of a certain event is a measure of the degree of our rational belief that the event will occur. For example, we say that the probability of a flipped coin landing heads up is 1/2 because we *believe* that there are two possible outcomes of flipping the coin (heads and tails) and we *believe* that these two possible outcomes are equally probable. According to the *a priori* theory, the probability of a certain event occurring in given circumstances is computed by dividing the number of ways in which that event can occur by the total number of possible outcomes of those circumstances, assuming that there is no reason to believe that any one outcome is more probable than any other. Thus, the probability of drawing a club from a standard deck of cards is 13/52 because there are thirteen ways of drawing a club and there are fifty-two possible outcomes of drawing a card, all of which are assumed to be equally probable. The *a priori* theory derives its name from the fact that a probability can be assigned *prior* to any trial runs; that is, one need not first flip a coin many times to see how frequently it lands heads up, and one need not draw many cards from a deck to see how frequently a club is drawn.

On the other hand, according to the **relative-frequency theory,** the probability of a certain event occurring is a measure of the relative frequency with which that event has been found to occur in the past. For example, we say that the probability of a twenty-five-year-old woman surviving her twenty-sixth birthday is 0.971 because it has been found through past experience that the relative frequency with which twenty-five-year-old women survive their twenty-sixth birthday is 0.971. The relative-frequency theory thus bases a prediction of the future on a knowledge of the past. According to the relative-frequency theory, the probability that a particular member of a given class will have a certain attribute is defined as the relative frequency with which members of that class have been found in the past to have that attribute.

In both the *a priori* theory and the relative-frequency theory, the probability of a certain event occurring is always determined relative to the "evidence" at hand. But the "evidence" in the two cases is different. In the case of the *a priori* theory applied to the flipped coin, the evidence is that the coin has two sides and that we have no reason to believe that one of these sides is more likely to turn up than the other. Whereas in the case of the relative-frequency theory applied to twenty-five-year-old women surviving their twenty-sixth birthday, the evidence is that the relative frequency with which twenty-five-year-old women have been found to survive their twenty-sixth birthday is 0.971, and the conclusion is that the probability of a particular twenty-five-year-old woman surviving her twenty-sixth birthday is 0.971. In the cases of both the *a priori* theory and the relative-frequency theory, the probability of a certain event occurring is determined by the "evidence" used.

In the next section of the text you will study the **probability calculus,** which consists of formulas for computing the probability of a complex event from the probabilities of its component events.

READ PAGES 514–518 OF THE TEXT

14.2 The Probability Calculus

The **probability calculus** can be used to compute the probability of a complex event from the probabilities of its component events.

1. ***Joint Occurrences.*** Suppose that we are interested in computing the probability of the complex event of getting two heads in a row in two tosses of a coin. The complex event in question is composed of the two component events of getting a head on the first toss of the coin and then getting a head on the second toss. These

two component events are said to be **independent** because what happens on the first toss is assumed to have no effect on what happens on the second toss. If the probability of getting heads on a single toss is 1/2, then we can compute the probability of getting two heads in a row on two tosses of a coin as follows: The probability of getting heads the first time is 1/2. In other words, 1/2 of the time, on average, the outcome of the first toss will be heads, and on 1/2 of these occasions, on average, the outcome of the second toss will be heads also, so that 1/2 of 1/2 of the time (or 1/4 of the time), on average, the joint outcome will be two heads in a row, which means that the probability of getting two heads in a row is 1/4.

In general, the probability of any two *independent* events occurring *jointly* is the *product* of the probability of the first event occurring and the probability of the second event occurring. Thus,

$$P(a \text{ and } b) = P(a) \times P(b)$$

where a and b stand for the two *independent* events in question, $P(a)$ and $P(b)$ stand for the probabilities of a and b respectively, and $P(a \text{ and } b)$ stands for the probability of the joint occurrence of a and b.

Another example should help to make clear the application of the preceding **product theorem.** Suppose that we are interested in computing the probability of the complex event of drawing a spade from each of two decks of cards. Here the complex event in question is composed of the two component events of drawing a spade from the first deck of cards and then drawing a spade from the second deck. These two component events are assumed to be *independent,* so that the preceding product theorem applies. If the probability of drawing a spade from a deck is 13/52 or 1/4, then the probability of drawing a spade from each of two decks can be computed as follows: 1/4 of the time, on average, the outcome of the draw from the first deck will be a spade, and on 1/4 of these occasions, on average, the outcome of the draw from the second deck will be a spade also, so that 1/4 of 1/4 of the time (or 1/16 of the time), on average, two spades will be drawn, which means that the probability of drawing two spades is 1/16. Notice that the probability is the same if just one deck of cards is used and the first card drawn is replaced before the second card is drawn.

There is a **general product theorem** which can be used to compute the probability of the joint occurrence of any number of independent events. For example, suppose that we are interested in computing the probability of drawing three spades in a row from a deck of cards (replacing each card drawn before the next card is drawn). The probability of drawing a spade the first time is 1/4. The probability of then drawing a spade the second time (assuming that the first card drawn has been replaced in the deck) is again 1/4, which makes the probability of drawing two spades in a row $1/4 \times 1/4$ or 1/16. The probability of subsequently drawing a spade the third time (assuming that the second card drawn has also been replaced in the deck) is again 1/4, which makes the probability of drawing three spades in a row $1/4 \times 1/4 \times 1/4$, or 1/64. The formula for the probability of the joint occurrence of three independent events is

$$P(a \text{ and } b \text{ and } c) = P(a) \times P(b) \times P(c)$$

and in general the probability of the joint occurrence of any number of independent events is the product of the separate probabilities of the independent events.

The preceding product theorems require only slight modification in the case of **dependent events.** Suppose, for example, that we are interested in computing the probability of the complex event of drawing two spades in a row from a deck of cards, where the first card drawn is *not* replaced in the deck before the second card is drawn. Here the complex event in question is composed of the two component events of drawing a spade the first time and then drawing a spade the second time (without having replaced the card drawn first). These two component events are **dependent,** because the probability of drawing a spade on the second draw is dependent on the outcome of the first draw. If a spade is *not* drawn on the first draw, then the probability of drawing a spade on the second draw is 13/51, whereas if a spade is drawn on the first draw, then the probability of drawing a spade on the second draw is 12/51. Now it is the latter probability which enters into the computation of the probability of drawing two spades in a row (without replacing the first card drawn). We can argue as follows: The probability of drawing a spade on the first draw is 1/4. In other words, 1/4 of the time, on average, the outcome of the first draw will be a spade, and on 12/51 of these occasions, on average, the outcome of the second draw will be a spade also, so that $1/4 \times 12/51$ of the time (or 1/17 of the time), on average, two spades will be drawn, which means that the probability of drawing two spades (without replacing the first card drawn) is 1/17. The formula for this computation is as follows

$$P(a \text{ and } b) = P(a) \times P(b \text{ if } a)$$

where $P(b \text{ if } a)$ stands for the probability of b occurring when a has already occurred. Thus, in this example, a is the event of drawing a spade on the first draw, and $P(a)$ is 1/4; whereas b if a is the event of drawing a spade on the second draw from among the remaining fifty-one cards, of which twelve are spades, and $P(b \text{ if } a)$ is 12/51; that is, the probability of drawing a spade on the second draw, assuming that a spade has already been drawn on the first draw, is 12/51.

There is also a **general product theorem for dependent events,** which is analogous to the general product theorem for independent events and which can be used to compute the probability of the joint occurrence of any number of dependent events. For example, suppose that we are interested in computing the probability of drawing three spades in a row *without* replacing each card drawn before the next card is drawn. The probability of drawing a spade on the first draw is 13/52. The probability of then drawing a spade on the second draw (assuming that a spade has been drawn on the first draw and *not* replaced) is 12/51, which makes the probability of drawing two spades in a row $13/52 \times 12/51$, or 1/17. The probability of subsequently drawing a spade on the third draw (assuming that two spades have already been drawn and not replaced) is 11/50, which makes the probability of drawing three spades in a row $13/52 \times 12/51 \times 11/50$, or 11/850. The formula for the probability of the joint occurrence of three dependent events is

$$P(a \text{ and } b \text{ and } c) = P(a) \times P(b \text{ if } a) \times P(c \text{ if both } a \text{ and } b)$$

and in general the probability of the joint occurrence of any number of dependent events is the product of the separate probabilities of those *dependent* events.

SOLUTIONS
to selected exercises on pages 518–519

Page 518, #2: Under assumption (a) the events are independent and the probability is $4/52 \times 4/52 \times 4/52$. Under assumption (b) the events are dependent and the probability is $4/52 \times 3/51 \times 2/50$.

Page 518, #6: Let the patients be named a, b, and c. It does not matter which of the five doors a enters so long as b and c enter that same door. Thus, we are interested in the probability of b and c entering the same door as a. Now the probability of b entering the same door as a is 1/5, and the probability of c entering the same door as a is 1/5, so that the probability of b and c both entering the same door as a is $1/5 \times 1/5$.

READ PAGES 519–523 OF THE TEXT

2. ***Alternative Occurrences.*** A new formula is required when we wish to compute the probability of a complex event from the probabilities of its component events where those component events are **alternative events** or **mutually exclusive events.**

Suppose, for example, that we are interested in computing the probability of the complex event of getting the same outcome on two tosses of a coin, that is, getting either two heads in a row or two tails in a row. Here the complex event in question (getting the same outcome on two tosses of a coin) is composed of two *mutually exclusive alternative events:* the event of getting two heads in a row and the event of getting two tails in a row. The complex event in whose probability we are interested is said to occur if *either* of the two component events occurs. The two component events are said to be **mutually exclusive** because either one or the other of them can occur, but *not both.* We can now compute the probability of getting either two heads in a row or two tails in a row as follows: We know from the product theorem developed in the previous section of the text that the probability of getting two heads in a row is 1/4 and that the probability of getting two tails in a row is 1/4. These are mutually exclusive events, so that 1/4 of the time, on average, the outcome of two tosses of the coin will be two heads in a row, and *another* 1/4 of the time, on average, the outcome of two tosses of the coin will be two tails in a row, which means that $1/4 + 1/4$ of the time (or 1/2 of the time), on average, the outcome of two tosses of the coin will be either two heads in a row or two tails in a row, which means that the probability that the outcome of two tosses of the coin will be either two heads or two tails is 1/2.

In general, the probability of one or the other of two mutually exclusive events occurring is the *sum* of the probability of the first event occurring and the probability of the second event occurring. Thus,

$$P(a \text{ or } b) = P(a) + P(b)$$

where a and b stand for the two *mutually exclusive* events in question, $P(a)$ and $P(b)$ stand for the probabilities of a and b, respectively, and $P(a \text{ or } b)$ stands for the probability of the *alternative occurrence of a or b,* that is, the occurrence of either a or b.

Another example should help to make clear the application of the preceding **addition theorem.** Suppose that one urn contains two white balls and four black balls and a second urn contains three white balls and nine black balls. We draw one ball from each urn. What is the probability of drawing two balls of the same color? The complex event in question (drawing two balls of the same color) consists of the alternative occurrence of either of two mutually exclusive events: the event of drawing two white balls, and the event of drawing two black balls. The addition theorem applies to this situation because the complex event in whose probability we are interested is said to occur if *either* of the two mutually exclusive events occurs. Therefore, the probability of drawing two balls of the same color is the sum of the probability of drawing two white balls and the probability of drawing two black balls. According to the product theorem, the probability of drawing two white balls is $2/6 \times 3/12$, or $1/12$. And the probability of drawing two black balls is $4/6 \times 9/12$, or $1/2$. So the probability of drawing two balls of the same color is $1/12 + 1/2$, or $7/12$.

There is a **general addition theorem** which can be used to compute the probability of the alternative occurrence of any number of mutually exclusive events. For example, suppose that we are interested in computing the probability of the complex event of getting at least one heads in two tosses of a coin. Here we are interested in a complex event which is composed of the alternative occurrence of *three* mutually exclusive events, the event of getting heads on the first toss and tails on the second toss, the event of getting tails on the first toss and heads on the second toss, and the event of getting heads on both tosses. Note that the complex event in question is analyzed into these three *mutually exclusive* events because the addition theorem applies *only* to mutually exclusive events. Now according to the product theorem, the probability of each of these three mutually exclusive events is $1/4$, so that according to the addition theorem the probability of one or another of the three mutually exclusive events occurring is $1/4 + 1/4 + 1/4$, or $3/4$. The formula for the probability of the alternative occurrence of three mutually exclusive events is

$$P(a \text{ or } b \text{ or } c) \equiv P(a) + P(b) + P(c)$$

and in general the probability of the alternative occurrence of any number of mutually exclusive events is the sum of the separate probabilities of the mutually exclusive events.

Concerning the above problem of computing the probability of getting at least one heads in two tosses of a coin, notice that it would be *incorrect* to argue: The probability of getting heads on the first toss is 1/2, and the probability of getting heads on the second toss is 1/2, so the probability of getting heads on one toss or the other is $1/2 + 1/2$, or 1. The *error* here arises from applying the addition theorem to two events which are *not* mutually exclusive. The event of getting heads on the first toss and the event of getting heads on the second toss are not mutually exclusive because they can *both* occur together. Therefore, the addition theorem is not directly applicable in the way suggested above in this paragraph. In order to use the addition theorem to compute the probability of getting at least one heads in two tosses of a coin, the complex event in question (getting at least one heads in two tosses of a coin) *must* be analyzed or broken down into *mutually exclusive events,* as was done in the preceding paragraph, where it was pointed out that the complex event of getting at least one heads in two tosses of a coin can be analyzed into *three* mutually exclusive events: the event of getting heads on the first toss and tails on the second toss, the event of getting tails on the first toss and heads on the second toss, and the event of getting heads on both tosses. The point to be remembered is that the addition theorem can be applied *only to mutually exclusive events.*

There is another method for computing the probability of getting at least one heads in two tosses of a coin, and this method should be understood thoroughly, since it will be used repeatedly in the exercises. Let the complex event of getting at least one heads in two tosses of a coin be called a. And let the event of *not* getting a heads on either toss be called $\bar{a}$. Now, a and $\bar{a}$ are not only mutually exclusive but they are also jointly exhaustive, that is, together they exhaust all the possibilities; either a or $\bar{a}$ must occur, since there must be either at least one heads or else no heads in two tosses of a coin. Since a and $\bar{a}$ exhaust the possibilities we know that

$$P(a \text{ or } \bar{a}) = 1$$

And since a and $\bar{a}$ are mutually exclusive we know by the addition theorem that

$$P(a \text{ or } \bar{a}) = P(a) + P(\bar{a})$$

Now things equal to the same thing are equal to each other, so from the two equations above it follows that

$$P(a) + P(\bar{a}) = 1$$

which entails that

$$P(a) = 1 - P(\bar{a})$$

In other words, the probability of *a* occurring is equal to 1 minus the probability of *a* not occurring.

Applying this formula to the problem at hand, we can conclude that the probability of getting at least one heads in two tosses of a coin is equal to 1 minus the probability of not getting heads on either toss of the coin, which is 1 minus the probability of getting tails on both tosses of the coin, which is $1 - 1/4$, which is $3/4$.

The above formula should be used whenever one is interested in the probability of a complex event and it is difficult or cumbersome to analyze the complex event into a number of mutually exclusive alternative events. Under these circumstances it is often easier to compute the probability of the complex event *not* occurring and subtract this from 1.

Another example should help to make clear the application of the above formula. Suppose that one urn contains two white balls and four black balls and a second urn contains three white balls and nine black balls. We draw one ball from each urn. What is the probability of drawing at least one white ball? The problem can be solved most easily by computing the probability of not drawing any white balls and then subtracting this from 1. The probability of not drawing any white balls is the same as the probability of drawing two black balls, which is $4/6 \times 9/12$, or $1/2$. Therefore, the probability of drawing at least one white ball is $1 - 1/2$, which is $1/2$.

The game of **craps,** which was explained in detail in the text, contains good illustrations of the principles developed so far. If you did not understand every step of the calculations, you should, before going on to the exercises, restudy the explanation beginning on line 12 of page 522.

SOLUTIONS

to selected exercises on pages 523–524

Page 523, #2: The probability of getting at least one spade is 1 minus the probability of getting no spades on any of the three draws. Therefore, (a) if each card is replaced before making the next drawing, then the probability of getting at least one spade is $1 - (39/52 \times 39/52 \times 39/52)$. Whereas (b) if the cards drawn are not replaced, then the probability of getting at least one spade is $1 - (39/52 \times 38/51 \times 37/50)$.

Page 524, #6: There are twenty-one coins.

a. In order for two coins to add up to 50¢, they must both be quarters. The probability of shaking out two quarters is $3/21 \times 2/20$.
b. In order for two coins to add up to 35¢, they must be a quarter and a dime. Shaking out a quarter and a dime is a complex event com-

posed of the two mutually exclusive alternative events of shaking out a quarter first and then a dime or shaking out a dime first and then a quarter. The probability of the first of these mutually exclusive events is $3/21 \times 2/20$, which is $1/70$. And the probability of the second of these mutually exclusive events is $2/21 \times 3/20$, which is $1/70$. Therefore, the probability of shaking out 35¢ is $1/70 + 1/70$, which is $1/35$.

c. In order for two coins to add up to 30¢, they must be a quarter and a nickel. Following reasoning analogous to that in (b) above, the probability is $(3/21 \times 5/20) + (5/21 \times 3/20)$, which is $1/14$.
d. In order for two coins to add up to 26¢, they must be a quarter and a penny, whence the probability is $(3/21 \times 11/20) + (11/21 \times 3/20)$, which is $11/70$.
e. In order for two coins to add up to 20¢, they must both be dimes, whence the probability is $2/21 \times 1/20$, which is $1/210$.
f. In order for two coins to add up to 15¢, they must be a dime and a nickel, whence the probability is $(2/21 \times 5/20) + (5/21 \times 2/20)$, which is $1/21$.
g. In order for two coins to add up to 11¢, they must be a dime and a penny, whence the probability is $(2/21 \times 11/20) + (11/21 \times 2/20)$, which is $11/105$.
h. In order for two coins to add up to 10¢, they must both be nickels, whence the probability is $5/21 \times 4/20$, which is $1/21$.
i. In order for two coins to add up to 6¢, they must be a nickel and a penny, whence the probability is $(5/21 \times 11/20) + (11/21 \times 5/20)$, which is $11/42$.
j. In order for two coins to add up to 2¢, they must both be pennies, whence the probability is $11/21 \times 10/20$, which is $11/42$.

READ PAGES 525–528 OF THE TEXT

14.3 Expectation or Expected Value

The **expected value** of a bet can be thought of as the average yield of such bets in the long run. For example, if a bet of $1 is made that heads will turn up on a toss of a coin and the return is $2 if heads does turn up and nothing if tails turns up, then one half of the time, on average, the bettor will win such a bet and will receive a return of $2, whereas the other half of the time, on average, the bettor will lose and will receive nothing. Thus, the total return from two such bets will, on average, be $2, which means that the average return per bet will be $1, which means that the **expected**

value of such a bet is \$1. Notice that the expected value is to be computed in the following way: One half of the time the bettor receives a return of \$2 and one half of the time the bettor receives no return, so that the expected value is $(1/2 \times \$2) + (1/2 \times \$0)$, which is \$1.

Consider a slightly more complicated example. Suppose that two coins are tossed and that if two heads turn up then the return is \$3, and if a heads and a tails turn up then the return is \$2, and if two tails turn up then the return is nothing. What is the expected value of a bet in this situation? We can reason as follows: One fourth of the time, on average, two heads will turn up and the bettor will receive \$3. One half of the time, on average, a heads and a tails will turn up and the bettor will receive \$2. And one fourth of the time, on average, two tails will turn up and the bettor will receive nothing. Thus, the bettor's total return from four such bets will, *on average,* be \$7 (\$3 from winning once with two heads, and \$4 from receiving \$2 twice with a heads and a tails). Now if on average the bettor's total return from four such bets is \$7, then the average return per bet will be \$1.75, which means that the **expected value** of such a bet is \$1.75. Notice that the expected value is to be computed in the following way: One fourth of the time the bettor receives \$3 and one half of the time the bettor receives \$2 and one fourth of the time the bettor receives \$0, so that the expected value is $(1/4 \times \$3) + (1/2 \times \$2) + (1/4 \times \$0)$, which is \$1.75.

In general, the **expected value** of a bet can be computed by multiplying the return yielded on each possible outcome by the probability of that outcome occurring and then adding together all these products. This formula should be thoroughly understood and remembered, as it will be essential in the exercises.

The game of **chuck-a-luck,** which was explained in detail in the text, contains good illustrations of the above formula. If you did not understand every step of the calculations, you should, before going on to the exercises, restudy the explanation beginning in the middle of page 525 of the text.

You should also thoroughly understand why the expected value of a bet or a series of bets cannot be altered by doubling the amount of money wagered after each loss, or by any other technique of splitting the bet, or quitting after a certain number of bets, or quitting after a certain predetermined amount of money has been won. In each case the expected value is the same. This fact is explained in detail in the text, and it is unnecessary to repeat the details here. If the explanation was not completely understood when you read it in the text, you should now review it before going on to the exercises. The explanation begins at the top of page 527 of the text.

SOLUTIONS
to selected exercises on pages 529–530

Page 529, #2: If the bet is $1 on each of the six numbers in chuck-a-luck, then there is a return no matter what the outcome is, and we must consider all possible outcomes. The easiest way to do this is to arrange them in the three groups below. In the following table, all possible outcomes are listed in the left-hand column. The return from each outcome is then listed in the second column. The probability of each outcome is listed in the third column. And the product of the second and third columns is listed in the fourth column. The expected value is then the sum of all the fractions in the fourth column.

Outcome	*Return*	*Probability*	*Return × Probability*
1 1 1	$4	1/216	$4/216
2 2 2	"	"	"
3 3 3	"	"	"
4 4 4	"	"	"
5 5 5	"	"	"
6 6 6	"	"	"
1 1 2	$5	3/216	$15/216
1 1 3	"	"	"
1 1 4	"	"	"
1 1 5	"	"	"
1 1 6	"	"	"
2 2 1	"	"	"
2 2 3	"	"	"
2 2 4	"	"	"
2 2 5	"	"	"
2 2 6	"	"	"
3 3 1	"	"	"
3 3 2	"	"	"
3 3 4	"	"	"
3 3 5	"	"	"
3 3 6	"	"	"
4 4 1	"	"	"
4 4 2	"	"	"
4 4 3	"	"	"
4 4 5	"	"	"
4 4 6	"	"	"
5 5 1	"	"	"
5 5 2	"	"	"
5 5 3	"	"	"
5 5 4	"	"	"
5 5 6	"	"	"

6 6 1	"	"	"
6 6 2	"	"	"
6 6 3	"	"	"
6 6 4	"	"	"
6 6 5	"	"	"
1 2 3	$6	6/216	$36/216
1 2 4	"	"	"
1 2 5	"	"	"
1 2 6	"	"	"
1 3 4	"	"	"
1 3 5	"	"	"
1 3 6	"	"	"
1 4 5	"	"	"
1 4 6	"	"	"
1 5 6	"	"	"
2 3 4	"	"	"
2 3 5	"	"	"
2 3 6	"	"	"
2 4 5	"	"	"
2 4 6	"	"	"
2 5 6	"	"	"
3 4 5	"	"	"
3 4 6	"	"	"
3 5 6	"	"	"
4 5 6	"	"	"

The sum of the fractions in the right-hand column is $1,194/216, which is approximately $5.52. Since $6 was bet, the expected value of approximately $5.52 represents an expectation of approximately 92¢ on the dollar, which is the constant value for any method of betting at chuck-a-luck.

In case you are not certain of how to compute the probabilities in column 3, consider the last row of the table as an example. The probability of the three dice showing a 4, a 5, and a 6 is 6/216, because there are six different ways of getting 4–5–6 with three dice (4–5–6, 4–6–5, 5–4–6, 5–6–4, 6–4–5, 6–5–4) and there are 216 possible outcomes of rolling three dice.

Page 529, #6: Note that a horse which "pays even money" returns *twice* what you bet, whereas a horse at odds of 8 to 1 returns *nine* times what you bet (because you get back your original bet plus *winnings* of eight times your bet). Therefore, for a $2 bet, the expected value of betting on the favorite is 0.46 × $4, which is $1.84; whereas the expected value of betting on the dark horse is 0.1 × $18, which is $1.80. Therefore, the favorite is the better bet.

EXAMINATION
on Chapter 14

Write your answers on a separate sheet of paper, then check them against the answers given at the end of the examination. If you miss a question, restudy the appropriate part of the text. Part I of this exam contains questions on the theory of probability; part II contains exercises similar to those in the text.

Part I. Theory.

1. Which of the following theorems is designed to be used when one is required to compute the probability of a complex event which is constituted by the occurrence of at least one of two alternatives which are *not* mutually exclusive?
   a. $P(a \text{ and } b) = P(a) \times P(b)$.
   b. $P(a \text{ and } b) = P(a) \times P(b \text{ if } a)$.
   c. $P(a \text{ or } b) = P(a) + P(b)$.
   d. $P(a) = 1 - P(\bar{a})$.
2. According to the relative-frequency theory of probability, what is the probability of a tossed coin showing heads, assuming that you know the coin to be lopsided but know nothing of the exact nature of its lopsidedness?
   a. 1/2.
   b. Between 0 and 1, but not exactly 1/2.
   c. One cannot choose between (a) and (b) on the basis of the information given.
3. According to the classical or *a priori* theory of probability, which of the answers in the previous question is correct?
4. Is the following argument necessarily *valid*?

$$P(a \text{ or } b) = 1$$
$$P(a \text{ or } b) = P(a) + P(b)$$
$$\text{Therefore, } P(a) = 1 - P(b)$$

5. Is the following argument necessarily *sound*?

$$P(a \text{ or } \bar{a}) = 1$$
$$P(a \text{ or } \bar{a}) = P(a) + P(\bar{a})$$
$$\text{Therefore, } P(a) = 1 - P(\bar{a})$$

6. Is it true according to the classical or *a priori* theory of probability that the determination of the probability of a certain event occurring in certain circumstances is always *relative* to the knowledge about those circumstances which is possessed by the person making that determination?

7. Which of the following (possibly more than one) *must* be true of a and b in order for the following theorem of the probability calculus to be applicable: $P(a \text{ or } b) = P(a) + P(b)$?
   a. a and b must be independent events.
   b. a and b must be mutually exclusive events.
   c. It must be possible for a and b to occur together.
   d. Either a or b must occur (that is, a and b must be jointly exhaustive).
   e. a and b cannot occur together.
   f. The occurrence or nonoccurrence of a has absolutely no effect on the probability of the occurrence or nonoccurrence of b.
   g. a and b must be equipossible.
   h. It is possible for b to occur only if a occurs.
8. Is it true that the probability that at least one of two independent events will occur is always equal to the sum of their separate probabilities?
9. Is it true that if we multiply the return yielded on each possible outcome by the probability of the outcome occurring, the sum of all such products is the expectation or expected value of the bet or investment?
10. Is it true that the probability of the joint occurrence of two mutually exclusive events is always equal to the product of their separate probabilities?

Part II. Problems. An answer may be left in its original form without carrying out any of the arithmetical operations indicated.

11. A dentist has her office in a building with five entrances, all equally accessible. Four patients arrive at her office at the same time. What is the probability that they all enter the building by different doors?
12. Suppose that there are four houses built around a square and that the Smiths, who live in one of the houses, are entertaining the three couples who live in the other three houses. After the party each male guest staggers back to one of the three houses (no two men going to the same house) and each female guest staggers back to one of the three houses (no two women going to the same house). What is the probability that each of the three female guests will end up in the same house with her husband?
13. Three balls are drawn from an urn containing four white balls and five black balls. What is the probability that *exactly two* of the balls drawn will be white?
14. Roll three dice. What is the probability that the numbers showing will add up to 17?
15. In playing poker a flush consists of five cards in the same suit. If you

are dealt five cards including three cards in the same suit, what is the probability of completing your flush by drawing two new cards?

16. Three cards are drawn from a thoroughly shuffled standard deck of 52 cards. What is the probability that the three cards drawn will all be of different suits?
17. Roll three dice. What is the probability that a 3 or a 4 will show on at least one of the dice?
18. What is the ratio between the expected value of a wager which consists of betting $2 on each of the numbers 1, 2, and 3 at chuck-a-luck, and the expected value of a wager which consists of betting $1 on each of the six numbers at chuck-a-luck?
19. Five cards are drawn from a thoroughly shuffled standard deck of 52 cards. What is the probability that the five cards drawn will all be of different suits?

ANSWERS

1. d.
2. c.
3. a.
4. Yes.
5. Yes.
6. Yes.
7. b, e.
8. No.
9. Yes.
10. No.
11. $4/5 \times 3/5 \times 2/5$. (Let one patient enter any one of the five doors. The probability of a second patient entering a different door is 4/5; the probability of a third patient entering a door different from either of the first two is 3/5; and the probability of the fourth patient entering a door different from any of the first three is 2/5.)
12. $1/3 \times 1/2 \times 1/1$. (It does not matter to which houses the husbands went. We are interested only in the probability of the wives joining their husbands. The probability of one wife joining her husband is 1/3, and the probability of a second wife joining her husband would *then* be 1/2, and then the probability of the third wife joining her husband would be 1/1.)
13. $(4/9 \times 3/8 \times 5/7) + (4/9 \times 5/8 \times 3/7) + (5/9 \times 4/8 \times 3/7)$. (There are three mutually exclusive ways of drawing exactly two white balls: drawing first white, then white, then black; or drawing first white, then black, then white; or drawing first black, then white, then white.)
14. 3/216. (There are 216 possible outcomes of rolling three dice. A total of 17 can occur only if there are two 6's and a 5, and the 5 can occur on any one of the three dice.)
15. $10/47 \times 9/46$.
16. $39/51 \times 26/50$. (Let the first card drawn be of any suit. The probability of the second card being of a different suit is 39/51; and the

probability of the third card being of a suit different from either of the first two is 26/50.)

17. $1 - (4/6 \times 4/6 \times 4/6)$. (1 minus the probability that all three of the dice will show numbers other than 3 or 4.)
18. 1/1
19. 0.